Farmhouse cooking is renowned for its use of
traditional recipes and fresh, wholesome food –
making every meal a pleasure. Mary Norwak
and Babs Honey have culled the very best
recipes from the private cookery books of
English farmers' wives over the past two hundred
years, so as to make good country cooking
available to all.

Book Two includes delicious recipes for steamed
puddings, cakes and biscuits, bread and buns,
jams, pickles, chutneys and candied fruits. The
invaluable hints on bottling, preserving and
storing are enhanced by the old-fashioned
household tips and the advice on how to grow
herbs and make natural health and beauty
preparations.

This wonderful collection of recipes, both
traditional and unusual, reflects the return to
food fresh from the farm. Now everyone can
enjoy the delights of good English country
cooking.

*Also by Mary Norwak and available
in Sphere Books*

DEEP FREEZING MENUS AND RECIPES
DEEP FREEZING
CALENDAR OF HOME FREEZING
A-Z OF HOME FREEZING
MIXER AND BLENDER COOKBOOK

and by Mary Norwak and Babs Honey
FARMHOUSE COOKING Book One

Farmhouse Cooking

Book Two

MARY NORWAK and BABS HONEY

SPHERE BOOKS LIMITED
30/32 Gray's Inn Road, London WC1X 8JL

First published in Great Britain by Sphere Books Ltd 1973

Set in Monotype Plantin

Printed in Great Britain by
Hazell Watson & Viney Ltd
Aylesbury, Bucks

ISBN 0 7221 6447 5

CONTENTS VOLUME 1

CONTENTS VOLUME 2

* NOTE: All recipes serve 4 to 6 people (according to appetite), unless otherwise stated.

Introduction

Most of us have a child's eye view of farming. We imagine all farms are nice neat buildings, surrounded by orderly fields, grazing cows and scratching chickens. The farmer wears breeches and boots and a soft hat, and strides around with a dog at heel, and sometimes a horse in hand. His wife looks like Mrs Noah, permanently wrapped in a huge white apron, her hair in a bun, living her life in a vast well-scrubbed kitchen surrounded by home-baked bread, honeycombs and cabbages fresh from her well-ordered kitchen garden.

How different is the reality! There are tiny hill farms and vast estates; decrepit cottages and sparkling new bungalows; gloomy Victorian piles and tidy Georgian doll-houses; farmhouses in the centre of village streets and farmhouses miles from anywhere up rough tracks. Farmers and their wives come in different patterns too, but all the men have one thing in common—they like their womenfolk at home, working for and with them. They are traditionalists, bless their hearts, even when they drive sparkling new cars and go abroad for their holidays. Family life is still ruled by the farm. Holidays are taken at odd times of the year, regardless of school terms, because haymaking and harvest are paramount. No farmer's wife will commit herself to village activities between June and September, when her men work all hours of daylight, and food and home comforts are the only things that matter.

All through the year, farmers insist on their hearty breakfasts, potatoes with every meal, pies and puddings, lashings of cut-and-come-again cakes and mouth-watering helpings of their leisure-time game and fish which they dump on the kitchen table.

This collection of recipes reflects this interest in good hearty food during the past two hundred years. We have been sent still-used eighteenth-century recipes; notes of old favourites on the backs of envelopes; Victorian recipes written on black-edged mourning paper; and a number of fascinating scrap-books full of delicious goodies. We received a number of recipes that originated during the 1939–45 war, when many of today's farmers were newly married and struggling to keep up their high standard of food. We have included recipes from an evacuee who grew to love farm life, and from an Italian farmer's wife whose husband was a prisoner-of-war in this country. Some of the recipes reflect the poverty of the country between the two wars of this century; others of the richness of some Victorian farmers, and the 'carefulness' of the Edwardians building up

9

their holdings. Some mirror the interest of today's young wives in foreign dishes, and in labour-saving devices, together with a returning interest in natural foods which discards the synthetic and the standardised convenience product.

Sadly, many of our contributors are unknown to us, for they have left only their names in their friends' cookery notebooks. Three of them however left exceptionally interesting collections of recipes. Thomas Train of Gateshead left a bound copy of *The Female Instructor; or, Young Woman's Companion* whose contents ranged through 'Education, Religion, Conversation, Sensibility and the Government of the Passions, Courtship and Marriage, The Management of Children, FamilyReceipts' but his family had used the book hard, and had written their own recipes on the blank backs of the illustrative plates. They are nice homely recipes which contrast with the rather formal instructions in the book in which they are written.

A little later in time, during the first quarter of the nineteenth century, came Joseph Webb of Kent, who left a neat pocketbook full of recipes 'for horse or man'. There are cures for the mange, nourishing drinks for cows, remedies for milk fever or scab or inflammation of the lungs (often the same remedy seemed to be applied to Mr Webb's animals and children). There are household hints, and recipes for sauces, wines and soft drinks, methods for pickling fruit and vegetables, ways of improving cider and colouring cheese, and even the costs of preparing some recipes. A basic family cake cost $4/5\frac{1}{2}$d in 1823 (one shilling for 1 lb butter, 10 pence for 1 lb sugar, and eggs 1 penny each).

Mrs Garden, perhaps our most prolific source of Victorian recipes, left a notebook which shows clearly the importance of good country food even in a rich and smart household in the second half of the nineteenth century. Her book started life as an Eton College exercise book, full of Greek and Latin exercises. Later it was used to note down jokes about the clergy, household hints, knitting patterns, instructions for dancing the Lancers, lists of useful shops in London and Paris, and above all, recipes. A few of the recipes are rather grand and expensive, with French names, but the majority are friends' recipes, mainly from East Anglia, for harvest cakes, stewed fowl, surplus game, hashed mutton, gingerbread, apple pudding, and the like. The Gardens, like so many Victorian families, were in the transitional stage from their country origins to life in a town. Their staff would still have been mainly recruited from the country, probably from their own ancestral neighbourhood, and both above and below stairs, country food was normally eaten. This tradition of simple country food maintained by the staff was certainly still evident in well-to-do nurseries until the 1939–45 war, and middle-aged men tend to consider 'nursery food' the only sort worth eating. After a century of country people drifting towards the towns, there is an increasing tendency for middle-class families to seek country homes again, with a consequent revival of interest in wholesome farm-based food. Mrs Garden's note book is as usable today as the most up-to-date cookery manual.

As far as possible we have avoided the professional technicalities of such subjects as salting and cheesemaking, which can be found in official bulletins, but have included the many homely ways in which farmers' wives preserve their surplus produce. We have let our ancestors and our friends speak for themselves and as far as possible kept their original writing which adds such flavour to each dish. Many of them kept commonplace books in which they recorded their recipes, the names of the houses or friends from which they originated, their reliable household hints and medical remedies and their favourite bits of poetry. We hope that you will enjoy today's version of a commonplace book.

1 Steamed Puddings, Dumplings and Sweet Sauces

If you want a good pudding, to teach you I'm willing,
Take twopennyworth of eggs, when twelve for a shilling,
And of the same fruit that Eve had once chosen,
Well pared and well chopped at least half a dozen;
Six ounces of bread (let your maid eat the crust);
The crumbs must be grated as small as the dust;
Six ounces of currants from the stones you must sort,
Lest they break out your teeth and spoil all your sport;
Six ounces of sugar won't make it too sweet,
Some salt and some nutmeg will make it complete.
Three hours let it boil, without hurry or flutter,
And then serve it up – without sugar or butter.

Sydney Smith

13

The English have long been famous for their sweet puddings served after the meat course. The price of sugar fell with the opening up of trade with the East in the seventeenth century, and the serving of fruit tarts or puddings became increasingly popular with prosperous citizens about the middle of the century. These were commonly made of flour, milk, eggs, butter, suet, marrow and raisins.

SUSSEX WELL PUDDING (sometimes called POND PUDDING in some families)

½ lb self-raising flour
or ½ lb plain flour and 1
teaspoon baking powder
Pinch of salt

2–4 oz suet
1 egg (if liked)
Milk or water to mix
4–6 oz dried fruit
Filling:
Butter and brown sugar

Mix all dry ingredients, then mix to an elastic dough with milk or water. Turn on to a floured board and roll into a neat round about size of breakfast plate. Take generous portions of butter and brown sugar and place in middle of pastry. Gather edges together at the top and make secure. Tie in cloth or place in greased basin and boil for 2 hours. Serve on large dish deep enough to catch the delicious filling which comes out once the 'football' has been cut into.

LIVERPOOL PUDDING WITH LEMON SAUCE

¼ lb breadcrumbs or bread
(soaked)
¼ lb flour
¼ lb suet
2 good tablespoons treacle
1 saltspoon nutmeg (fresh
ground)
2 oz currants

1 teaspoon baking powder
2 oz brown sugar
Juice and rind of 1 lemon
2 eggs (beaten)
A little milk
¼ teaspoon salt
A little mixed peel or 1
tablespoon marmalade

Mix all dry ingredients together. Add rind and juice of lemon, and syrup. Add squeezed out bread (if soaked) and mix into other ingredients with egg and milk. Mix altogether briskly but well then pour into greased mould or bowl. Cover with greased paper and steam for 2 hours. Serve with lemon sauce if preferred or thin custard.

Lemon Sauce – Melt knob of butter or margarine in small warm saucepan. Pour into it ½ pint of lemon squash. To this add 1 good heaped teaspoon cornflour and stir till all is smoothly blended. Add ¼ pint of cold water and cook very carefully until thick and smooth. Add a little white sugar if needed.

GOLDEN LAYER PUDDING

½ lb self-raising flour
3–4 oz suet
½ teaspoon salt
Cold water to mix

Filling:
Golden syrup
Breadcrumbs
Lemon juice

Mix all dry ingredients then add sufficient water gradually to mix to an elastic dough. Roll out this dough thinly and cut into rounds to fit a 1½ pint pudding basin. Spread layer of filling-mixture in bottom of basin, then cover with layer of pastry, then filling and so on up the sides of basin finishing with pastry. Boil for 2½ hours and turn out carefully on to hot deep dish.

MARMALADE PUDDING (very light)

2 oz breadcrumbs
2 oz self-raising flour
1 oz castor sugar
2 oz chopped mixed peel
1 grated lemon rind

2 oz margarine
1 egg
1 tablespoon milk or water
2 tablespoons marmalade

Rub margarine or butter into flour. Add sugar and breadcrumbs. Next add marmalade and stir in beaten egg and milk adding more milk or (preferably) a little water if need be to make a nice soft consistency. Boil in lightly greased basin for 2 hours. Turn out onto hot plate.

HAMPSHIRE SIX-CUP PUDDING

1 cupful each of:
Self-raising flour
Breadcrumbs
Suet
Brown sugar

Milk
A mixture of raisins,
sultanas and currants
1 teaspoon bicarbonate of soda

Mix all dry ingredients together except the bicarbonate of soda. Warm the milk and dissolve bicarbonate of soda in it; allow to cool a little. Now add milk to other ingredients. Place in greased bowl and for 4 hours steam in just boiling water.

BERKSHIRE GINGER PUDDING

6 oz self-raising flour
3 oz golden syrup
3 oz lard

½ teaspoon ground ginger
½ gill milk
Pinch of salt

Mix flour, salt and ginger in bowl. Warm lard, syrup and milk in saucepan, taking care not to heat up too much (lukewarm if possible). Add contents of saucepan to dry ingredients and boil for 2 hours in a greased basin. Turn onto hot dish and serve with extra syrup if desired.

CHOCOLATE CRUMB PUDDING

1½ pints milk
2 level tablespoons cocoa
2 eggs, beaten
5½ oz stale breadcrumbs

2 oz sugar
½ teaspoon salt
1 teaspoon vanilla essence or
¼ teaspoon mixed spice

Heat milk to scalding point. Add breadcrumbs and let stand until soft. Combine cocoa, sugar and salt and add to eggs. Add egg mixture to breadcrumb mixture and stir well. Add flavouring Pour into greased pudding dish, place in a pan of hot water and bake in a moderate oven or steam about 1 hour until set. Serve hot or as party sweet, cold and decorated with whipped cream and chocolate peppermint crisps.

FRILSHAM FRUIT BATTER

2 oz margarine
4 oz self-raising flour
2 oz sugar

1 pint rhubarb—sliced,
fresh, bottled or deep frozen
can be used for this adaptable
recipe

Rub margarine into flour. Stir in salt, sugar, rhubarb and just enough milk to make a nice thick batter. Bake in a greased pie-dish for about ½ hour till batter is cooked through at 400°F (Gas Mark 6). Serve with cream or smooth thin custard.

A very simple pudding quickly made but delicious if unexpected visitors arrive.

GINGER SNAP WITH APPLE SAUCE

1½ cups ginger snap crumbs
2 oz sugar, preferably soft
brown

1 level teaspoon mixed spice
1 beaten egg
3 teacups milk

Grease a pie-dish and sprinkle in snap crumbs. Add sugar, spice and egg and milk. Mix till blended. Stand dish in baking tin to contain hot water reaching halfway up tin. Bake in a moderate oven, 350°F (Gas Mark 4) for about ½ hour until set. Serve with thinly sliced, stewed, sweetened apples.

GOOSEBERRY PUDDING

Make a suet crust with 4 oz suet, 1 oz butter and 8 oz self-raising flour, with a pinch of salt. Line a small greased pudding basin with crust, leaving enough for a lid. Top and tail gooseberries and fill basin, adding 2 oz sugar. Cover with crust, and seal edges. Cover with foil, and cook in a pan of boiling water for 2½ hours. Turn out and serve with hot apricot jam and cream.

CHERRY AND CURRANT PUDDING

Prepare a suet crust with ½ lb of flour, 4 oz of suet, 1 teaspoon of baking powder, a little salt, and about 1 gill of water. Mix the dry ingredients together, and mix them to a stiff paste with the cold water. Turn this on to a floured board, and roll it out to the size of the basin you are using, saving enough for the top. Line the basin closely with the suet crust, leaving no spaces or holes, and allow the crust to overlap the edges of the basin a little.

Half fill it with prepared cherries and currants, and then add 1 oz of brown sugar, and fill up with fruit. Turn the overlapping edges in towards the basin and fit on the piece of crust reserved for the top, tie the pudding down with a scalded and well-floured cloth, and boil for about 2 hours.

1911

CURRANT AND APPLE PUDDING

Rub together 4 oz of sugar and 2 oz of cooking butter until it is thick and creamy. Then add 1 unbeaten egg, 4 oz of flour and 1 good teaspoon of baking powder. Mix well together and add sufficient milk to form a rather stiff batter. Beat the ingredients thoroughly well together, adding 3 small chopped up apples (in dice) and ½ a cupful of prepared currants.

Turn the mixture into a well-buttered mould and steam it for not less than 1½ hours – custard sauce is the correct accompaniment.

1911

OXFORD PUDDING

6 oz self-raising flour
2 oz ground rice
4 oz chopped suet
4 oz thick marmalade

4 oz golden syrup
1 egg, beaten
2 tablespoons milk
2 oz soft brown sugar

Grease a 1½ pint basin and press the sugar round sides and on the base.
  Sift flour and rice, stir in suet, syrup and marmalade, and mix with egg and milk. Turn into basin, cover down and steam for 3 hours. Serve with warmed syrup.

STEAMED CARAMEL PUDDING

Caramel:
3 oz granulated sugar
3 tablespoons water

Sponge:
3 oz butter
3 oz castor sugar
2 eggs (separated)
6 oz self-raising flour
6 tablespoons milk

Put the sugar and water into a small pan over a very gentle heat, and leave until a light golden brown. Pour into a warmed 2 pint basin and coat the inside. Cream the butter and sugar together until light and fluffy and beat in the egg yolks. Add the flour and milk a little at a time. Whisk the egg whites until stiff and lightly fold into the mixture. Put into the basin. Butter a piece of greaseproof paper and make a pleat in it. Secure it over the basin and tie with string. Steam for 1½ hours. Turn out on to a warm plate and serve at once, with sugar.

BAKED GINGER FRUIT PUDDING WITH SYRUP SAUCE

4 oz butter
4 oz castor sugar
2 eggs
2 tablespoons milk
4 oz self-raising flour
Pinch of salt
½ level teaspoon ground ginger
1 oz stem or crystallised

ginger (chopped)
3 oz sultanas

Sauce:
6 rounded tablespoons golden syrup
1 tablespoon lemon juice

Cream butter, add sugar and beat together until light and fluffy. Beat in eggs, 1 at a time, with a little of the flour. Add milk. Sieve in remaining flour, with the salt and ground ginger. Add chopped ginger and sultanas, and fold into mixture lightly until well mixed. Turn mixture into a well-buttered 2-pint ovenproof dish and bake in a moderate oven, 350°F (Gas Mark 4) for about an hour. To make sauce, heat together the syrup and lemon juice, stirring. Turn out pudding, and serve with sauce.

SPICED ORANGE PUDDING

3 oz butter
2 oz soft brown sugar
Grated zest of 1 orange
3 oz black treacle
1 large egg

6 oz self-raising flour
1 teaspoon ground cinnamon
1½ oz chopped glacé cherries
2 oz seeded raisins or chopped dates

Grease 1½-pint pudding basin and line bottom with a circle of greased paper. Cream butter, sugar and orange zest until light and fluffy. Beat in treacle. Whisk egg and add gradually. Stir in sifted flour and cinnamon and lastly add fruit. Turn into pudding basin, cover with foil and steam 1½ to 1¾ hours. Turn out and serve with orange sauce.
Orange Sauce – Make up the juice of 2 oranges to ½ pint with water. Blend a little of this with 1 level tablespoon of cornflour and stir this into heated juice. Bring to boil, stirring. Sweeten to taste.

OLD-FASHIONED RHUBARB PUDDING

1 oz butter
Brown sugar

Suet Crust:
8 oz self-raising flour
1 teaspoon salt
3 oz suet
¼ pint water

Filling:
1½ lb young rhubarb
1 oz chopped candied peel
2 oz currants
Grated rind and juice of
½ lemon
4 oz sugar
Pinch of cinnamon
½ teacup water

Butter 2-pint pudding basin thickly and sprinkle plentifully with brown sugar. Make suet crust by sieving together flour and salt and working in suet and water. Knead pastry until smooth and cut off one-third pastry for lid. Line the basin with suet crust. Cut rhubarb into 1 inch pieces and put half into the basin. Sprinkle over peel, currants, lemon rind and juice, half the sugar, and the cinnamon. Add the rest of the rhubarb and sugar, and pour in water. Cover with suet crust lid, and a greased paper on top. Bake at 350°F (Gas Mark 4) for 1¼ hours. Turn out to serve, with cream or egg custard.

GREAT GRANDMA'S STIR-IN PUDDING

1 lb self-raising flour
7 oz lard
½ teaspoon salt

Rub together to fine crumbs
and add ½ lb sugar

Stir in prepared gooseberries, chopped apple, halved plums or chopped rhubarb. Mix with sufficient milk and water to make a soft dough which will drop easily but cleanly into a greased basin. Cover with butter paper and then foil. Steam 2 hours. Serve with fresh cream or smooth, creamy custard.

This is an old Dorset recipe, handed down from generation to generation; very adaptable and useful.

GINGER FRUIT PUDDING

8 oz self-raising flour
½ level teaspoon salt
2 rounded teaspoons ginger
4 oz butter or margarine
3 oz soft brown sugar

4 oz mixed dried fruit
2 large eggs, beaten
Approximately 6 tablespoons
milk to mix

Sift together dry ingredients, rub in fat, add sugar and fruit, then stirring briskly, mix to a soft dropping consistency with the beaten eggs and milk. Turn into a very well-greased fluted mould. Cover with greaseproof paper or aluminium foil, and steam steadily for 1½ hours. Turn out on to a warm dish and serve with Marmalade Sauce.

Marmalade Sauce – Blend 4 tablespoons marmalade with 2 tablespoons water in a saucepan. Heat gently until boiling.

BLACKCURRANT JAM PUDDING

6 oz self-raising flour
3 oz butter or margarine
2 oz soft white breadcrumbs
2 oz castor sugar
1 level teaspoon salt

2 tablespoons blackcurrant
jam
2 eggs, well beaten
2 tablespoons milk

Rub fat into flour, then add breadcrumbs, sugar and salt. Stir in the jam and eggs, then mix to a slack consistency with the milk. Well-grease a pudding basin or mould, put a little jam in the bottom, then fill with the pudding mixture. Cover with greased paper or aluminium foil, and steam for 1½ hours. Turn out and serve warm with additional jam and sour cream, sweetened to taste with icing sugar and sprinkled with nutmeg.

SYRUP SPONGE PUDDING

4 oz butter or margarine
4 oz sugar
4 level tablespoons golden
syrup

2 standard eggs
6 tablespoons milk
8 oz self-raising flour
Pinch of salt

Cream fat, sugar and 2 tablespoons syrup till light and fluffy. Beat in eggs, one at a time, then fold in sifted dry ingredients alternatively with the milk, to make a fairly slack mixture. Well-grease a 2 pint fancy mould or pudding basin and pour in remaining syrup. Top with pudding mixture, spread evenly, then hollow out centre slightly. Cover with aluminium foil or with 2 sheets of greased greaseproof paper. Steam for 2 hours. Turn out on to a warm dish.

APPLE SUET ROLL

Sift 8 oz self-raising flour, a pinch of salt and a pinch of mixed spice into a bowl and stir in 4 oz shredded suet. Mix well and add enough cold water gradually to form a pliable dough. Roll out ⅛ inch thick into an oblong. Peel, core and chop 1 large cooking apple and put on pastry, leaving 1 inch uncovered at each side. Sprinkle with 2 oz cleaned currants, 2 oz soft brown sugar, grated rind of 1 lemon and 2 tablespoons golden syrup. Roll up pastry and tie in a piece of clean cloth, securing firmly. Put into top of steamer or into a large pan of boiling water, and cook for 2 hours.

BAKEWELL PUDDING

Yolks of 5 eggs
Whites of 3 eggs
6 oz castor sugar

4 oz butter
Almond essence
Strawberry jam

Line flan ring or baking tin with puff pastry, spread with jam. Melt together butter and sugar, mix in egg yolks and whites and essence, bake in hot oven, 350°F (Gas Mark 4) for 25 minutes.

The first Bakewell Pudding was the result of a misunderstanding between the mistress of the Rutland Arms Inn, Mrs Greaves, and her cook. Mrs Greaves was the wife of William Greaves, who kept the inn in the coaching days of the last century. On a day when important visitors were expected Mrs Greaves instructed her cook how she wanted the pastry made for the strawberry tart; the egg mixture was to be mixed into the pastry. The cook misunderstood her mistress and poured it on top of the jam and what should have been a tart went to the table as a pudding. When the guests complimented Mrs Greaves on her pudding she was mystified and questioned her cook who confessed what she had done. Mrs Greaves' very words to her cook were 'Continue to make them in that way', and so they have been made for 100 years.

Mrs Burton, Kirk Langley, near Derby

GRANNY'S SIX CUP PUDDING

1 teacup flour
1 teacup sugar
1 teacup breadcrumbs
1 teacup grated suet (from the butcher if possible)

1 teacup currants
1 teacup raisins
2 large eggs
Allspice to taste
Candied peel if liked

Beat eggs. Sieve flour and spice, add dry ingredients together then eggs and mix well. Almost fill basins with mixture. Steam 3 hours. The longer the steaming the darker the pudding. These puddings can be reheated as desired.

Mrs Naylor's grannie came to Lancashire almost 100 years ago as a nurse maid. This recipe was used at the house where she was employed. She used it herself for Christmas puddings and Mrs Naylor prefers it for Christmas and usually makes about half a dozen.

Mrs Naylor, Cowpe, Rossendale

BROWN BREAD PUDDING

6 oz brown breadcrumbs
½ pint milk
3 oz butter
4 oz sugar
3 eggs

2 oz raisins (or chopped candied peel)
Grating of nutmeg
1 teaspoon cinnamon
Pinch of salt

Put breadcrumbs in a bowl and pour on hot milk. Add the spices, raisins, salt. Cream butter and sugar, and add the eggs one at a time. Gradually work in the breadcrumb mixture. Put into a well-buttered mould, cover with foil or buttered paper and steam for 2 hours. Serve with jam, fruit syrup or custard.

LEMON PUDDING

Take 4 oz each of breadcrumbs, suet, flour and sugar. Mix with this a teaspoon of baking powder, the grated rind and juice of 1 lemon, and

2 well-beaten eggs. Stir all well together, place in a buttered mould, and steam for 3 hours. Serve with any sweet sauce preferred. Tried with great success.

Mrs F. Arden, Swinton, Manchester, 1911

TREACLE PUDDING

2 teacups of flour, 2 teacups of breadcrumbs, 4 oz of beef suet, 1 teaspoon of ground ginger, 4 tablespoons of treacle, and a little milk. Chop the suet fine, then mix with the other dry ingredients. Put the treacle and milk in a basin, and stir until thoroughly mixed. Then pour into the dry ingredients, and mix well. Put into a greased basin, and steam about 3 hours. Serve with sweet sauce.

Miss Kathleen Brooks, Hove, 1911

SYRUP SPONGE

1 heaped breakfastcup flour	*2 eggs*
1 teacup sugar	*3 tablespoons syrup*
¼ lb butter	*A little milk*
2 tablespoons baking powder	

Butter a basin, and pour in the syrup. Mix flour and baking powder together, and rub in butter with hands till it has the appearance of breadcrumbs; add sugar. Well beat eggs and sufficient milk to make a nice consistency. Pour into basin, and steam for 3 hours.

1911

SUSSEX PLUM DUFF

1¼ cups pastry flour	*1 cup raisins*
⅔ cup suet	*1 cup currants*
⅔ cup brown sugar	*Pinch of mixed spice*
Milk to mix	

Chop the suet finely, then rub into the flour. Mix in the sugar, raisins, currants, and spice and mix to a stiff paste with a little milk. Put the paste into a floured cloth, tie up like a ball and drop into a pan of boiling water. Boil for 1½ hours.

CHOCOLATE CHIP SPONGE PUDDING

4 oz chocolate or chocolate
chips
4 oz margarine
4 oz castor sugar
2 eggs

8 oz plain flour
2 level teaspoons baking
powder
Milk to mix

If you are using block chocolate, use the plain variety, and cut it into neat pieces with a sharp knife before starting to make the pudding. Cream margarine and sugar and beat in each egg separately. Fold in sieved flour and baking powder, and add milk to give a soft dropping consistency (if liked, add a little orange or lemon essence too). Stir in chocolate, and put into a greased pudding basin or a fireproof oven dish. Steam for 1 hour, or bake at 425°F (Gas Mark 7) for 15 minutes, then lower heat to 375°F (Gas Mark 5) for 30 minutes. Serve with jam sauce or chocolate sauce.

SPICED APPLE AND RAISIN PUDDING

½ lb cooking apples
2 tablespoons water
12 oz self-raising flour
1 level teaspoon cinnamon
½ level teaspoon mixed spice
3 oz butter

1 oz walnuts
3 oz stoned raisins
4 oz soft brown sugar
2 eggs
4 tablespoons milk

Lightly grease a 1½ pint pudding mould or basin. Peel, core and slice apples and stew in water. Cool and sieve. Sieve flour, cinnamon and spice, rub in butter, and add chopped walnuts and raisins and sugar. Lightly beat eggs and fold into dry ingredients, together with apple purée. Blend well, adding enough milk to make a soft dropping consistency. Put into the mould and cover with greased greaseproof paper and foil. Steam for 2½ hours. Serve with a jam or honey sauce.

KISS ME QUICK PUDDING

2 eggs and their weight in
flour, sugar and butter

2 tablespoons raspberry jam
1 small teaspoon soda (bicarb)

All beaten up. Steam it 1 hour and ½.

Mrs Garden, 1847

MRS TOWNLEY'S FULBOURN APPLE PUDDING

Peel 2 dozen russetts, remove the cores and cut them in slices. Put them into a deep saucepan with 4 oz butter, the rind of 2 lemons, 12 oz pounded sugar and 1 lb apricot jam. Toss the whole over a slow stove fire until the apples begin to dissolve and then set them aside to cool. Next, line a good-sized basin with some light-made suet paste. Fill this with the prepared apples – place a covering of paste on the top and fasten it down securely and steam it for about 2 hours. It may also be served up with some warm apricot jam poured over it. This apple preparation is also best for apple Charlottes or for apples served with rice, or whipped cream.

Mrs Garden, 1847

DRIPPING PUDDINGS

The weight of 3 eggs in their shells in dripping, $\frac{1}{2}$ teacup currants, tablespoon powdered sugar, flour to thicken. Beat up the 3 eggs, add the sugar and currants also the dripping (melted if too hard); beat up all together, thickening it with flour, but do not make it too stiff or they will not be light. Bake in small tins.

Mrs Garden, 1847

MANOR HOUSE MARROW PUDDING

Take 1 pint of breadcrumbs, $\frac{1}{2}$ pint of currants, $\frac{1}{2}$ lb of raisins, lemon and orange peel, $\frac{1}{2}$ lb suet cut very fine – the marrow out of a round of beef bone is the best if you have it. Mix all together then take a small piece of puff paste and line the dish you intend to bake it in with the paste. Fill the dish half full of the mixture. Take 6 eggs beaten well, as much sugar as will sweeten to your taste, 1 quart of new milk and mix with the eggs, nutmeg according to fancy. Put in $\frac{1}{2}$ glass of brandy. Pour this custard in the dish with the other mixtures. It will take $1\frac{1}{4}$ hours to bake. From the Manor House, Brentwood.

Mrs Garden, 1847

BAKED APPLE PUDDING

Take 6 apples cut small and simmer them in a pan with lemon peel, lump sugar and cinnamon and cloves according to your taste. Boil a lemon whole till quite soft, beat it up and mix it with the apples. Take 6 yolks and 4 whites of eggs, beat them up and when the apples are quite cold, stir them together. Then have it baked with a paste round it. Strew almonds on the top. This recipe, and variations on it, appear in a number of old manuscript books, but Mrs Garden's version is the easiest and clearest. Possibly it was copied from a popular book or magazine of the period.

Mrs Garden, 1847

1898 CUP PUDDING

1 *breakfastcup flour*
½ *cup sugar*
1 *teaspoon baking powder*
1 *oz lard*

1 *oz butter*
1 *egg*
A little milk

Butter basin and fill half full of jam. Put in mixture and steam for 2 hours.
Miss Jeffrey, Hambledon, Hants.

1898 JAM SPONGE

2 eggs, their weight in flour and butter, the weight of one in sugar; 3 tablespoons strawberry jam. Mix altogether. Butter a basin well and fill it 3 parts full. Steam it for 2 hours.

Miss Jeffrey, Hambledon, Hants

1898 TREACLE SPONGE

½ *lb treacle*
1 *teacup milk*
¾ *lb flour*

2 *oz suet*
2 *teaspoons baking powder*

Warm milk and treacle. Boil 3 hours.   *Miss Jeffrey, Hambledon, Hants*

COTTAGE PUDDING

2½ *oz shredded suet*
8 *oz flour*
4 *oz stoned raisins*
4 *oz sugar*
1 *egg*

4 *tablespoons milk*
½ *tablespoon cream of tartar*
¼ *teaspoon bicarbonate of soda*
Pinch of salt

Mix the suet, flour, raisins, sugar, cream of tartar and salt together. Dissolve the soda in the milk, add it to the well-beaten egg, mix well, and stir into the dry ingredients. The mixture must be rather stiff, but at the same time, thoroughly moistened. Turn into a greased Yorkshire pudding tin, and bake in a moderate oven from 30 to 40 minutes. Cut the pudding into squares, and serve, after dusting it over with white sugar.

GERMAN PUDDING

1 *lb flour*
½ *lb golden syrup*
½ *lb suet*
1 *oz sugar*

½ *oz spice*
½ *oz ground ginger*
Pinch of salt

Mix the syrup with a little milk slightly warmed. Mix all together, put into a greased basin, tie down and boil 3½ hours.

Lewis' Mother's Cookbook, Mary Horrell, Exeter

HIGH CHURCH PUDDING

Take ½ lb fine flour and nearly ½ lb chopped suet, 1 teacup of jam, 1 of milk, 1 teaspoon of bicarbonate of soda. Mix together, put in a buttered basin and tie loosely, and boil slowly 2 hours as the pudding will swell Serve with wine sauce.

Lewis' Mother's Cookbook, Mary Horrell, Exeter

PRUSSIAN PUDDING

Stew very slowly until quite dry and tender 3 oz of well-washed rice in rather more than a pint of milk. Let it cool a little, then mix it with 3 oz of finely rolled and rubbed suet. Add a little finely shredded candied peel, 3 oz of raisins or sultanas carefully picked over, and a couple of well-beaten eggs. Boil in a well-greased basin for 2 hours. Serve with custard sauce.

Lewis' Mother's Cookbook, Mary Horrell, Exeter

SPICED HONEY PUDDING

Boil ¾ pint milk and stir in 2 oz semolina. Cook for a few minutes, stirring all the time, then pour into a basin. To this add 4 oz honey, 4 oz bread-crumbs, the juice and grated rind of a lemon, 1 teaspoon ground ginger, 4 egg yolks and 2 oz butter. Beat well, then fold in well-beaten whites of 3 eggs. Put in a buttered dish and steam for an hour. Serve with melted redcurrant jelly.

BOILED BATTER PUDDING

Take a quart of milk, beat up the yolks of 6 eggs, and the whites of 3, and mix them with a ¼ pint of milk. Then take 6 spoonfuls of flour, a teaspoon of salt, and 1 of ginger. Put to these the remainder of the milk, mix all well together, put into your cloth, and boil it 1¼ hours. Pour melted butter over it when you serve it up. A batter pudding may be made without eggs, in which case proceed thus: take a quart of milk, mix 6 spoonfuls of flour with a little of the milk first, a teaspoon of salt, 2 of beaten ginger, and 2 of the tincture of saffron. Then mix all together, and boil it an hour.

Thomas Train, Gateshead, 1812

JEAN'S STEAMED PUDDING

2 oz breadcrumbs
2 oz castor sugar
2 oz suet
2 tablespoons golden syrup

1 egg
Milk mixed with small
½ teaspoon bicarbonate of soda
Add ginger if liked

Pouring mixture. Steam for 1½–2 hours.

Pat Smith, Keynsham, Somerset

DATE PUDDING

¾ cup plain flour
1 teaspoon bicarbonate soda
¾ cup boiling milk
1 tablespoon sugar or golden syrup

¼ lb dates or other dried fruit
1 tablespoon fat (suet, lard, margarine or dripping)
Small teaspoon vanilla essence

Put sugar, fat, soda, dates in greased basin, pour over boiling milk, quickly stir in flour, add essence. Mix well. Steam at once for 1 hour or a little less.

NEWCASTLE PUDDING

2 oz butter
2 oz castor sugar
3 oz flour
¾ teaspoon baking powder

2 eggs
1 teaspoon vanilla essence
4 oz glacé cherries

Beat butter and sugar to a cream. Sift flour with baking powder, and add flour and eggs alternately. Beat well and add essence. Grease a mould and decorate with halved cherries. Pour in mixture and steam 1¼ hours. Pour *Jam Sauce* round dish. Make this by boiling 2 tablespoons raspberry jam and 2 oz sugar with 1 gill water. Add ½ teaspoon arrowroot mixed with a little water. Bring to the boil and serve.

GYPSY PUDDING

12 oz shredded suet
1 lb currants
1 lb raisins
1 lb breadcrumbs
1 lb sugar
8 oz mixed peel
8 oz apples
8 oz flour

8 oz grated carrots
4 oz chopped blanched almonds
6 eggs
½ oz mixed spice
1 teaspoon baking powder
1 teaspoon vanilla essence

Add a silver thimble for the old maid, a button for the old bachelor, a nut for wealth, a ring for marriage, and a sixpence for good luck. Steam for 6 hours when made and 3 hours more when wanted. Will keep for months if well steamed at making.

WELCOME GUEST PUDDING

1½ oz almonds
2 oz shredded suet
4 oz breadcrumbs
2 oz sugar

1½ oz candied lemon peel
1 gill milk
2 eggs
1 teaspoon vanilla essence

Blanch the almonds and chop roughly. Mix the suet, breadcrumbs, sugar and peel. Beat together the milk, eggs and essence, and mix into dry ingredients. Pour into greased basin, cover with greased paper and steam for 1 hour 20 minutes.

SOUTHPORT PUDDING

6 oz apples (weighed after peeling)
6 oz breadcrumbs
3 oz suet

6 oz brown sugar
Good pinch of nutmeg
1 oz candied peel
2 eggs

Grate the apples and mix with breadcrumbs, suet, sugar, nutmeg and peel. Mix with beaten eggs and pour into a greased basin. Steam for 2 hours. Serve with a sweetened apple sauce flavoured with cloves.

APPLE DUMPLINGS

8 oz flour
4 oz suet
1 level teaspoon salt
2 level teaspoons baking powder

1 gill water
3 lb Bramley's Seedling apples
3 oz sugar

Sift flour and baking powder, add salt, mix in suet. Mix to a soft dough with water. Divide pastry in 2 pieces of ⅓ and ⅔. Grease a 2 pint basin, line it with ⅔ of the suet crust. Peel, core and slice the apples. Put half the apples into the lined basin, add the sugar then the rest of the apple. Cover the pudding with the remaining ⅓ of the suet crust and seal edges. Cover basin with greased greaseproof paper or kitchen foil. Steam for 2 to 3 hours until fruit and pastry are cooked. Turn out and serve very hot.

FRUIT DUMPLINGS

Three-quarters fill a small basin or stone jam jar with any fresh fruit.
Sprinkle with sugar, cover with saucer. Place in a large saucepan with
water coming half-way up basin. Cover, boil till fruit is soft.

Rub ½ teaspoon butter or margarine into 2 tablespoons self-raising
flour and a pinch of salt. Mix quickly with water to soft dough, divide into
4, drop on top of fruit. Cover closely. Simmer for 10–15 minutes. Serve
straight from basin.

Mrs L. Ward, London

QUICK FRUIT DUMPLINGS

2 cups flour
2 teaspoons baking powder
½ teaspoon salt
1 tablespoon sugar

1 cup milk
2 tablespoons fat
Large bottle cherries or
blackberries

Rub fat into flour and other dry ingredients and make into very soft dough
with milk. Bring the fruit and juice to boil, using pan that has tight lid.
When boiling, drop dumpling mixture by tablespoons on to fruit, cover at
once, very tightly, cook without raising lid 15 minutes. Serve hot.

CLOOTIE DUMPLING (1)

3 oz plain flour
3 oz breadcrumbs
3 oz chopped suet
2 oz sugar
1 tablespoon golden syrup
¾ cup milk or sour milk

1 teaspoon ground cinnamon
1 teaspoon ground nutmeg
2 oz currants
2 oz sultanas
1 level teaspoon bicarbonate
of soda

When mixed, tie in a cloth. Boil for at least 2 hours. Serve with sauce or
custard. This is from a farmer's widow with many grandchildren, who still
rears calves for her son.

Mrs Corrie, Burnside of Auchengool, Kirkcudbright

CLOOTIE DUMPLING (2)

4 teacups flour
1½ teaspoons baking powder
2 teaspoons cinnamon
1 teaspoon mixed spice
¼ lb chopped suet

1 cup sugar
½ lb raisins (blue)
½ lb sultanas
¼ teaspoon salt
(Peel if desired)

Mix dry ingredients, add fruit and enough milk to mix to fairly stiff consistency. Have pot boiling with a plate on the bottom. Dip cloth in boiling water. Sprinkle cloth with flour; shape dumpling into round on cloth and tie securely. Put into boiling water and make sure water does *not* cover dumpling. Keep at boiling point for $3\frac{1}{2}$–4 hours.

A very old recipe – can be eaten hot as a pudding or sliced cold and fried with bacon. Mrs Usher says she finds this 'disastrous for one's figure, but very useful for filling the bottomless holes inside our seven grandchildren'.

Mrs Antonia Usher, Argyll

FLUFFY BRANDY SAUCE

1 egg separated
4 oz icing sugar

$\frac{1}{4}$ pint whipped double cream
3 tablespoons brandy

Beat the egg white until it is foamy. Add 2 oz of the icing sugar, a little at a time, beating well after each addition until the mixture is stiff enough to stand up in peaks. In a second bowl, beat the egg yolk and remaining 2 oz sugar until the mixture thickens. Fold into the egg white and sugar mixture together with the whipped cream and brandy.

This sauce can be made in advance and kept in the refrigerator until needed. It is good with rich fruit puddings.

SPICED APPLE SAUCE

1 lb cooking apples
4 oz granulated sugar
2 tablespoons water

$\frac{1}{4}$ teaspoon cinnamon
$\frac{1}{8}$ teaspoon grated nutmeg

Wash, core and peel apples. Cut into quarters, and place in a medium-sized saucepan with granulated sugar, water, cinnamon and nutmeg. Simmer gently for 20 to 25 minutes, stirring occasionally. Serve with light fruit puddings.

2 Pies and Tarts

'Miss Bates, let Emma help you to a little bit of tart – a very little bit. Ours are all apple tarts. You need not be afraid of unwholesome preserves here. I do not advise the custard.'

'Emma', Jane Austen

KENTISH APPLE TART

Grate 2 large cooking apples in basin, add 3 oz sugar, 1 beaten egg, 2 oz butter, rind and juice of lemon. Mix well. Pour into pastry case and bake about ½ hour in quick oven.

Mrs Padgham, Minehead, Somerset

NORFOLK APPLE PIE

Roll out 12 oz short pastry and line a deep pie plate or an 8 inch sandwich tin with half of it.

2 lb cooking apples
Small knob of butter
1 tablespoon granulated sugar

2 tablespoons orange
marmalade
1 tablespoon cleaned currants

Peel, core and slice the apples and cook them without any water, adding the small knob of butter to prevent burning. When they are soft, stir in the sugar and beat them to a pulp. Pour half of this into the pastry case, spread over the marmalade, and sprinkle on the currants. Put the remaining apple pulp on the top. Make a lid from the other piece of pastry and put on top. Trim and decorate the edges. Bake in a hot oven, 400°F (Gas Mark 6) for about 15 minutes, then reduce heat to 350°F (Gas Mark 4) for a further 20–25 minutes. Dredge the top with castor sugar and serve hot with custard or cream.

BLACKBERRY PIE

1½ lb large ripe blackberries
2 tablespoons butter
1 lb sugar

4 tablespoons cornflour
8 oz short pastry

Butter a deep pie dish and put in 1 lb of blackberries. Dot with butter and stir in 6 oz sugar. Cook remaining blackberries with the rest of the sugar and very little water until soft, and put through a sieve. Thicken with cornflour blended with 6 tablespoons water. Pour over the raw berries and cover with pastry. Bake at 400°F (Gas Mark 6) until lightly brown, then reduce heat to 350°F (Gas Mark 4) and cook for 30 minutes. Serve cool with cream.

FEN COUNTRY APPLE CAKE

1½ lb cooking apples, peeled,
cored and sliced
Juice of ½ lemon
1 oz butter
2 oz castor sugar
2 rounded tablespoons
semolina

6-8 oz short pastry or rough
puff pastry
1 oz currants, washed and
dried
3 level tablespoons black
treacle

Put apples, lemon juice and butter into a pan, cover, then simmer slowly till soft and pulpy. Add sugar and semolina, bring very slowly to the boil, then cook gently for 5 to 7 minutes or till mixture has thickened. Remove from heat and leave till completely cold.

Divide pastry in two. Roll out 1 portion and with it line a 7–8 inch heatproof plate. Spread with half apple filling to within ½ inch of edges, sprinkle with currants and add treacle then top with remaining filling. Roll out rest of pastry into an 8–9 inch round, moisten edges with water and cover pie. Press edges well together to seal and knock up with the back of a knife. Brush top with beaten egg or milk then bake towards top of a hot oven, 425°F (Gas Mark 7) for 25–30 minutes or till pale gold.

RAISIN PASTRY

12 oz short pastry
2 level tablespoons oatmeal

2 tablespoons black treacle
3 oz raisins

Roll out the pastry thinly and use half to line 1 inch plate. Cover with the oatmeal and pour on the treacle. Sprinkle the raisins evenly over the tart. Moisten the edges of the tart with water and cover with the rest of the pastry. Press edges together to seal, and trim off surplus pastry. Flute the edges. Bake in a hot oven, 425°F (Gas Mark 7) for 20–30 minutes. Serve hot or cold.

ELDERBERRY PIE

1 lb elderberries (use ripe elderberries, stripped from stalks)
1 tablespoon golden syrup

Warm water
2 or 3 cloves
½ lb pastry

Nearly fill pie-dish with berries, add cloves. Sweeten with syrup. Pour over 2 or more tablespoons water according to size of pie. Cover with pastry. Bake in brisk oven till crust is browned. Then lower heat and allow fruit to simmer for a further 10–15 minutes.

PEACH PIE

Flaky pastry
1 lb fresh peaches or large can peach halves

4 oz ground almonds
4 oz icing sugar
3 eggs

Line a pie plate with pastry. Arrange peach halves (strain if using canned). Add almonds and icing sugar to the well-beaten eggs and pour over the peaches. Bake in a moderate oven until brown.

FRUIT AND ALMOND TART

8 oz plain flour
1 teaspoon cinnamon
2 oz castor sugar
4 oz lard
1 egg yolk
2 tablespoons cold water

4 egg whites
6 oz castor sugar
4 oz ground almonds
1½ lb cooked fruit (plums, gooseberries, rhubarb)

Sift flour with a pinch of salt, cinnamon and 2 oz castor sugar, and rub in lard until mixture is like fine breadcrumbs. Beat egg yolk with water and use to make a stiff dough; leave in cold place for 15 minutes. Whisk egg whites until stiff and fold in sugar and ground almonds. Roll out pastry and line 9 inch flan ring. Spread egg mixture in pastry case and arrange well-drained fruit over filling. Bake at 400°F (Gas Mark 6) for 10 minutes, then at 350°F (Gas Mark 4) for 35 minutes. This is a party pie which is particularly good with early rhubarb or cooked dried apricots.

RASPBERRY PIE

Lay into a tart dish a border of puff paste and 1½ pints of fresh raspberries well mixed with 3 oz sugar. Beat thoroughly 3 large eggs with 3 oz more sugar and pour over the fruit. Bake the pudding 25–30 minutes in a moderate oven 350°F (Gas Mark 4).

MRS C'S SPECIAL FLAN

1 × 8 inch flan case	*4 oz currants*
2 oz castor sugar	*1 oz glacé cherries*
2 oz butter	*½ teaspoon mixed spice*
4 eggs	*2 drops vanilla essence*
4 oz sultanas	*1 wineglass sherry*

The pastry case should be about 2 inches deep. Bake the flan case until it is just set but not coloured. Beat together butter and sugar, the egg yolks, and 2 of the egg whites. Add the sultanas and currants, cherries, spice, essence and sherry. Whip the remaining egg whites until very stiff and fold in carefully. Pour into the pastry case. Bake at 350°F (Gas Mark 4) for about 25 minutes until set and golden brown. Serve with cream. It makes a change from mince pies.

AUNT LUCY'S OPEN APPLE TART

2 oz butter	*Almonds and raisins, if liked*
1 cup sugar	*Pastry*
1 good-sized lemon	*1 egg*
1 large apple	

Melt butter, stir in sugar and beaten egg. Add finely chopped apple, the grated rind and juice of the lemon and almonds and raisins if liked (but these are only for festive occasions). Stir all ingredients well together. Line a pie-dish with sweet pastry. Pour in the mixture and bake.

STRAWBERRY FLAN

4 oz plain flour	*2 oz castor sugar*
Pinch of salt	*1 lb strawberries*
Yolk of 1 large egg	*6 tablespoons raspberry*
2 oz butter	*jelly or jam*

Sieve flour and salt on to pastry board, and shape into a circle. In the centre of the circle, put the egg yolk, sugar and butter, and use the tips of the fingers to pinch these ingredients together. Gradually work in the flour, using a palette knife to push in the flour from the outside ring. When the dough is made, knead lightly until free of cracks. The mixture is soft and delicate but should not be made too dry with additional flour. Wrap the dough in greaseproof paper and leave to rest in a cool place for an hour before using. Roll mixture and put into a flan ring (handle it very carefully), and bake blind at 400°F (Gas Mark 6) for 30 minutes. Remove flan ring and allow pastry to finish until it is light golden in colour. Cool completely. Arrange strawberries in neat circles on pastry. Melt jam or jelly with 3 tablespoons water (sieve if jam is used) until a smooth syrup is achieved. Glaze the strawberries by spooning this syrup lightly over them, starting in the centre of the flan and working outwards, and being careful to avoid the pastry edge.

ALMOND FRUIT TART

½ lb plain flour	Filling:
Good pinch of salt	4 egg whites
1 teaspoon cinnamon	6 oz castor sugar
2 oz castor sugar	4 oz ground almonds
4 oz lard	1½ lb cooked fruit (plums,
1 egg yolk	gooseberries, rhubarb,
1-2 tablespoons cold water	apricots)

Sift flour, salt, cinnamon and sugar and rub in lard until the mixture resembles fine breadcrumbs. Beat egg yolk with a little cold water and use to form a firm dough. Allow to relax for 15 minutes.

Whisk egg whites until stiff and fold in sugar and ground almonds. Roll out the pastry to line a 9 inch flan ring and spread the egg mixture in the pastry case. Drain the fruit thoroughly and arrange over the filling. Bake at 400–425°F (Gas Mark 6–7) for about 10 minutes: then reduce temperature to 350°F (Gas Mark 4) and cook for a further 30–35 minutes until the pastry is browned.

RHUBARB AND ORANGE TART

For the flan:	1 teaspoon castor sugar
4 oz plain flour	Lemon juice
1 tablespoon cornflour	Pinch of salt
1¼ oz lard	Cold water to mix
1¼ oz margarine	1 egg yolk

Sieve the flour, cornflour and salt. Rub in the fats. Add the sugar, stir in the beaten egg yolk and a few drops of lemon juice. Mix to a stiff dough with cold water. Roll out thinly and line a large flan case with it.

For the filling:

1½ lb rhubarb
3 dessertspoons castor sugar

1 heaped teaspoon cornflour
A little boiling water
2 oranges

Wipe the rhubarb and cut into very small pieces. Keep the skin on unless it really is stringy and tough. Arrange in the pastry case in circles. You may have to pile it up a bit in the middle. Sprinkle with sugar. Now heat up the juice of the oranges with a little boiling water and a little sugar. Mix cornflour to a smooth paste with a little water and pour the boiling fruit juice over it, stirring constantly. Return to pan and stir till boiling. Pour over the rhubarb, covering it all if possible. Bake in a fairly hot oven for about 25 minutes.

ORANGE TART

½ pint milk
2 eggs
1 tablespoon flour
1 dessertspoon cornflour
2 tablespoons sugar

2 or 3 oranges
2 tablespoons marmalade
A few drops rum essence or
1 dessertspoon rum (optional)
Flaky pastry

Bring the milk to the boil. Meanwhile separate the egg yolks from the whites. Mix the egg yolks with the flours and sugar, blend thoroughly. Slowly add the boiled milk. Return to the saucepan over a low heat, stirring all the time until the mixture thickens. Remove from heat. Add the grated rind of 1 orange and stir in the marmalade. Leave to cool. Add the rum or essence and fold in the stiffly beaten egg whites.

Have ready the pastry case on a plate, fill with orange cream and cover with thinly sliced orange. (I have seen it with the peel left on – although it looks prettier that way, it is also more indigestible, so I prefer to peel the oranges before slicing.) Bake in a moderate oven, 350°F (Gas Mark 4) for 35–40 minutes.

KATIE'S TART

Puff or flaky pastry
3 egg yolks
2 oz sugar
1 tablespoon flour
½ pint milk, boiled

Topping:
10 oz castor sugar
5 tablespoons water
6 oz soaked desiccated
coconut

Thoroughly blend the egg yolks with the sugar and flour. Slowly add the boiled milk. Return to the saucepan over a low heat, stirring constantly until the mixture thickens. Do not allow to boil. Allow to cool.

Meanwhile, line a pie plate with the pastry. Prepare the topping by melting the sugar with the water in a saucepan over a low flame. Stir until it begins to thicken. Add the strained coconut and boil until transparent. Pour the filling into the pastry case and cover with the coconut topping. Bake in a moderate oven until the pastry is cooked and the top brown.

MINCEMEAT AND APPLE TART

Pastry:
6 oz flour
¼ teaspoon salt
1 level dessertspoon castor sugar
4 oz butter or margarine
1 egg yolk

Filling:
Mincemeat
Apple purée
Juice of 1 orange
2 oz ground almonds

Sieve the flour, salt and sugar together. Rub in the fat very lightly. Mix to a stiff dough with the egg yolk. Leave in a cool place for at least an hour. Knead well, roll out thinly and line a shallow pie-dish. Prick well. Fill this case with alternate layers of mincemeat and apple purée. Pour over the orange juice and cover with ground almonds. Bake in a moderate oven, 350°F (Gas Mark 4) for 35–40 minutes.

NORFOLK TREACLE TART

Line a 9 inch pie plate with short pastry. Take 1 egg, 2 tablespoons of golden syrup, the rind and juice of half a lemon. Beat the egg. Warm the syrup and beat the egg into it. Stir in the lemon-rind and juice. Pour into the pastry case and bake at 375°F (Gas Mark 5) for about 35 minutes. Eat cold, when the mixture will have set like a jelly.

TREACLE CUSTARD PIE

6 oz short pastry
1 level dessertspoon semolina or rolled oats
1 level tablespoon black treacle
½ pint milk
2 eggs
1 oz castor sugar

Roll out pastry and with it line a 7–8 inch heatproof pie plate. Sprinkle base with semolina or oats then pour in treacle. Combine milk and eggs and beat till well blended. Stir in sugar then pour custard into lined pie plate. Bake in the centre of the oven, at 450°F (Gas Mark 8) for 10 minutes, then at 325°F (Gas Mark 3) for 30 minutes or till firm to the touch. Serve warm or cold.

CINNAMON PLUM TART

4 oz butter
6 oz plain flour
10 oz castor sugar
1 egg yolk

1½ dessertspoons lemon juice
1½ lb plums
1 teaspoon cinnamon

Rub 3 oz butter into flour and stir in 3 oz castor sugar. Mix to a dough with egg yolk, 1 teaspoon lemon juice and 3 tablespoons iced water. Chill pastry well, then roll out to fit a 9 inch pie plate or sandwich tin, fluting the edges. Halve and stone plums and arrange in a pattern, cut side up all over the pastry. Mix together remaining sugar and cinnamon and sprinkle half on plums. Pour over remaining lemon juice and dot with remaining butter. Bake at 350°F (Gas Mark 4) for 40 minutes, then sprinkle with remaining cinnamon sugar. Serve warm or cold.

LEMON PIE

Short crust. Take slice of bread 1 inch thick, remove crusts, pour ¾ cup granulated sugar on it, and pour 1 breakfast cup of boiling water over it, the grated rind and juice of 1 lemon, 2 egg yolks, and beat all together, then boil for 2 or 3 minutes. Whip whites of eggs with a little sugar put on top of filling in open tart and brown under grill.

Mrs Beck, Felixstowe

SUFFOLK PIE

2 egg yolks
1 oz sugar
1½ gills milk
1 oz breadcrumbs
2 oz ground almonds

1 oz butter
Almond or vanilla essence
1 egg white
1 tablespoon raspberry jam

Make a custard by blending the egg yolks with the sugar and pouring the warm milk over, mixing well. Return to the pan and cook over gentle heat, stirring all the time, until the custard just coats the back of the spoon. Do not allow it to boil. Stir in the crumbs, almonds, butter and flavouring, then fold in the stiffly whisked egg white. Spread the jam over an 8 inch pastry case, pour in the filling and bake for 35–40 minutes in a fairly hot oven, 350°F (Gas Mark 4).

COUNTRY GOOSEBERRY AMBER PIE

1½ lb green gooseberries   1 oz butter
4 oz sugar   2 eggs

Sufficient short crust pastry rolled thinly to line a pie-dish or enamel plate. Have this ready and 'resting' in cool place while preparing and cooking the fruit, etc.

Prepare the fruit by topping and tailing and washing if necessary. Place them in a saucepan with ½ a teacup of water and cook until softened a little, then add sugar and let it dissolve. Continue simmering gently until fruit is pulped. Remove from stove. When fruit has cooled a little, beat in butter and egg *yolks* only. Fetch pastry case from the cool and fill it with the fruit and egg mix. Bake in good oven for 35–40 minutes until filling is 'setting' or firming to the touch. Beat whites of egg until stiff with, if liked, a little extra sugar. Spread over the pie and return to oven to colour and crisp just to brown.

LOUGHBOROUGH LEMON PIE or
GRANNY-KNOWS-BEST

1 egg   1 oz sugar
1 oz plain flour   Short crust pastry
½ pint milk   1 lemon (or orange or
¼ oz butter   equivalent pure lemon juice)

Make a thin sauce by blending the flour with the milk and sugar, then adding butter. If preferred the butter can be melted first, the flour and sugar stirred carefully into this and the milk gradually added to make smooth paste. Cook gently stirring all the time. Separate yolk from the egg white and beat the yolk with the lemon juice (and rind if whole fruit used – the rind improves flavour). Blend egg-lemon mixture with the sauce, being careful to see that the sauce is not too hot at the time. Pour into the pastry case. Beat egg white until very stiff and 'peaky' and cover top of pie with it. Bake in moderate oven until top is golden brown. Serve hot or cold with cream.

For using that odd scrap of left-over pastry to make an easy and yet 'special' pudding suitable for lunch or Sunday tea.

POULTON MORELLO CHERRY PIE

½ lb short pastry
¼ pint water
¾ pint milk
½ lb Morello cherries (other
varieties will do, or black
eating cherries)
½ teaspoon almond essence

2¼ level dessertspoons custard
powder
1-2 tablespoons sugar,
according to variety of cherry
¼ oz gelatine with
2 tablespoons cold water

Roll out the pastry thinly and line a pie plate. Trim the pastry so that it just overlaps the edge, double it under so that it rests on top of the plate's rim, then pinch into flutes. Prick pastry at base and sides with a fork and line it with a round of greased paper, and weigh it down with a few clean stones. Place to chill in a very cool place for ½ hour before cooking it in a hot oven.

When nearly cooked, remove the paper and weighting and return the case to a cooler oven for a while to dry off the pastry base. Then leave to get cold. Wash and stalk the cherries and stew until tender with the water with ¾ of the sugar or to taste. Then drain off juice, and measure it. Thicken the juice with cornflour allowing 1 level dessertspoon to ¼ pint juice. Cook this for 2 or 3 minutes and, when cool, turn it out into the pastry shell and let it set. Make a custard with the milk and custard powder and add the remainder of the sugar and the almond flavouring. Leave this until cold but stirring at frequent intervals. Stone ¼ pint of the cooked cherries and add it to the custard. Soften the gelatine in the cold water then dissolve it gently over a low heat and strain into the custard. Add more sugar or flavouring if required and, when it is beginning to set, turn it out into the pastry shell. When it is quite set, decorate pie with the remainder of the fruit. Serve with cream.

APRICOT PIE

Coddle 6 large apricots very tender. Break them very small, sweeten them to your taste. When they are cold add 6 eggs (only 2 whites) well beaten. Mix them well together with a pint of good cream. Lay a puff paste all over ye dish and pour in your ingredients. Bake it ½ an hour. Don't let the oven be too hot. When it is enough, throw a little fine sugar over it, and send it to the table hot.

Mrs Garden, 1847

41

BAKED APPLE DUMPLINGS

8 oz short crust pastry
4 small cooking apples
1 oz seeded raisins

¾ oz brown sugar
¾ oz butter
¼ teaspoon cinnamon

Make shortcrust pastry and roll out, cutting 4 circles round a saucer. Peel and core apples and put one in the centre of each piece of pastry. Fill centre of apples with mixture of raisins, sugar, butter and cinnamon. Enclose apples completely in pastry and invert on baking sheet. Brush pastry with egg or milk and bake at 425°F (Gas Mark 7) for 25 minutes. Sprinkle with castor sugar as they come out of the oven and serve hot or cold with cream. They are also very good served with heated sieved apricot jam, and make a pleasant variation of apple pie.

APPLE AND GINGER DUMPLINGS

Make 8 oz of your usual short crust pastry. Divide it into 4 equal pieces and roll out each to a round large enough to enclose a peeled and cored cooking apple (a Bramley Seedling, for preference). Place each apple on a piece of pastry. Drop a piece of crystallised ginger or ginger in syrup into each core cavity and fill up with demerara sugar. Wet a margin half-way round the inner rim of each piece of pastry, fold over and pinch the joins firmly together.

Place, join sides down, on a baking sheet and brush with milk. Form the rolled-out pastry trimmings into 'leaves', place them in position and brush them, too, with milk.

Bake for 10 minutes at 425°F (Gas Mark 7), then lower the heat to 350°F (Gas Mark 4) and bake for a further 30 minutes. Serve warm and pass the cream with the apples.

HEREFORD ORANGE AND APPLE DUMPLINGS

4 good cooking apples, peeled
and cored. Take care to keep
them whole, cover with water.
A few dates, raisins or
sultanas

1 medium egg
Cold water to mix
A little milk and sugar to
glaze
Grated rind from 1 large
orange

For Pastry:
8 oz plain flour or ½ plain and
½ self-raising flour
4 oz fat, either all lard or lard
and margarine mixed
1 teaspoon sugar

Orange sauce:
Juice of an orange
Water
1 heaped tablespoon sugar
1 level tablespoon cornflour

Make pastry by rubbing fat into flour until like breadcrumbs; then stir in the grated rind of the orange. Add sugar. Then beat egg with a little water and mix with rest to make a firm dough. Divide pastry into 4 and roll out each piece on floured board. Drain apples and fill with dried fruit. Mould pastry covers over each apple bringing any surplus up to top. Dampen inside and pinch well together, cutting off overflow to use for leaves for garnishing. Turn dumpling upside down and press gently but firmly on to a greased baking sheet. Arrange pastry leaves around top of dumpling. Brush with milk and press in a little sugar, taking care not to spill around bases. Put well down in oven and cook for 40–50 minutes or until apples are cooked inside, if this takes longer than 50 minutes reduce heat for last few minutes. Meanwhile make sauce. Using juice from the orange and enough water to make this up to $\frac{1}{2}$ pint, mix cornflour in a saucepan with a little of this liquid. Add sugar and rest of liquid and stir well. Cook gently over heat until boiling point is reached but taking care to stir all the time. Continue cooking for 1 minute. Pour into warmed sauceboat and serve with the dumplings.

D'ARCY APPLE CRISPS

6 oz short pastry
1 lb apples
6 tablespoons apricot jam

5 tablespoons soft breadcrumbs

Roll out the pastry and line a tin about 10 × 8 inches. Sprinkle with half the crumbs. Warm the jam slightly and spread half of it over the crumbs. Peel the apples and cut them in neat slices, and arrange them in lines on the pastry. Brush with remaining jam and scatter on the rest of the crumbs. Bake at 425°F (Gas Mark 7) for 20 minutes, and then at 350°F (Gas Mark 4) for 10 minutes. Serve hot or cold with cream. Rather crisp eating apples are nicest to use for this.

APRICOT TURNOVERS

8 oz plain flour
1 teaspoon salt
5 oz lard
3 dessertspoons cold water

2 oz sugar
2 breakfastcups cooked apricots

Sieve flour and salt together, cut in lard and add cold water a little at a time until the dough just holds in a ball. Roll out thinly and cut into 5 inch squares. Place a few apricots on each square. Moisten edges with cold water, fold to make a triangle and press edges with a fork. Bake at 375°F (Gas Mark 5) for 40 minutes. This mixture makes about 12 turnovers. These are a good variation on the usual apple pie, and are very easy to carry for a picnic.

APPLE TURNOVERS

12 oz short crust or flaky
pastry
1½ lb cooking apples

4 tablespoons brown sugar
1 oz raisins
2 oz butter

Roll out pastry and cut into 4 inch circles (cut round a saucer for the shape). Peel and slice apples and cook gently with sugar, raisins and butter until soft. If you like a pinch of cloves or cinnamon, add during the cooking. Put a spoonful of mixture on to half of each circle, fold over and press edges together, damping them a little first. Bake at 425°F (Gas Mark 7).

APPLE TREACLE SQUARES

Short crust pastry:
8 oz plain flour
4 oz butter or margarine
Pinch of salt
Water to mix

Apple filling:
1½ lb cooking apples
2 tablespoons black treacle
1 oz brown sugar
1 level teaspoon cinnamon

Place long strips of greased greaseproof paper along the length of the bottom of a 7 × 11 inch swiss roll rin. Let the paper come well over the shorter sides of the tin.

Sieve together the salt and the flour. Rub in the butter until the mixture resembles fine breadcrumbs. Sprinkle on the water and lightly mix with a round bladed knife until the pastry holds together. Turn on to a floured board and knead very lightly until smooth. Divide into 2 and roll each piece into an oblong shape to fit the tin. Line the tin with one half of the pastry and lightly prick with a fork.

Peel, core and slice the apples. Mix together the apple slices, black treacle, sugar and cinnamon and spread over the pastry. Moisten the edges of the pastry with water and top with the second piece of pastry. Press down gently along the edges to seal.

Bake in a hot oven at 425°F (Gas Mark 7) for 15 minutes, and then at 350°F (Gas Mark 4) for approximately 30 minutes, until the pie is evenly brown and the apple is tender.

Allow to cool slightly. Carefully lift the pie out of the tin by gently raising the greaseproof paper strips. Sieve the icing sugar over the top. Cut into squares and serve with brown sugar and fresh dairy cream. Makes 12 squares.

ALMOND TARTS

Line tart tins with pastry. Put spot jam in each. Beat 2 egg whites with 5 oz sugar. Add 4 oz ground almonds. Put spoonful in each case and bake in moderate oven.

BALMORAL TARTS

1 oz butter
1 oz castor sugar
1 egg
1 oz sponge cake crumbs

1 oz glacé cherries, peel, etc.
½ oz cornflour
A little lemon rind
A little lemon curd

Make flaky or short pastry. Line patty pans with very thin pastry and place a little lemon curd in each. Cream butter and sugar. Beat in egg yolk and a little lemon rind. Fold in crumbs, cornflour and fruit. Whisk egg white stiffly, fold into mixture. Place a little filling in each tart. Bake in a moderate oven, 375°F (Gas Mark 5) for 25 minutes.

RASPBERRY-CURRANT TARTS

Line some deep patty pans with short pastry, prick well with a fork and bake in a hot oven for 12 minutes or till golden. Leave to cool. In a saucepan, mix together ¼ lb raspberries, ½ lb red currants and 8 oz sugar, and stir over a low heat for 10 minutes. Mix together 2 tablespoons of cornflour and 2 tablespoons of cold water, stir into the fruit, and continue cooking till thick and clear. Chill well, and just before serving fill pastry cases and garnish with sweetened cream.

MRS GORONWY'S MARMALADE TART

2 oz butter
2 oz sugar
2 tablespoons marmalade

1 egg
Flaky or puff pastry

Line a dish with pastry. Cream together the butter, sugar, well-beaten egg and marmalade, and use as filling. Bake for a ½ hour in a warm oven.

OPEN TART

Make short pastry, roll out fairly thinly and put in round flat tin about 1½ inches deep. Put a layer of purée of prunes (stewed and sieved), a layer of apples cut in thin slices and arranged nicely in rings. Bake for about 30 minutes till apples are golden brown.

3 Hot Sweets

I've done it, said brave Mr Banting,
And so may each overfed Briton,
If he'd only adopt resolution severe
And avoid—if he would not grow fatter and fatter—
All bread, butter, sugar, milk, 'taters and beer.

William Banting published *A Letter on Corpulence addressed to the Public* in 1863, telling his own story. He had adopted a diet consisting mainly of meat, fish and fruit, giving up milk, butter, sugar and potatoes. He lost 2½ stone in nine months and gained better health than before. His name is still used as a slang term for slimming.

FLAMING PEARS

4 large pears
4 oz sugar

½ pint water
8 tablespoons brandy

Peel the pears, but leave on the stems. Put into a casserole and cover with the sugar and water. Cover and bake at 350°F (Gas Mark 4) for 45 minutes. Arrange pears on a serving dish, and pour a little of the syrup round them. Sprinkle each with a little sugar and the brandy, and set on fire at the table.

BAKED PEARS

2 lb cooking pears (or hard
eating pears)
4 oz castor sugar
½ pint cider

½ pint water
Shredded almonds
A twist of lemon peel

Peel the pears, leaving the stems on, and arrange them upright in a deep casserole. Sprinkle on sugar and pour over cider and water and add lemon peel. Cook at 300°F (Gas Mark 2) until pears are tender and can be pierced with a fork. Leave to cool in the juice, then reduce this juice until thick and syrupy. Spike with almonds and serve with thick cream. The pears may also be cooked in red wine. Quinces are excellent cooked this way in cider, using honey instead of sugar.

MRS BROWN'S PEARS IN WINE

2 lb firm eating pears
½ pint cheap red wine
4 oz brown sugar

1 teaspoon ground ginger
2 pinches saffron
1 tablespoon wine vinegar

Mix together wine, sugar, ginger, saffron and wine vinegar and simmer until the sugar melts. Peel the pears and cut in quarters or eighths. Poach in the sauce until tender. Drain off sauce and put pears in a serving dish. Thicken the sauce with a little cornflour or arrowroot and pour over the pears.

FANCY STEWED APPLES

Peel and core 7 or 8 apples, place them in a syrup and stew until soft, turning occasionally so they are cooked through. The syrup should be made of ½ lb castor sugar, the juice of 2 lemons and enough lemon rind to flavour simmered till thick. Dish the apples carefully so as to keep them whole. Colour the syrup with cochineal and pour around. Have ready some blanched sweet almonds. Stick the apples thickly with these, and on the top of each put a piece of redcurrant jelly.

Lewis' Mother's Cookbook, Mary Horrell, Exeter

APPLE CANDY CRUMBLE

1 lb peeled and sliced apples
½ pint water
4 oz plain flour

4 oz butter
8 oz sugar
1 teaspoon cinnamon

Put apples into a buttered baking dish. Pour over water. Rub together flour, butter, sugar and cinnamon till the mixture is like breadcrumbs. Pat down firmly on top of apples and bake at 350°F (Gas Mark 4) for 30 minutes until crust is brown. Serve warm with cream.

GOOSEBERRY TANSY

Simmer 1 lb gooseberries in 4 oz fresh butter until cooked. Stir in 2 beaten egg yolks and ¼ pint lightly whipped cream. Add 4 oz sugar and boil gently. Turn into dish and sprinkle with the juice of 1 lemon and a little sugar. Serve hot or cold.

APPLE CHARLOTTE (1)

Butter a pie-dish and coat with 1½ tablespoons of brown sugar mixed with a little ground cinnamon, or ground cloves, nutmeg or ginger. Line the dish with slices of bread and butter and fill it with peeled, cored and sliced apples. Sprinkle each layer with the chosen spice and another dessert-spoon of brown sugar. Warm ½ a cup of golden syrup with ½ a cup of water and pour it over the apples. Put another layer of bread and butter on top, sprinkle another tablespoon of sugar over it and dot with butter. Bake at 350°F (Gas Mark 4) for 45 minutes. Turn out and serve with cream.

APPLE CHARLOTTE (2)

2 lb apples (firm or soft as   *Bread and butter*
preferred)   *3 tablespoons brown sugar*
A little grated lemon rind   *3 tablespoons syrup*
¼ pint water

Stew the apples with the lemon rind and water until very soft. Butter a fireproof dish, and line the sides with bread and butter, buttered side inwards. Pour in the apple pulp and cover with buttered bread, buttered side uppermost. Dredge thickly with sugar, pour on the syrup, bake in a good oven, 400°F (Gas Mark 6) for ½ an hour.

GOOSEBERRY MARMALADE CHARLOTTE

3 slices bread, butter   *gooseberries*
and marmalade   *½ pint milk*
½ lb lightly stewed   *1 egg*

48

Remove crusts from bread, cut into fingers and line the base and sides of a pie-dish. Put the gooseberries (no juice) inside. Mix the milk and egg together and pour over the gooseberries. If time, leave for 30 minutes. Bake near the bottom of a moderately hot oven, 375°F (Gas Mark 5) for 1 hour.

SOMERSET LOGANBERRY AND APPLE CHARLOTTE

Basketful loganberries-
about ½ lb
3 large or 4 medium cooking
apples

2 oz butter
Saltspoon cinnamon
4 oz white breadcrumbs
4 oz demerara sugar

Peel core and slice thinly the apples. Wash loganberries if need be. Melt butter in pan; mix breadcrumbs with cinnamon and sugar and throw into hot butter. Sprinkle thin layer of well-stirred crumbs onto bottom of a lightly greased pie-dish (1½ pint size). Cover with a layer of apple, then a layer of crumbs. Do this twice. Cover with loganberries, then crumbs, apple and lastly crumbs, as thick a layer as possible. Bake in a gentle oven for about an hour until top is golden brown. If apple is not quite done, reduce heat and continue gently cooking until it is soft. Serve with cream or creamy custard.

This pudding can be made with blackberries or raspberries, whortle-berries or mulberries substituted for loganberries.

BLACKBERRY SPONGE

Small bowlful blackberries-
about ½ lb
3 oz butter
2 standard eggs

Wineglass milk
3 oz sugar
6 oz self-raising flour

Douse blackberries with cold water and quickly get out to drain off. Layer them in bottom of a pie-dish. Cover with a little of the sugar—1 heaped tablespoon. Cream the rest of the sugar with the butter, gradually add well-beaten eggs and milk. Fold sifted flour into this creamy mixture using metal spoon and flicking wrist right over quite awkwardly.

Spread soft mixture evenly over fruit and smooth off top with the back of the spoon. Bake in a moderately hot oven, 400°F (Gas Mark 6) for 40–45 minutes using lower shelf. Sponge will be well risen and golden brown. Serve with Cornish cream.

RASPBERRY OMELETTE

Clean and sugar a $\frac{1}{2}$ lb of fresh raspberries. Beat 4 egg yolks till pale lemon-coloured, and slowly add $1\frac{1}{2}$ oz of castor sugar and a $\frac{1}{2}$ teaspoon of grated lemon rind. Beat the egg whites with a pinch of salt till stiff peaks form and gently fold into yolk mixture. Melt butter in an omelette pan, pour in mixture and cook over a low heat with a lid until browned at the edges. Put in a moderate oven (350°F, Gas Mark 4) for 5 minutes till centre is well done. Drain fruit, place on $\frac{1}{2}$ the omelette, fold over and serve dusted with icing sugar.

1915 TREACLE SLIPS

4 oz of flour, a little salt, 1 egg, and $\frac{1}{2}$ a pint of milk. Sieve the flour and salt, break the egg into it, and beat well without letting it get lumpy. Add $\frac{1}{2}$ the milk, stirring it in gradually, and then beating with the back of a wooden spoon to put plenty of air into the mixture. Beat it until bubbles appear.

Add the rest of the milk, and stand the batter aside for $\frac{1}{2}$ hour if possible. Then fry it as for pancakes, only make them a shade thicker. As each one is cooked turn it on to a sugared paper, sprinkle with lemon-juice, and spread with golden syrup.

HONEY, NUT AND DATE PUFF

1 lb puff pastry
Castor sugar for dusting
4 oz chopped dates
1 heaped tablespoon flaked almonds
Finely grated rind of 1 orange

A little egg white
$\frac{1}{4}$ lb cream cheese
1 heaped tablespoon thick honey
2 teaspoons orange juice

Cut the pastry in half and roll out into 2 squares of equal size, and $\frac{1}{4}$ inch thick. Mix all the remaining ingredients except egg white and castor sugar, until smooth and thick. Put one square of pastry onto baking sheet and spread with nut and date mixture. Wet the surface of second square and with wet side downwards, press over mixture. Brush all over with egg white, dust with castor sugar. Bake at 375°F (Gas Mark 5) for 25–30 minutes until golden brown. Serve with custard or cream.

MIDFORD APPLE CAKE

4 peeled apples   2 eggs
3 oz butter   2 oz flour
¼ pint milk   3 tablespoons sugar

Slice apples and fry in hot butter. Mix milk, eggs and flour. Stir in apples and butter and bake for 20 minutes at 375°F (Gas Mark 5). Turn out, sprinkle with sugar, and brown in oven or under grill.

AUNT TOMMY'S ORANGE SWEET

5 oranges   3 eggs
3 oz castor sugar   1 tablespoon cornflour
1 pint milk   2 tablespoons icing sugar

Peel the oranges and cut them in thin slices. Put into a fireproof dish and scatter the sugar over the fruit. In a double saucepan, bring the milk to the boil. Pour a little milk on to the egg yolks and mix well. Return to the remaining milk, together with the cornflour mixed with a little water. Stir constantly until it thickens, and then pour over the fruit. Whisk the egg whites to stiff peaks. Fold in the icing sugar, and spread the mixture over the custard. Bake at 325°F (Gas Mark 3) for 15 minutes.

QUAKING PUDDING

Take a quart of cream, boil it and let it stand till almost cold; then beat up 4 eggs very fine, with 1½ spoons of flour: mix them well with your cream; add sugar and nutmeg to your palate. Tie it up close in a cloth well buttered. Let it boil an hour and then carefully turn it out. Pour over it melted butter.

Thomas Train, Gateshead 1812

BOILED RICE PUDDING WITH RAISINS

1 pint milk   2 oz sultanas or raisins
2 oz Carolina rice   Nutmeg
2 oz sugar

Add rice to the milk and bring to the boil. Add the sugar and dried fruit. Simmer for ½ hour stirring occasionally. Add grated nutmeg.

Mrs Biggar, Kirkcudbrightshire

CRUSTY PLUMS

Cut thick slices of bread and spread with butter and black treacle on one side. Press into this side stoned, raw half plums. Put a little butter and brown sugar into each half plum and place slices in a buttered fireproof dish. Cover with buttered paper and bake for 30 minutes in a moderate oven, 350°F (Gas Mark 4). Serve with cream.

RHUBARB TANSY

1 *lb rhubarb*	2 *egg yolks*
4 *oz butter*	$\frac{1}{4}$ *pint double cream*
2 *oz sugar*	2 *tablespoons lemon juice*

Prepare and chop the rhubarb into $1\frac{1}{2}$ ins. pieces. Simmer gently in the butter until cooked. Add the beaten egg yolks and the lightly whipped cream, sweeten to taste, then gently boil the mixture until it is just firm. Turn out at once on a serving dish. Sprinkle with lemon juice and a little castor sugar to taste. Serve hot or cold.

LEMON SPONGE

1 oz butter beat well with 3 oz sugar; add juice and rind of 1 lemon and yolk of egg; add 1 large tablespoon of flour and $\frac{1}{4}$ pint milk. Whisk white of egg and add last. Put in well-greased pie-dish; stand in pan of water. Bake at 400°F (Gas Mark 6) for 25 minutes.

Mrs Beck, Felixstowe

HOT STRAWBERRY PUDDING

Hull 2 lb strawberries and put them in a fireproof dish with 1 lb sugar and a pinch of cinnamon. Put in a very low oven until the sugar has melted, then drain off the syrup. Stir in 2 wineglasses of red wine, pour the liquid over the fruit and return to the oven until hot. Just before serving, add a dessertspoon of honey and a dessertspoon of lemon juice, and serve very hot with thick cream.

FRESH PLUM PUDDING

1 *egg*	*Sugar*
Butter	$\frac{1}{2}$ *lb small ripe plums*
Flour	*Soft brown sugar*

AUDLEY END SAUCE

2 oz cornflour
1 pint milk
2 oz butter
1½ oz sugar

1 egg
½ gill top milk or cream
1 tablespoon moist brown
sugar

Weigh the egg and weigh out the equivalent in butter, flour and sugar. Remove stones from plums and cut them in half. Cream butter and sugar, add beaten egg and flour. Spread a layer of this sponge mixture in a greased oven dish, add the plums face down and sprinkle lightly with sugar, then add the rest of the sponge mixture. Bake at 350°F (Gas Mark 4) for 30 minutes until golden and firm. Make the sauce by mixing cornflour with a little water then cooking gently for 5 minutes with the boiling milk, butter and sugar. Gradually whisk in the egg and top milk or cream. Put sauce into a buttered dish, sprinkle sugar on top and caramelise under a hot grill. Serve sauce either hot or cold.

VICTORIA PLUM SPONGE

1 lb Victoria plums, halved
and stoned
2-3 oz sugar
2 tablespoons water, or
1 lb 3 oz can plums, drained
1 oz hazelnuts, roasted and
husks removed

Sponge:
4 oz self-raising flour
1 level teaspoon baking
powder

4 oz softened butter
2 eggs

Topping:
2 oz plain flour
1 level teaspoon mixed spice
1 oz butter
2 oz demerara sugar
1 oz hazelnuts, roasted, husks
removed, roughly chopped
2 tablespoons plum jam,
warmed

Place plums, sugar, water and hazelnuts in a greased 2½ pint ovenproof dish, and add hazelnuts.

Sift flour and baking powder together. Add remaining sponge ingredients and beat for 2 minutes. Spoon mixture over plums and spread evenly. Bake at 375°F (Gas Mark 5) for 30–35 minutes until sponge is risen and golden.

Meanwhile prepare topping, sift flour and mixed spice together. Rub in butter and mix in sugar and nuts. Remove pudding from oven and quickly spread top of sponge with jam. Sprinkle topping evenly over sponge. Return pudding to oven for a further 10–15 minutes until topping is lightly browned. Serve hot with cream, custard or ice cream.

LEMON DREAM

2 oz butter
4 oz castor sugar
2 eggs

1 oz plain flour
1 lemon
¼ pint milk

Cream butter and sugar, and beat in egg yolks. Stir in flour and juice and grated rind of lemon. Add the milk (the mixture will look curdled). Whisk egg whites stiffly and fold in. Pour into well-buttered 1½ pint oven dish, stand in a shallow pan of warm water and bake at 350°F (Gas Mark 4) for 35 minutes. This gives a delectable lemon pudding with its own sauce underneath.

Loraine Honey, Harewood End

ORCHARD PUDDING

1 lb apples
¾ pint milk
½ oz butter
1 teaspoon almond essence
Rind of ½ lemon

4 oz sugar
3 oz fresh white
breadcrumbs
2 eggs
1 oz chopped almonds

Bramley's Seedling apples are best for this. Peel and core the apples. Cut four rings and slice the rest. Put the apples into a pan with the milk, butter, essence, lemon rind and 1 oz sugar. Heat very gently just to soften the apples slightly. Remove the apple slices and rings carefully. Pour the milk mixture on to the breadcrumbs and leave to soak for 20 minutes. Separate the eggs and mix the yolks into the breadcrumb mixture. Put into a fireproof dish and put the dish into a tin of warm water. Cover the dish with a piece of wet greaseproof paper. Bake at 325°F (Gas Mark 3) for 30 minutes. Top with the apple slices. Whisk the two egg whites stiffly and fold in the remaining sugar. Stir in the nuts and pile on top of the pudding. Decorate with the four apple rings set into the meringue. Bake at 250°F (Gas Mark ½) for 30 minutes and serve hot.

OATMEAL PUDDING

1 tablespoon fine oatmeal
1 dessertspoon flour
1¼ pints milk
1 egg

Pinch of salt
1 oz sugar
Butter

Mix the oatmeal and flour together into a smooth cream with a little of the milk, then add the rest of the milk to the oatmeal and flour. Stir and simmer for five minutes. Add the salt and sugar and cool slightly. Add the beaten egg and turn into a dish which has been greased well with butter. Bake at 325°F (Gas Mark 3) for 20 minutes. Serve with syrup or brown sugar and cream.

QUEEN ANNE'S SEMOLINA

1 pint milk
Pinch of salt
8 level tablespoons fine
semolina

2 eggs
8 oz castor sugar
3 tablespoons redcurrant jelly

Warm milk and sprinkle in salt and semolina, bring just to boil and simmer for 2 minutes. Remove from heat and stir in beaten egg yolks and half the sugar. Turn into 1½ pint heatproof dish, cool slightly and spread thinly with redcurrant jelly. Whisk the egg whites until stiff, add 3 tablespoons of remaining sugar and whisk again to firm peaks. Fold in rest of the sugar and pile lightly on top of pudding. Place in a very hot oven, 450°F (Gas Mark 8) for 3 minutes, until pale golden. Dot with small blobs of redcurrant jelly and serve hot or cold.

CHOCOLATE FUDGE PUDDING

2 oz castor sugar
1 oz cocoa
¼ teaspoon cinnamon
2 oz fine semolina
1 teaspoon baking powder
1 oz butter

½ teaspoon vanilla essence
2 eggs
1 tablespoon walnuts
½ pint hot water
3 oz brown sugar
½ oz extra cocoa

Sift sugar, cocoa, cinnamon, semolina and baking powder. Melt butter and blend with vanilla essence and beaten eggs, and stir into dry mixture. Add chopped walnuts, and put into well-greased 1½ pint pie dish. Blend hot water, brown sugar, and extra cocoa, and pour gently in circular movement over top. Bake at 375°F (Gas Mark 5) for 30 minutes. Serve warm. This recipe makes a spiced chocolate pudding with its own sauce in one dish.

DEBDEN CHOCOLATE PUDDING

6 oz sugar
4 oz flour
2 teaspoons baking powder
Pinch of salt
1 oz plain chocolate
2 tablespoons butter

Scant ¼ pint milk
3 oz brown sugar
4 oz castor sugar
3 tablespoons cocoa
⅓ pint cold water

Stir together 6 oz sugar, flour, baking powder and salt, and blend with melted chocolate, butter and milk. Pour into a buttered baking dish (about 1½ pint size). Over the top scatter brown and castor sugars and cocoa, without mixing, and pour on cold water. Bake at 325°F (Gas Mark 3) for 1 hour. Leave to stand at room temperature for 1 hour, and serve cool but not chilled. The pudding makes its own fudge sauce beneath a cake-like top, and is for a person who likes a really rich chocolate confection. Whipped cream or ice cream are delicious as a topping, but only possible for the iron digestion of the schoolboy.

BLACKBERRY PUDDING CAKE

This can be eaten as a cake, but it is also excellent when served as a pudding with cream or custard. Cream together 4 oz butter and 4 oz sugar, and beat in 1 egg. Gradually add 8 oz plain flour sifted with 2 teaspoons baking powder and ¼ teaspoon salt, and beat to a smooth batter with ¼ pint milk. Pour into a buttered square or rectangular tin, and sprinkle thickly with well-washed and drained blackberries. Cream together 2 oz butter with 4 oz sugar, 2 oz plain flour and ½ teaspoon cinnamon until the mixture is of a crumble consistency. Sprinkle on blackberries, and bake at 350°F (Gas Mark 4) for 1 hour.

DEVONSHIRE PUDDING

3 eggs
3 oz soft brown sugar
3 oz flour

1 large tin apricots
Grated rind of ½ lemon

Separate eggs and beat yolks with sugar until pale and creamy. Mix in flour and blend well. Beat egg whites until stiff and fold into the mixture. Drain off juice from apricot halves, mix them with the lemon peel into the sponge base and turn into a buttered baking dish. Bake at 350°F (Gas Mark 4). Serve with cream.

CHERRY PUDDING

Take 1 lb of cherries, 4 oz sugar, 2 oz plain flour, 2 oz castor sugar, 3 eggs, 1 gill of thick cream, 2 or 3 tablespoons of milk, the grated rind of a lemon and a pinch of mace.

Cook the cherries with a little water and 4 oz of sugar until tender. Allow to cool and remove the stones. Mix the flour and milk together, then add the castor sugar, and cream, and mace, and warm slowly before beating in the egg yolks. Add the grated lemon rind and lastly the egg whites beaten stiffly. Well butter a mould or basin and fill with alternate layers of cherries and the mixture until full. Cover with greased paper or foil and bake in a moderate oven for $\frac{3}{4}$ of an hour.

LEMON SAUCE PUDDING

8 oz castor sugar
$1\frac{1}{2}$ oz plain flour
$\frac{1}{2}$ teaspoon baking powder
Pinch of salt
2 eggs
$1\frac{1}{2}$ teaspoons grated lemon rind
1 tablespoon melted butter
$\frac{1}{8}$ pint milk
4 tablespoons lemon juice

Sift 6 oz of the sugar with flour, baking powder and salt. Beat egg yolks until light and creamy. Fold in melted butter, milk and lemon juice, and stir into flour mixture. Beat egg whites, fold in remaining sugar and beat well, then fold into lemon mixture. Put into buttered pie-dish and bake at 350°F (Gas Mark 4) for 1 hour. Serve warm with cream. The pudding is a light sponge with a lemon sauce underneath.

BREAD AND BUTTER PUDDING

1 oz butter
4 slices white bread
4 oz raisins
2 oz chopped dried apricots
2 oz sugar
2 eggs
1 pint milk
1 tablespoon granulated sugar

Butter a baking dish. Remove crusts from the bread, butter the slices and cut into 1 inch wide fingers. Arrange half the bread, butter side up, in the bottom of the dish and cover with dried fruit and 2 oz sugar. Top with remaining bread. Beat eggs with the milk and pour over the pudding. Leave to stand for 15 minutes, sprinkle the surface with 1 tablespoon granulated sugar and bake in a moderate oven, 300°F (Gas Mark 2) for $1\frac{1}{2}$ hours.

RHUBARB BUTTERSCOTCH CRUMBLE

3 cups rhubarb
Pastry of your choice
3 oz brown sugar
2 tablespoons flour (level)

Pinch of salt
1 egg, beaten
2 tablespoons cream

Chop up rhubarb and put into a pastry-lined pie plate. Now mix together the brown sugar, flour, salt, egg and cream. Spread this mixture over the rhubarb, and bake the pie in a hot oven for 10 minutes. Then reduce the heat to moderate and bake for 20 minutes more. Serve warm or cold.

RHUBARB BROWN BETTY

4 oz fresh white breadcrumbs
2 oz suet
2 oz sugar

1 lb young rhubarb
2 tablespoons golden syrup
½ teacup water

Mix breadcrumbs with suet and sugar and put in a thin layer at the bottom of a greased basin. Cover with a layer of chopped rhubarb. Dissolve syrup in water, and use half of this to pour over the rhubarb. Add another layer of crumb mixture, then rhubarb and syrup, and finally top with crumbs. Cover and steam for 1½ hours, or bake at 325°F (Gas Mark 3) for 1½ hours. Serve with cream or egg custard.

RHUBARB PUDDING

2 lb rhubarb
3 oz sultanas or currants
3 oz butter
1 egg, large
½ teaspoon mixed spice
Lemon peel (about a 4-inch

strip)
3 tablespoons golden syrup
6 tablespoons plain flour
3 teaspoons baking powder
Pinch of salt
1½ breakfastcups milk

Cut the rhubarb into 1 inch pieces and put in a fireproof dish with the sultanas or currants. Add 1 tablespoon syrup dissolved in warm water, the spice and the lemon peel. Cream the butter, add the well-beaten egg, and the rest of the syrup. In another basin sieve the flour, baking powder and salt together. Add to this the milk and the egg mixture alternately till all is mixed. Pour over fruit. Bake in moderate oven for about 50 minutes.

GINGERBREAD PLUM PUDDING

1½ lb yellow plums	1 egg
6 oz castor sugar	4 oz plain flour
2 oz butter	1 oz granulated sugar
3 oz black treacle	1 teaspoon mixed spice
1 oz golden syrup	1 teaspoon ground ginger
5 tablespoons milk	½ teaspoon bicarbonate of soda

Mix plums and castor sugar and put into a buttered oven dish. Warm together butter, treacle and syrup, then add milk and beaten egg and leave to cool. In a bowl, mix sieved flour, granulated sugar, spices and soda, add cooled treacle mixture and blend well together. Pour over fruit, spreading evenly. Bake in the middle of a low oven, 325°F (Gas Mark 3) for 1¼ hours.

TOSSED APPLES

Peel very small eating apples, but leave on stalks. Heat some butter in a thick pan and toss apples in it until brown. Drain and arrange on thick layer of castor sugar. Serve warm or cold.

Mrs Georgina Hill, 1864

APPLE SLICES

Butter thin bread on both sides and put in a baking dish. Halve apples without peeling, but remove cores. Put half an apple on each piece of bread, hollow side up, and put thick cream in each hollow. Scatter soft brown sugar on bread and fruit. Cook at 325°F (Gas Mark 3) for 45 minutes, renewing cream and sugar half way through cooking. Serve warm.

Mrs Georgina Hill, 1864

DEEP-FRIED APPLES

Make a thick batter with 3 eggs, ½ a pint of milk, a pinch of nutmeg, a liqueur glassful of brandy and enough flour to give the consistency of thick cream. Dip in apple slices and deep-fry in hot lard. Drain and sprinkle with sugar.

Mrs Georgina Hill, 1864

APPLE CHARTREUSE

Boil 8 oz of Carolina rice in 2 pints of milk until the rice is tender and has absorbed milk. Peel and core 9 medium pippins; put raspberry jam in holes and fill up with cream.

Line a deep pie-dish with rough puff pastry. Put in apples and fill in spaces with rice. Brush over apples and rice with egg yolk, dust with sugar and decorate with candied peel. Bake at 400°F (Gas Mark 6) for 20 minutes, then at 375°F (Gas Mark 5) for 25 minutes. Serve hot.

Mrs Georgina Hill, 1864

APPLE OMELETTE

Slice eating apples thinly and dip in brandy. Dust with grated lemon peel and fry quickly on both sides in hot lard. Beat up eggs (allow 2 for each person) and pour into a little hot butter in an omelette pan. Spread apple slices over eggs and cook until eggs are just set.

Fold over omelette, dust with icing sugar and glaze under grill or in oven.

Mrs Georgina Hill, 1864

APRICOT DELIGHT

6 oz breadcrumbs	*¾ oz ground almonds*
3 oz sugar	*2 oz bitter almonds*
3 oz suet	*1 or 2 eggs*
Some apricot jam	*Squeeze lemon juice*

Beat the egg, stir in the sugar, the jam and the lemon juice, add the finely chopped almonds. Mix suet with breadcrumbs. Grease a pie-dish and put into it alternate layers of the breadcrumbs and the jam mixture, beginning and ending with crumbs. Bake in a moderate oven for about an hour or until firm. Serve with cream or custard.

BASIC BATTER

4 oz plain flour	*1 egg*
Good pinch salt	*½ pint milk and/or water*

Sieve the flour and salt into a basin. Make a well in the centre and drop in the egg. Add about ½ the liquid, bit by bit, and mix from the middle outwards. Beat well until the mixture is smooth like cream. If possible give it time to 'rest' for ½ an hour by covering and leaving in the cool. Finally add the rest of the liquid and beat again. Some people add 1 tablespoon of boiling water just before they pour into the cooking dish but this takes courage.

PANCAKES

(The basic recipe makes 8 pancakes.)
Heat a little lard in a frying pan. Pour in a little batter, tilt the pan until covered evenly, cook quickly until the pancake is golden brown underneath. Then toss or turn and brown the other side. Turn out on to sugared paper, roll up and sprinkle with lemon juice.

JAM PANCAKES

Spread a little warm jam on the pancakes before you roll them up.

APPLE BATTER

Add 2 tablespoons of sugar to the basic batter. Peel, core and slice 2 or 3 medium-sized apples. Heat a knob of butter in a baking tin. Add the apples and the batter. Sprinkle with cinnamon or nutmeg. Cook like a Yorkshire pudding.

PANCAKES WITH HONEY AND WALNUT SAUCE

8 pancakes
1 rounded tablespoon thick
honey

10 oz chopped walnuts
Juice of 1 lemon
1 oz butter

The pancakes can be made fresh or made before the meal. Place the butter in a shallow pan, and when it has melted add honey, nuts and lemon juice. Stir until blended. Slide one pancake into the mixture fold in halves and into quarters in the pan and then slide in next pancake until all pancakes are in the pan. Remove pancakes and arrange on a heated serving dish, pour remaining mixture over the top.

BLACKBERRY PANCAKES

Blend together 4 oz flour, 2 tablespoons sugar, 1 egg yolk, $\frac{1}{2}$ pint milk, and $\frac{1}{2}$ lb blackberries to a smooth batter. Add 1 tablespoon melted butter and fold in the stiffly beaten white of the egg. Fry small pancakes of this mixture in butter browning on both sides. Serve very hot with plenty of vanilla ice-cream.

SOMERSET FRITTERS

8 oz *plain flour*
1 egg
Enough milk to make a stiff batter
2 tablespoons sugar

2 tablespoons currants
4 apples
1 teaspoon mixed spice
½ teaspoon bicarbonate of soda

Make a batter with flour, egg and milk just stiff enough to drop from a spoon. Mix in sugar, currants, grated apples, spice, and the bicarbonate of soda mixed with a little milk. Melt some lard in a frying pan. Put in spoonfuls of batter and brown on both sides. Pile on to dish and sprinkle with sugar.

GERMAN PUFFS

2 tablespoons flour, 2 eggs well beaten, ½ pint new milk, 2 oz butter just melted. Stir all together add a little nutmeg and sugar, put the mixture into teacups, half filling them. Bake in a quick oven ¼ of an hour, turn into a dish, and strew sugar over.

Lewis' Mother's Cookbook, Mary Horrell, Exeter

1911 SUNDERLAND PANCAKES

2 eggs, 2 oz of butter, 2 oz of sifted sugar, 2 oz of flour, and ½ a pint of new milk. Beat the eggs thoroughly, and put them into a basin with the butter, which should be beaten to a cream. Stir in the sugar and flour, and when these ingredients are well mixed, add the milk, which should be slightly warm. Keep stirring and beating the mixture for a few minutes; put it on buttered plates, and bake it in a quick oven for 20 minutes. Serve with a cut lemon and sifted sugar, or pile the pancakes high on a dish, with a layer of preserve or marmalade between each layer.

NORTHALLERTON PUDDING

4 oz *plain flour*
1 egg
½ pint milk

1 tablespoon castor sugar
2 drops vanilla essence
1 oz lard

Sieve flour into a mixing bowl. Make a well in the centre, add the egg and sugar and gradually beat the egg into the flour, adding a little milk to make a smooth paste. Add vanilla essence and beat in remaining milk until small bubbles rise to the surface. Leave to stand for 30 minutes.

Heat lard in a baking dish until smoking, add batter and bake, 425°F (Gas Mark 7) for 30 minutes. Serve with golden syrup and cream.

APPLE BATTER

4 small cooking apples
4 dessertspoons mincemeat
3 eggs
1 oz sugar

2 oz flour
¼ pint milk
Pinch of salt

Peel and core apples and put into a buttered oven dish. Put mincemeat into each one. Beat together egg yolks, sugar, flour and milk with a pinch of salt, then fold in stiffly beaten egg whites. Pour over apples and bake at 350°F (Gas Mark 4) for 1 hour. Sprinkle with sugar and serve at once.

APPLE AND OATMEAL CAKES

3 oz oatmeal
6 apples (large, firm)
2 oz sugar

1 oz flour
Butter for frying

Cook the oatmeal in water until well swollen, then strain and turn into a basin. Peel and core the apples, chop into small pieces. Mix the apples, the oatmeal and the sugar together, binding with the flour. Form into small balls with the hands, and fry in hot butter until just brown. Sprinkle with sugar and serve very hot with custard.

APPLE FRITTERS

2 apples (firm)
2 tablespoons flour
½ teaspoon baking powder

1 egg
A little milk

Peel and core the apples, and cover with a little sugar to prevent them browning. Make a batter of the flour, baking powder and milk, with the yolk of egg. Whisk the white and fold it in to the batter. Dip slices of apple into the batter, then drop in very hot fat, and fry until golden brown. Sprinkle with castor sugar and serve very hot.

APPLE CRISPS

Some large apples (firm)
2 or 3 thick slices of white bread

Butter
Sugar

Peel and cut up the apples, cut the crusts off the bread, and cut it into cubes. Fry the apples in butter in a frying pan, and as soon as they are cooked, lift out and put into a dish, and sprinkle them with sugar. Fry the bread cubes in the remaining butter, lift out to drain, then mix with the apples and serve with custard or cream.

4 Cold Sweets and Ices

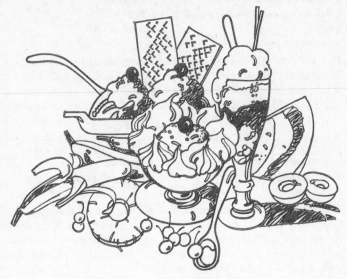

Things sweet to taste prove indigestion sour.
William Shakespeare

A perpetual feast of nectared sweets
Where no crude surfeit reigns.

Milton

AUTUMN PUDDING

1 lb blackberries	**4 oz sugar**
2 large apples	**White bread**

Simmer blackberries with peeled and sliced apples, sugar and $\frac{1}{2}$ pint water until soft. Strain, keeping the juice, and rub the fruit through a sieve. Add half the juice to the fruit pulp and sweeten with more sugar to taste. In the bottom of a soufflé dish or straight-sided casserole, put a layer of thinly-sliced white bread without crusts. Cover with a layer of blackberry purée, then another layer of bread and purée until the dish is filled, making sure each layer of bread is well-soaked with the fruit, and finishing with a layer of bread. Put a plate on top with a heavy weight, and leave overnight. Turn out to serve, with the rest of the blackberry juice thickened with cornflour to make a sauce and with cream if liked.

64

BLACKBERRY PUDDING

1 lb blackberries　　　　　　　*8 oz castor sugar*
½ pint cider　　　　　　　　*5 slices white bread*

Simmer the blackberries with cider and sugar. Take the crusts from the bread, and use some of the bread to line a pudding basin. Pour the hot fruit into the basin and cover with bread. Put a plate and a weight on top and leave in a cold place for 24 hours. Turn out and serve with cream.

BLACKBERRY MOULD

Line a mould with pieces of bread and put a layer of blackberries and apples previously boiled, then a layer of bread and so on until the mould is full. Set to cool overnight, turn out and serve with custard or cream.

Lewis' Mother's Cookbook, Mary Horrell, Exeter

POLKA PUDDING

Mix 2 teaspoons of arrowroot in ½ pint of cold milk. Beat 2 eggs well, add to them 1½ oz of fresh butter cut into small pieces, a dessertspoon of rosewater, a few drops of any essence you like, ½ a teacup of powdered sugar. Boil ½ pint of milk in a stewpan. When boiling stir in these ingredients without taking the pan off the fire. Boil 5 minutes keeping it well stirred, then put into a mould and serve cold.

Lewis' Mother's Cookbook, Mary Horrell, Exeter

FUDGE PUDDING

2 oz butter　　　　　　　　*teaspoons coffee essence*
2 oz plain flour　　　　　　*2 tablespoons golden syrup*
1 pint milk　　　　　　　　*2 oz plain chocolate*
½ teaspoon vanilla or 2

Make a plain white sauce with the butter, flour and milk, and add essence. Grease a small thick saucepan, put in the golden syrup and heat it to a rich brown colour. Be careful that it does not burn, or it may curdle the milk. Stir this quickly into the sauce and mix well. When cool, pour into a pretty serving dish. Just before serving, grate chocolate on top.

NO-BAKE RHUBARB CRUMBLE

1 lb young rhubarb　　　　　*water and sugar)*
2 tablespoons water　　　　　*2 oz butter*
4 oz sugar (or use 4 oz　　　*6 oz fresh white breadcrumbs*
raspberry jam instead of　　*2 oz soft brown sugar*

Cut rhubarb into 1 inch lengths and cook gently with water and sugar (or jam) until tender, then cool. Melt butter, remove from heat and mix in crumbs and sugar. Fill a serving bowl with alternate layers of rhubarb and crumb mixture. Top with whipped cream. Add a grating of lemon or orange, a pinch of ginger, or a few shreds of angelica for extra flavour.

POPLAR COTTAGE RAISIN FLAN

8 oz digestive biscuits
4 oz melted butter
6 oz seedless raisins
8 fluid oz water

1 tablespoon cornflour
½ teaspoon ground cloves
½ teaspoon ground cinnamon
4 oz brown sugar

Crush the biscuits into crumbs and mix with the melted butter. Press into a flan dish and chill. Cook the raisins in the water for 10 minutes until plump and soft. Stir in cornflour mixed with a little water, and simmer until thick. Add spices and sugar and stir until the sugar has dissolved. Cool and fill the flan case. Serve with thick cream.

BETTY'S ORANGE MERINGUE

1 tin mandarin oranges
1 lemon
Sugar to taste

2 tablespoons cornflour
2 eggs

Drain oranges and put in bottom of buttered Pyrex dish, saving some to decorate. Make liquid up to ½ pint with water and lemon juice. Make blancmange with liquid and cornflour and sugar. Grate lemon rind finely and add. Cool and add 2 egg yolks. Whisk whites stiffly and fold on top. Add sugar. Cook 1 hour in slow oven. Decorate with oranges.

STRAWBERRY SHORTCAKE

10 oz plain flour
4 teaspoons baking powder
2 tablespoons castor sugar
½ teaspoon salt
3 oz butter

1 egg
5 tablespoons milk
1½ lb strawberries
Whipped cream

Heat oven to 425°F (Gas Mark 7) and grease and flour an 8 inch cake tin. Mix flour with baking powder, sugar and salt, and cut in butter until mixture looks like breadcrumbs. Make a well in centre, add beaten egg and milk and stir quickly until well mixed. Spread in cake tin and bake for 15 minutes until golden and firm. Leave in the tin until partly cool, then turn out on to rack. While the shortcake is still warm, split and butter the bottom layer. Cover with halved berries, sprinkle with sugar and top with the second half. Spoon on more sliced berries and whipped cream, and garnish with whole berries. Serve at once.

ORANGE CREAM ROLL

¼ *pint double cream*
2 *level tablespoons icing sugar*
3 *level tablespoons orange juice*
2 *level teaspoons grated orange rind*
15 *ginger biscuits*

Whip cream, fold in sugar, orange juice and rind. Mix gently until mixture is dropping consistency. Sandwich ginger biscuits together with cream and place in a roll on a dish. Cover roll completely with remaining cream. Cover roll with a lid and leave to chill in refrigerator overnight. To serve, cut diagonally into slices.

ANGIE'S GINGER ROLL

Dip ginger nuts in sherry (quite quickly or else they almost disintegrate) sandwich with whipped cream into a long shape. Then cover with cream and chill. Then before serving decorate with chopped stem ginger. The ginger nuts can also be put together with leftover brandy butter, instead of cream.

Mrs Hollest, Saffron Walden, Essex

RICE SOLID

6 *oz rice*
Quart of milk
Sugar to taste
Lemon rind for flavouring
Filling

Boil the rice until cooked in the milk, which has been sweetened, and flavoured by adding a strip of lemon rind. Turn it into a pretty mould, and leave it until cold and set. Then turn it out gently scoop out 2 tablespoons of rice from the centre, and fill the cavity with baked apple, putting a little strawberry jam on the top. Put the scooped out rice round the base of the mould, and stand it in some whole fruits from the jam for decoration.

Mrs Lowelle, Birmingham, 1915

AN ECONOMICAL JELLY

Take two calves' feet, when thoroughly cleaned cut them into pieces, place in a stewpan, with 2 quarts of cold water; let them boil, skin, then gently simmer for 5 or 6 hours, when the liquor should be strained through a wire sieve, and set aside until the next day. Remove every particle of fat, warm the jelly in an enamel saucepan, with the rind and juice of 2 lemons, loaf sugar to sweeten, 4 cloves, a small stick of cinnamon, the whites and shells of 2 eggs, a pinch of dried saffron. Let it all come to a boil, strain through a jelly-bag into a basin; when cool add 2 wine-glasses of sherry, and pour into damp moulds.

Mrs Thorne, 1911

APPLES IN RED JELLY

Choose rather large apples, peel and take out the cores with a scoop and put into each apple 2 cloves, then fill them up with sifted sugar, place them in a pie-dish and add more sugar, the juice of 1 lemon and 2 teacups of water. Bake ½ hour, do not let the apples break. Lift them out carefully, then strain the liquor in which they have been stewing into a lined sauce-pan, add the rind of a lemon and 1 tablespoon of gelatine, which has been dissolved in cold water, and if not sweet enough, add more sugar and 6 cloves. Boil till quite clear. Colour with a few drops of cochineal and strain the jelly through a double muslin into a jug and let it cool a little, then pour it into the dish around the apples. When quite cold put on the top of each apple the white of an egg beaten to a stiff froth. A very pretty supper dish.

Lewis' Mother's Cookbook, Mary Horrell, Exeter

APPLE CUSTARD

Boil 1½ lb loaf sugar in a pint of water until it hardens when poured into cold water. Then add 2 lb of apples pared and cored, the peel and a little of the juice of 2 lemons. Boil till quite stiff, put into a mould. When cold, put into a glass dish and pour custard around.

Lewis' Mother's Cookbook, Mary Horrell, Exeter

APPLE FOAM

2 lb apples   *2 egg whites*
Sugar to taste   *2 cartons natural yoghurt*

Peel and core apples and cook gently with sugar to taste but no water. When fruit is tender, sieve and cool. Whip egg whites and fold into pulp with yoghurt. Chill well.

BLACKBERRY AND APPLE COMPÔTE

1 lb blackberries   *8 oz sugar*
2 large apples   *4 tablespoons water*

Wash blackberries, and add peeled and sliced apples, sugar and water.
Bring to the boil, cover and simmer for 5 minutes until apple is tender.
Chill thoroughly, and serve with cream.

SOFT APPLES

Use small eating apples, peel them and prick with a coarse needle. Put
into a jar inside a saucepan of boiling water. Put in 2 tablespoons of honey
for 8 oz apples. Tie brown paper over jar and shake frequently but gently.
When soft, put in dish and pour on liquid from cooking. When cold,
top with thick cream.

Mrs Georgina Hill, 1864

RASPBERRIES WITH RED CURRANT SAUCE

Simmer a ½ lb red currants with 6 oz sugar for 15 minutes. Strain the
liquid and chill; serve over raspberries.

COLD RASPBERRY SOUFFLÉ

Sieve ½ lb fresh raspberries, measure the purée and make up to a ½ pint
with water. Sprinkle 1 tablespoon gelatine in 4 tablespoons of cold water
and leave to soften. In a double boiler, cook together 4 egg yolks with
4 oz sugar and cook over hot but not boiling water until thickened (about
10 minutes). Add the softened gelatine and stir till dissolved, then let the
mixture cool for 15 minutes. Stir the raspberry purée into the cool
gelatine mixture. Beat 4 egg whites till stiff peaks form. Whip a ½ pint
cream stiffly, fold into the meringue and gradually add the raspberry
mixture. When thoroughly combined, turn into a soufflé dish and chill
for at least 2 hours. Decorate with whipped cream and a few raspberries.

MRS D.G.'S APPLE JELLY

To 1 lb apples pared and cored add 1 lb sugar powdered and ¼ pint water.
Boil it until it is stiff with some strips of lemon peel. It may then be
put into a mould and turned out when cold.

Mrs Garden, 1847

VICTORIAN APPLE MARMALADE JELLY

2½ lb peeled and cored 'good' cooking apples, stewed in only sufficient water to prevent burning. Beat them to a smooth pulp. For each lb of pulp take ¾ lb sugar and boil it to a thick syrup adding as little water as necessary for making the sugar boil. Add this syrup to the apple pulp with about ½ teaspoon of minced or grated lemon peel. Stir over a good heat for about 25 minutes or till the apples cease to stick to the bottom of the pan. The jelly may now be poured into moulds which have been dipped in cold water. This will turn out into a nice stiff jelly, which may be stuck with blanched almonds, and a custard poured round it on the dish. The apples will take about ¾ hour to reduce to pulp, and 25 minutes to boil after the sugar syrup has been added.

VICTORIAN LEMON JELLY

Take a clean saucepan and put into it 1½ pints of water, the juice of 8 lemons and the rind of 2, pared very thinly, ½ lb sugar, 1 inch stick of cinnamon, 3 oz leaf gelatine (see instructions on side of modern packets of powdered gelatine for equivalent quantity) and 4 cloves.

Stir this over the fire with a wooden spoon until the gelatine is entirely dissolved, then add the crushed shells of 2 eggs and the whites well beaten up, but not the yolks. Whisk the contents in the stewpan until it comes to the boil, then stop, let the scum rise and remove it. Turn a chair upside down on another chair, take a cloth and tie a corner of the cloth to each of the 4 legs, place a basin underneath the cloth and first of all pour some boiling water through the cloth to make it hot. Empty the basin and replace it; now pour the contents of the pan through the cloth so that it will run through into the basin. Repeat this operation 3 times, each time rinsing the basin first in hot then in cold water, leaving it cold and wet each time. After the third operation the jelly will become very brilliant, and brilliancy in a jelly is to be aimed at. When the jelly is nearly cold it may be poured into an ornamental mould, which has been previously scaled and rinsed in cold water and left wet.

WINE JELLY

Any kind of wine jelly may be made from the preceding recipe by substituting a pint of wine in lieu of water, and using only 2 lemons.

GLOUCESTER GOOSEBERRY MOULD

1½ lb prepared gooseberries	*Sugar to taste*
½ oz gelatine	½ pint water

Soak the gelatine for 1 hour in a gill of water. Cook fruit in rest of water until tender. Add sugar and dissolve. Bring fruit again to the boil, just, stirring all the time. Beat in the softened gelatine and when quite dissolved, turn all into a wetted mould or basin and leave to set. Turn onto fancy plate and serve with cold, creamy custard or real cream.

RHUBARB THING

8 oz digestive biscuits   *1 pint stewed rhubarb*
2 oz butter   *1 orange jelly*
Castor sugar to taste

Crumble the biscuits and mix with melted butter and sugar. Press into a flan dish and chill. Melt the jelly in a little hot water and add to the rhubarb. Whisk well, or whirl in the blender. Just before setting, pour into the biscuit case. Chill before serving.

Jean Clark, Cherington, Glos.

OATMEAL FLUMMERY

Steep 3 large handfuls of very fine oatmeal in cold water for 24 hours, then add the same quantity of water again and leave for a further 24 hours. Strain through a fine sieve and boil until very thick, stirring well, and working in 1 tablespoon castor sugar and 2 tablespoons orange flower water. Pour into shallow dishes and serve with cream and sugar, and fresh fruit in season.

RICE FLUMMERY

Scald 1 pint of milk with a piece of lemon peel and a pinch of cinnamon, and stir in 2 oz castor sugar. Mix 3 oz ground rice with a little cold milk, then stir in the boiling milk with 1 oz fresh butter and 4 drops almond essence. Cook gently, stirring all the time, until the mixture thickens and leaves the sides of the saucepan. Pour into a wetted mould and leave until cold. Turn out and serve with cream, custard, jam, or fresh fruit.

EDWARDIAN FLUMMERY

Soften 2 oz gelatine in $1\frac{1}{2}$ pints warm water, and add a wineglass of sherry and $\frac{1}{2}$ wineglass brandy, with the juice of 3 lemons and sugar to sweeten lightly. Leave until cold, then stir in 1 pint lightly whipped double cream. Put into a wet mould and leave until set. Turn out, and decorate with split blanched almonds and glacé cherries. (The original recipe says this will make 2 moulds for a cost of 3/– (15p). One mould would be enough for a modern family, though the cost is far higher!)

SUMMER FLUMMERY

In a saucepan, put $\frac{1}{2}$ pint water with 5 tablespoons white wine, cider or lemon juice. Heat gently and scatter 6 level tablespoons fine semolina on the warm but not boiling liquid. Bring just to boil and reduce heat. Stir and cook for 3 minutes, then add 4 level tablespoons castor sugar. Continue stirring for 5 minutes, then remove from heat and cool. Beat 2 egg whites very stiffly and fold into lukewarm mixture. Pour into well-oiled 1-pint mould to chill and set firmly. Turn out and decorate with a few strawberries or raspberries, and serve with a sauce made from $\frac{1}{2}$ lb strawberries or raspberries which have been sweetened, crushed and very lightly cooked.

LEMON FLUMMERY

Boil $\frac{1}{2}$ pint water with $\frac{3}{4}$ oz butter and the grated peel of 1 lemon. Mix in a bowl 1 oz plain flour and 4 oz castor sugar. Make a well in the centre and put in the hot liquid, whisking to avoid lumps. Blend 1 egg yolk with a little of the hot mixture, then return all the liquid to the pan. Bring slowly to the boil and cook gently for 10 minutes. Whisk 1 egg white until stiff, add the juice of the lemon to the saucepan, then pour into a bowl and fold in the egg white. Cool, then scatter top with crushed macaroons or digestive biscuits. Serve cold with cream.

GOOSEBERRY FLUMMERY

Stew 1 lb green gooseberries with 8 oz sugar and very little water in a covered saucepan until the skins burst and the fruit is pulpy. Remove from heat and add 1 teaspoon lemon juice. Warm $\frac{1}{2}$ pint milk and sprinkle in 4 level tablespoons fine semolina. Bring just to boil, then simmer 3 minutes to thicken. Remove from heat and stir in cooked gooseberries. Tint a pale green if liked. then pour into a bowl to chill and set. Stewed rhubarb may be used instead of gooseberries, tinted lightly pink.

SIMPLE GOOSEBERRY FOOL

This is one of the few old recipes which recommend sieving the fruit. Top and tail 1 lb green gooseberries, and boil with 12 oz sugar and $\frac{1}{3}$ pint water. Put through a coarse sieve, and mix very gradually with 1 pint milk or 1 pint cream. Serve very cold.

RICH GOOSEBERRY FOOL

Stew 1 lb green gooseberries in ¼ pint water with 8 oz sugar, until soft and pulpy. Whisk them well, then blend with 1 dessertspoon orange-flower water and ¾ pint cream.

SUFFOLK MIXED FRUIT FOOL

This recipe is about 150 years old, and very rich, but well worth while for a special occasion. Bruise together ½ pint strawberries and ½ pint raspberries, and put them through a fine sieve. Mix pulp with 4 oz castor sugar and 1 dessertspoon orange-flower water. Scald ¾ pint cream and stir until cold, then mix the fruit pulp and cream well together. Cool in a bowl, and decorate with whole fresh strawberries or raspberries.

STRAWBERRY OR RASPBERRY FOOL

Put 1 quart strawberries or raspberries in a pan with 4 oz castor sugar and heat them just enough to draw the juice. Sieve and mix with as much creamy milk as will give the consistency of custard. Serve very cold. A richer mixture may be made if the yolks of 2 eggs are mixed with the milk and gently stirred over a low heat (preferably in a double boiler) until the custard has thickened.

APPLE FLUMMERY

Put 4 tablespoons pearl barley in 2 pints water and bring to the boil. When boiling, add 1½ lb peeled and sliced sweet apples and cook until barley and apples are soft. Sieve them and put back into the pan with 1½ oz castor sugar and the juice of 1 lemon. Bring to the boil, cool and stir in 3 tablespoons of cream. Serve very cold.

BLACKBERRY FOOL

Stew 1 lb blackberries in just enough water to cover them, and sweeten with castor sugar to taste. Put through a fine sieve, and mix with 1 pint cream. Serve cold in small glasses with shortbread biscuits.

BLACKBERRY FLUMMERY

Simmer 1 lb well-washed blackberries with 8 oz sugar till soft. Put through a sieve, and thicken with 2 tablespoons cornflour and a pinch of salt. Continue to cook for 5 minutes, stirring well. Add 1 teaspoon lemon juice, and cool. Serve with sugar and cream.

BLACKCURRANT FLUMMERY

1 lb blackcurrants
1 pint water
1 dessertspoon cornflour

4 oz castor sugar
2 teaspoons lemon juice
2 eggs

Remove stalks and wash currants; stew gently in the water until tender, then sieve them. Mix the cornflour to a smooth paste with a tablespoon of the blackcurrant purée. Put rest of purée on to boil with the sugar. When boiling, add the blended cornflour and the lemon juice, and cook for 2 minutes, stirring all the time to prevent sticking. Leave to cool. Separate the eggs, beat the yolks, and add to the cooled blackcurrant-cornflour mixture, mixing well. Whip egg whites to a stiff foam and fold into the mixture when cold. Pour into glass serving bowl; serve with cream or egg custard.

RHUBARB FOOL

2 cups stewed rhubarb
½ pint whipped evaporated milk

Sugar to taste
Lemon juice to flavour

Sweeten the stewed fruit to taste and allow to become cold. Scald the tin of evaporated milk in a pan of boiling water for ½ an hour, cool and then chill thoroughly. Beat the milk and then fold in the stewed fruit. Flavour with a little lemon juice.

LEMON FLUMMERY

4 eggs
4 oz castor sugar
2 lemons

½ oz gelatine
½ pint cream

Separate eggs. Beat egg yolks and sugar until creamy; add rind and lemon juice slowly. Add gelatine previously dissolved in 2 tablespoons hot water. Beat ¼ pint cream until half thick. Stir in, fold in egg white. Decorate with ¼ pint thickly whipped cream, violets and angelica.

Pat Brown, Keynsham, Somerset

RASPBERRY CREAM

Rub a quart of raspberries, or raspberry jam, through a hair sieve to take out the seeds, and then mix in well with cream. Sweeten it with sugar to your taste; then put it into a stone jug, and raise a froth with a chocolate mill. As your froth rises, take it off with a spoon, and lay it upon a hair sieve. When you have got as much froth as you want, put what cream remains into a deep china dish, or punch bowl, pour your frothed cream upon it as high as it will lie on.

Thomas Train, Gateshead 1812

DAMASK CREAM

1 *pint cream*   *Rosewater*
Blade of mace   *Pinch of salt*
1 *cinnamon stick*   *Rennet*
Icing sugar

Heat the cream gently with the mace and cinnamon stick, but do not let it boil. When the cream is well-flavoured, remove the pan from the heat, take out spices, and sweeten to taste with icing sugar. Add rosewater to taste and salt. Cool to bloodheat and set with rennet (using the amount required for 1 pint milk). When it is cold, pour on a layer of fresh cream flavoured with rosewater, about $\frac{1}{4}$ inch thick. Decorate with rose petals.

Eighteenth-Century Recipe

POLLY'S STRAWBERRY CREAM

1 *lb strawberries* $\frac{1}{2}$ *pint cream*
$\frac{1}{2}$ *pint milk*   1 *miniature bottle Kirsch*
2 *eggs*   3 *drops rosewater*
5 *tablespoons castor sugar*

If the strawberries are large, cut them in half. Leave small ones whole. Put strawberries into a bowl with half the Kirsch. Make a custard with the milk, egg yolks and 1 tablespoon sugar. Chill and mix in remaining Kirsch. Whip the cream and the rosewater. Into the cream, fold the custard, stiffly whipped egg whites, strawberries and Kirsch, and the remaining sugar.   Serve very cold.

STONE CREAM

Cover the bottom of a glass dish about an inch thick with apricot jam. Plum or Strawberry will do. To a pint of cream put a little white powdered sugar and just enough isinglass to make it a *very* little stiff. *Nearly* boil it and when the isinglass is dissolved strain it. When nearly cold, pour over the preserves in the glass dish. You can put any ornaments you please on the top.

Mrs Garden, 1847

GERANIUM CREAM

½ pint double cream
6 oz cream cheese
4 tablespoons castor sugar

2 sweet-scented rose
geranium leaves

Put the cream into a double saucepan with the sugar and geranium leaves and heat over boiling water until the cream is hot but not boiling. Cool, leaving in the geranium leaves. Mix with the cream cheese until smooth and put into a bowl. Chill with a cover on for 12 hours. Remove the leaves just before serving. Serve with fresh sugared raspberries or blackberries.

CARAMEL CUSTARD

For the custard:
½ pint milk
3 eggs
1½ oz castor sugar
Vanilla flavouring

For the caramel:
4 tablespoons sugar and
2 of water

Make caramel by boiling sugar and water in a pan until golden-brown. Pour the caramel into the greased mould, or moulds. Leave until quite cold. Mix the custard, pour on top of the caramel, steam gently until set. Cool slightly before turning out. Serve hot or cold.

FROZEN APPLE CREAM

½ pint apple sauce
Cinnamon and nutmeg
1 teaspoon melted butter

2 teaspoons lemon juice
½ pint whipped cream

Put apple sauce through a sieve and add a pinch each of cinnamon and nutmeg. Stir in butter and lemon juice, and chill in refrigerator for 1 hour. Fold in cream and put into freezing tray. Freeze at lowest refrigerator setting until firm.

SCOTS CREAM-CROWDIE

1 pint double cream
2 oz coarse oatmeal
2 oz castor sugar

1 tablespoon rum
4 oz fresh raspberries or
blackberries

Cast the oatmeal in a thick-bottomed saucepan over the fire until crisp. Beat the cream to a thick froth and stir in the oatmeal, sugar, rum and fresh fruit. Serve at once.

GOOSEBERRY CREAM

Cover 2 lb prepared gooseberries with cold water and boil until tender. Sieve, and reheat the pulp, sweetening to taste. Add 1 oz butter, then 2 beaten eggs, and stir gently, but do not boil. When the mixture is thick, remove from heat, and when nearly cold add 1 teaspoon orange-flower water and a little green colouring. Stir well and put into small serving glasses. Serve with cream and sponge fingers.

GINGER CREAM

½ *pint double cream*
¼ *pint cold custard (the same consistency as the cream)*
1 *oz sugar*
½ *oz gelatine*
3 *tablespoons water*
1 *oz chopped crystallised ginger*

Dissolve the gelatine and sugar in the water. Whip cream until thick (don't overwhip) and fold into custard. Add the gelatine and stir until the mixture begins to set. Stir in the ginger. Pour into a mould to set.

ALMOND CREAM

½ *pint double cream*
1 *oz sugar*
¼ *oz gelatine*
3 *tablespoons water*
2 *oz almonds*
Almond essence

Blanch and skin almonds. Chop them coarsely (leaving a few for decoration) and toast till light brown. Cool. Add almond essence to the water and dissolve the sugar and gelatine in it. Whip the cream until thick (don't overwhip). Add gelatine mixture and cold chopped almonds. Mix lightly. Pour into individual moulds. Leave to set. Turn out and decorate with the whole almonds.

STRAWBERRY CREAM

2 *lb strawberries*
1 *tablespoon lemon juice*
6 *oz castor sugar*
2 *envelopes gelatine*
¼ *pint double cream*

Clean strawberries and press through a sieve, then combine with lemon juice and sugar, and stir until sugar dissolves. Melt gelatine in a little cold water, and stand bowl over hot water until gelatine becomes syrupy. Blend gelatine into strawberry mixture, then refrigerate until mixture is like unbeaten egg white. Whip cream until just stiff, fold in strawberry mixture and pour into mould. Refrigerate 2 hours before unmoulding.

COMMON SYLLABUB

Put a pint of cyder and a bottle of strong beer into a large bowl; grate in a small nutmeg and sweeten it to your taste. Then milk from the cow as much milk as will make a strong froth. Let it stand an hour, and then strew over it a few currants, well washed, picked and plummed before the fire, and it will be fit for use.

Thomas Train, Gateshead, 1812

EVERLASTING SYLLABUB

This is a very old country recipe, with a rather misleading name. The syllabub will certainly not last as long as the recipe has.

Place ½ pint thick cream in a deep bowl. Pour in about ½ pint wine. Traditionally raisin wine was used, but the cream can be flavoured with brandy, sherry, or what you will. Having added the wine, add 4 oz castor sugar and the grated rind of a lemon. Whip up the mixture briskly. As the cream rises, remove the top with a fish slice. Place the cream so sliced off in a wide glass. Continue until you have filled as many glasses as there are diners. Set aside in a cool larder or a refrigerator.

NORFOLK SYLLABUB

4 fluid oz white wine
1 tablespoon sherry
2 tablespoons brandy

1 lemon or 1 bitter (Seville) orange
2 oz castor sugar
½ pint double cream

Put the wine, sherry and brandy into a basin. Peel the lemon or orange very thinly and squeeze out the juice. Put peel and juice into the wine mixture. Leave overnight, and remove peel. Stir in the sugar until it dissolves. Add the cream and whip until the mixture forms soft peaks. Put into tall wine glasses, jelly glasses or custard cups. This syllabub will hold its shape for 12 hours. Originally a syllabub was made by milking the cow into the wine mixture and skimming off the froth which arose into serving glasses.

HONEYCOMB MOULD (1)

1 pint of milk, 2 eggs, ½ oz of gelatine, and sugar and flavouring to suit taste. Put the milk on to boil, and beat the whites and the yolks of the eggs separately. Stir the yolks into the hot milk with the sugar and the gelatine. Let it cook until it is just thick, and then add the whites of the eggs. Then turn it into a mould to set.

Mrs Lavelle, Birmingham 1913

HONEYCOMB MOULD (2)

Juice and rind of 2 lemons $\frac{1}{2}$ *oz gelatine*
3 egg yolks $\frac{3}{4}$ *pint milk*
3 stiffly-beaten egg whites   *3 tablespoons cream*

Beat the egg yolks in a large basin. Add the thinly-pared lemon rind, gelatine, sugar, milk and cream, and stir to a thick custard over a pan of simmering water. Mix in the lemon juice, and fold the custard into the stiffly-beaten whites. Pour into a jelly mould.

MY FRIEND'S LEMON SOLID

Put 1 quart of milk in a saucepan with $\frac{3}{4}$ lb of loaf sugar and 2 oz of gelatine. Let it get hot enough to dissolve the gelatine, then stand aside to cool, and when cool, stir in the juice of 1 good-sized lemon. Pour into a wetted mould and leave till next day, when it will turn out $\frac{1}{2}$ a solid-looking custard and the other $\frac{1}{2}$ a clear jelly.

Miss R. Harding, 1913

LEMON SOLID

$1\frac{1}{2}$ *pints milk*   *2 lemons*
$\frac{1}{2}$ *pint single cream*   *5 oz granulated sugar*
1 oz gelatine

Put gelatine to stand in 1 pint of milk. Put remaining milk and cream mixed in a pan with the sugar. Warm until melted and bring to near boil. Add the rind of the lemons. Pour in the other milk and slowly stir in the juice of the lemons. It should slightly curdle. Pour into mould, set and turn out.

Pat Brown, Keynsham, Somerset

CAFÉ MOUSSE

Make a teacup of strongest and clearest coffee; use $\frac{1}{4}$ lb to a teacup water. When made put coffee with 2 yolks of eggs and 1 oz sugar in a gallipot into a saucepan boiling water and stir over the fire until the mixture thickens. Then let it get cold. Whip a pint of cream quite stiff and add the mixture by degrees so that it is smooth and thick. Serve in china cups and saucers.

Mrs Garden, 1847

LEMON MOUSSE

3 *eggs*   1 oz *gelatine*
3 oz *castor sugar*   4 oz *tin evaporated milk*
1 *large lemon*   or ½ *pint cream*

Separate the eggs. Whisk the egg whites to a stiff peak in one basin. Whisk
the evaporated milk or cream to soft peaks in another basin. Put egg
yolks and sugar into a double saucepan and whisk over heat until creamy.
Add the lemon juice and grated lemon rind. Pour into the whipped cream
and whisk gently, gradually adding the gelatine melted in a little hot water.
Fold in the egg whites, mix well and chill. As a change, use 4 oz grated
chocolate, a little coffee and rum instead of the lemon juice and rind.

Jean Clark, Cherington, Glos.

ICE CREAM

To 1 lb of preserved fruit, which may be of what kind you choose, add a
quart of good cream, the juice of 2 lemons squeezed into it, and some
sugar to your palate. Let the whole be rubbed through a fine hair sieve,
and if raspberry, strawberry, or any red fruit, you must add a little
cochineal to heighten the colour. Have your freezing pot nice and clean,
and put your cream into it, cover it and put it into your tub with ice beat
small, and some salt, turn the freezing pot quick, and as the cream sticks
to the sides scrape it down with your ice-spoon, and so on till it is frozen.
The more the cream is worked to the sides with the spoon, the smoother
and better flavoured it will be. After it is well frozen, take it out, and
put it into ice shapes, with fresh salt and ice; when you serve it, carefully
wash the shapes for fear any salt should adhere to them, dip them in
water lukewarm, and send them up to table.

Thomas Train, Gateshead, 1812

FRUIT ICES

These may be made either with water or cream. If water, 2 lb of fruit,
1 pint of spring water, 1 lb of clarified sugar, and the juice of 2 lemons.

Thomas Train, Gateshead, 1812

NO-BEATING ICE CREAM

4 *eggs*   ½ *pint double cream*
4 oz *sifted icing sugar*   *Flavouring to taste*

This will fill one 2½ pint or 2 × 1½ pint refrigerator containers with lids
if the freezing compartment is big enough. If not, use an ice tray and

cover with a lid of foil. Set the refrigerator to coldest setting. Separate the eggs and whisk the egg yolks in a small bowl until well blended. In a larger bowl, whisk egg whites until they form stiff peaks. Beat in the sifted icing sugar a spoonful at a time until it has all been included. Slowly whisk the blended egg yolks with the white meringue mixture. Lightly whip cream until it is frothy and will form stiff peaks. Fold this into the egg mixture and add any flavouring. Mix thoroughly and pour into container. Cover and freeze for at least 2 hours before serving.

Joan Gay, Marlborough, Wilts

IVY COTTAGE ICE CREAM

Make a custard with ½ pint milk, 2 eggs, 3 oz sugar. Cool a little. Add 4 oz plain chocolate or chocolate chips. Now add 1 level teaspoon gelatine dissolved in 1 tablespoon of water. Cool this chocolate-custard-gelatine mixture. Take ½ pint evaporated milk and whisk it till it doubles in volume. Now add the other mixture and chill together in freezer. *Note for evaporated milk*—Boil if for 20 minutes in *unopened* tin. Store in refrigerator until needed.

This recipe is quite successful for coffee flavouring.

For best results turn the refrigerator to COLDEST setting ½ hour before making the ice cream, as the faster it sets the creamier it will be.

ICE CREAM

Whip ¼ pint of cream, stir in 4 level tablespoons icing sugar. Fold into two stiffly beaten egg whites, add flavouring. No need to stir while freezing.

M. Shepherd, Tywardreath

BLACKBERRY ICE

Boil together 4 oz castor sugar and ¼ pint water for 5 minutes to make a syrup. 2 rose geranium leaves steeped in the syrup or a tablespoon of rosewater will greatly improve the flavour of the ice. Sieve 1 lb blackberries very finely, and blend into the syrup. Pour into refrigerator freezing tray, cover with aluminium foil, and freeze at normal ice-making temperature for 2 hours.

STRAWBERRY ICE

8 oz strawberries
Juice of 1 orange
¼ pint water

12 oz sugar
1 egg white

Sieve strawberries with orange juice. Dissolve sugar in water and boil for 10 minutes. Cool and add strawberries and orange juice. Freeze at lowest setting of refrigerator until mushy. Put into chilled bowl, add stiffly-whipped egg white and beat well. Return to freezer for a further hour.

HONEY ICE CREAM

1 lb fresh or frozen
raspberries
¼ pint double cream
1 small carton plain yoghurt

10 level tablespoons honey
2 tablespoons lemon juice
Pinch of salt
4 egg whites

Put raspberries through a sieve and add cream, yoghurt, honey, lemon juice and salt. Mix thoroughly, put into ice trays and freeze. Put into a mixing bowl and stir until smooth, then fold in stiffly whisked egg whites. Return mixture to ice trays and refreeze. Serve in chilled glasses.

This is a delicious, light and refreshing ice with a distinctive flavour of honey and raspberries, which is very good after a heavy meal.

MICHAEL'S BIRTHDAY PUDDING

Years ago there was a BBC competition for summer sweets. Being self-confident in those days, I composed this recipe and sent it up without ever actually making it. When I collected first prize and had it demonstrated on television I could not confess and had to think quickly to avoid awkward questions. Subsequently I have frequently made it, as it is easy and keeps for ages in the deep freeze.

Make your favourite ice cream (I use blackberry with ½ pint of frozen pulp). Put some lightly crushed meringues in the bottom of a ring mould. Fill up with ice cream and cover with more crushed meringue. Press them firmly into the ice cream. Turn out and serve with more meringues and whole blackberries in the centre.

Joan Dampney, Christchurch, Hants

5 Cheesecakes

The calves then that come betwene new yere and lent:
save gladly for store lest thou after repent.
For all thing at that time that colde feleth some:
shall better beare colde when the next winter come.
Weane no time thy calfe under xl daies olde:
and lay for to save it as thou savest golde.
Yet calves that doe fal betwene change and the prime:
has seldome to rere them, but kill them in time.

Thomas Tusser

MRS SHUTTLEWORTH'S YORKSHIRE CHEESECAKE

About a quart of beastings
3 oz sugar
1 egg, beaten
Lemon rind
Short crust pastry (10 oz flour to 4½ oz lard and 1½ oz butter or margarine)

Pinch of freshly grated nutmeg
Baking powder
A little melted butter

83

To make the curd: put the beastings into a heavy-based pan and stand over a gentle heat (a double saucepan could be used). You must be careful to avoid letting it burn—it quickly turns solid in the pan as it is *very high in protein.*

When it is solid, turn it out into a large basin, straining it through a sieve. Before the curd is quite cold, break it up with a fork, not too finely. To make the cheesecakes line a deep saucer or tin with a good short crust pastry and fill it with the following mixture: to ½ lb curds add 3 oz sugar, the egg and nutmeg. Stir in the currants and lemon rind. Finally stir in 1 teaspoon of baking powder and a scant oz of melted butter. Bake at about 400°F (Gas Mark 6) for 30 minutes or until golden brown.

From Mrs Shuttleworth comes this recipe which 'could never be found in any modern cookbook'. She says it is a recipe which has been handed down to her through the tattered pages of her husband's grandmother's cookery book. In the West Riding, she says, they usually just call them curd tarts, but in some districts they are known as 'beastings' tarts. You will need to know a diary farmer to procure the 'beastings' or first milk. or colostrum, of a freshly calved cow. Once procured, however, it will keep in a freezer for a while. She says 'I guarantee that this will disappear like magic, before your very eyes, which is just as well because *they should be eaten while fresh* to be at their best.'

HONEY AND WALNUT CHEESECAKE

Short pastry
3 tablespoons sultanas
1 tablespoon chopped
candied peel
8 oz cottage cheese
2 tablespoons double cream

1 tablespoon honey
2 eggs
1 dessertspoon lemon juice
1 level teaspoon cinnamon
3 oz walnut kernels

Line a pie plate with pastry and sprinkle the bottom with sultanas and peel. Blend sieved cottage cheese with cream, honey, egg yolks and lemon juice. Whisk egg whites stiffly and fold in mixture. Put into pastry case and sprinkle with cinnamon. Bake at 425°F (Gas Mark 7) for 10 minutes, then reduce the heat to 375°F (Gas Mark 5) and bake for 30 minutes. Sprinkle thickly with very finely-chopped walnuts before serving.

HONEY CHEESECAKE

4 oz cottage cheese
2 oz honey
2 oz castor sugar
½ level teaspoon cinnamon

2 beaten eggs
Short pastry
Cinnamon
Castor sugar

Blend together sieved cottage cheese, honey, sugar, cinnamon and eggs. Line a pie plate with short pastry and fill with the cheese mixture. Sprinkle thickly with a mixture of cinnamon and extra castor sugar, and bake at 375°F (Gas Mark 5) for 35 minutes.

SONIA'S CHEESECAKE

2 oz butter
4 oz castor sugar
4 eggs
1 lb cottage cheese
2 tablespoons whipped cream

1 level tablespoon cornflour
2 tablespoons lemon juice
1 teaspoon grated lemon rind
Sweet biscuit crumbs

Cream butter and sugar and beat in egg yolks. Add sieved cottage cheese, whipped cream, cornflour, lemon juice and rind. Blend all ingredients thoroughly and fold in stiffly whisked egg whites. Butter an 8 inch tin, and sprinkle with crushed sweet biscuit crumbs. Pour in cheese mixture and bake near the top of oven at 325°F (Gas Mark 3) for $1\frac{1}{4}$ hours. Leave to cool slightly in the turned-off oven before serving.

ALMOND CHEESECAKE

2 oz butter
2 oz castor sugar
Grated rind of 1 lemon
3 egg yolks
1 lb cottage cheese

2 oz ground almonds
1 oz sultanas
2 oz soft breadcrumbs
Pinch of salt

Cream butter and sugar with lemon rind. Beat in egg yolks. Stir in sieved cottage cheese, ground almonds, sultanas, breadcrumbs and salt. Put into a buttered 8 inch tin, and bake at 400°F (Gas Mark 6) for 40 minutes. Leave to cool with the oven turned off. Sprinkle with sugar before serving.

OLD-FASHIONED CHEESECAKES

8 oz cottage cheese
6 oz castor sugar
6 egg yolks
2 oz butter
Finely grated rind of 2 lemons
Pinch of salt

Pinch of nutmeg
Puff pastry
Chopped mixed peel
Currants
Sultanas

Blend together sieved cottage cheese, sugar, egg yolks, butter, lemon rind salt and nutmeg. Line tartlet tins with puff pastry, and spoon the cheese mixture into the cases. Sprinkle with peel, currants and sultanas. Bake at 375°F (Gas Mark 5) until the pastry is light and golden.

COVENTRY TARTS

8 oz cottage cheese
4 oz castor sugar
Pinch of salt
Pinch of nutmeg
1 tablespoon orange juice

4 oz butter
1 egg
Short pastry
Apple, cranberry, quince or currant jelly

Blend together sieved cottage cheese, sugar, salt, nutmeg, fruit juice, butter and beaten egg. Line tartlet tins with short pastry and fill with mixture. Bake at 375°F (Gas Mark 5) until pastry is light and golden. Top each tart with jelly before serving.

There seem to be several traditional English cheesecakes, some dating from the seventeenth century, usually made from cottage or curd cheese. The name 'cheesecake' was also given to those made with fresh cream and fruit juices, since the mixture formed a curd. The famous Yorkshire curd cakes were made with new cheese curd rubbed into a custard with milk and eggs, and baked in a pastry case, sometimes with currants.

Today, curds are not often obtainable, and pasteurised milk is not suitable for making our own soft cheese, but cottage cheese is widely available. This is best sieved for use and mixed with a little fresh cream. Soured cream is also available in cartons, or fresh cream may be soured with a little lemon juice. Traditionally cheesecakes have a pastry base and are cooked in a slow moderate oven. Some modern versions which masquerade under the same name are unbaked and set in the refrigerator; they make delicious puddings but won't please the husband who wants a cheesecake 'just like Mother made'.

TRADITIONAL YORKSHIRE CHEESECAKE

4 oz plain flour
Pinch of salt
2½ oz butter
Juice of 1½ lemons
8 oz curd cheese (or cottage cheese)
2 tablespoons castor sugar

2 eggs
Grated rind of 1 lemon
2 teaspoons cornflour
2 tablespoons double cream
1 tablespoon melted butter
Raisins

Sift flour and salt, rub in butter, and add juice of ½ lemon and enough water to bind. Roll out thinly and use to line 10 inch plate. Bake blind at 425°F (Gas Mark 7) for 10 minutes. Sieve cheese and mix with sugar, eggs, lemon rind and remainder of lemon juice. Beat until smooth and add cornflour mixed with cream to a smooth paste. Fold in melted butter and blend well. Pour into pastry case and sprinkle with raisins. Bake at 350°F (Gas Mark 4) for 30 minutes. Serve cold.

Black Bull Hotel, Freath, Yorks

NINETEENTH-CENTURY CHEESECAKES

8 oz puff pastry
8 oz cottage cheese
6 oz sugar
6 egg yolks

2 oz butter
Pinch of nutmeg and salt
Grated rind of 2 lemons

Line small tart tins with pastry. Sieve cheese and mix with all ingredients, and put into tart cases. Sprinkle top of each with a mixture of chopped candied peel, currants and sultanas. Bake at 375°F (Gas Mark 5) until pastry is golden, about 20 mintues.

RAISIN AND PINEAPPLE CHEESECAKE

8 oz plain flour
Pinch of salt
5 oz butter
1 oz castor sugar
1 egg yolk
2 pineapple rings

2 oz seeded raisins
8 oz cottage cheese
10 oz soured cream
2 oz castor sugar
2 eggs and 1 egg white
1 teaspoon grated lemon rind

A flan ring is best for this cheesecake, but if you are uncertain about using one successfully, a china flan dish will look decorative. Grease the container well. Sieve flour and salt and rub in butter until the mixture is like breadcrumbs. Add sugar and bind together with the egg yolk blended with 1 teaspoon water. Line flan ring and chill, saving trimmings for lattice strips. Chop pineapple and put with raisins on the bottom of the pastry case. Sieve cottage cheese and beat in remaining ingredients. Pour into pastry shell. Bake at 425°F (Gas Mark 7) for 20 minutes. Remove from oven, lattice top with strips, sprinkle with extra castor sugar and bake at 325°F (Gas Mark 3) for 35 minutes.

CHRISTMAS CHEESECAKE

8 oz rich short pastry
16 oz cottage cheese
1 oz ground almonds
2 eggs and 2 egg yolks
4 oz castor sugar
Grated zest of 1 large lemon
5 oz soured cream

2 oz sultanas
1 oz chopped candied peel
5 oz soured cream
1 oz castor sugar
Candied lemon and orange slices

Line Swiss roll tin with pastry and bake blind at 425°F (Gas Mark 7) for 7 minutes. Mix together sieved cottage cheese, ground almonds, eggs, yolks, sugar, lemon zest, soured cream, sultanas and chopped candied peel. Fill pastry case and bake at 300°F (Gas Mark 2) for 1 hour 10 minutes. Mix together soured cream and sugar for topping and spread on top of cheesecake 15 minutes before end of baking time. Turn off oven and leave cheesecake in oven for 1 hour. Chill and remove from tin. Decorate with halved slices of candied orange and lemon. This makes a delicious contrast to traditional Christmas foods.

6 Bread and Yeast Cakes and Buns

Sainct James willeth husbandes, get reapers at hande:
the corne being ripe doe but shead as it stande.
Be saving and thankfull, for that god hath sent:
He sendeth it theee, for the selfe same entent.

Reape well, scatter not, gather cleane that is shorne:
binde fast, shock a pase, pay the tenth of thy corne.
Lode salfe, carry home, lose no time, being faier:
golfe just, in the barne, it is out of dispaier.

                                 Thomas Tusser

There is no mystery about breadmaking. The rules are simple, but these are the basic instructions for preparing the best possible bread.

Warm basin and flour to avoid chilling the dough, which slows up the working of the yeast.

Make the dough on the soft side for a light loaf; if it's too stiff it cannot expand under the influence of the yeast.

Work the dough thoroughly to ensure an even distribution of yeast to allow it to work properly in raising the dough.

Keep the dough warm and warm the tins.

Don't make the dough too hot or it will produce a coarse, breakable crumb of irregular texture.

Don't try to shorten the rising or proving time of the dough. Under-proving or under-fermentation will give a heavy, soggy loaf with a crust breaking away from the top.

Don't let the dough rise for too long. Over-proving or over-fermentation results in a loss of strength, colour, scent and flavour.

Don't bake the bread at too low a temperature, or it will be pale, moist and flavourless.

Yeast products freeze particularly well and you can keep a good supply of bread, buns and yeast pastries which will taste just as delicious as they were fresh from the oven. Uncooked yeast mixtures can also be frozen for future baking.

Equipment

Any type of cooker can be used, and the oven must be preheated before baking. You need a large mixing bowl, a wooden spoon, a clean cloth to cover the dough, and loaf tins and/or baking sheets. Once these tins have been greased and used regularly, they should not be washed but wiped clean, greased and floured for each using.

A dough hook for an electric mixer is cheap and will save a lot of hard work.

Ingredients

Large quantities of flour can be stored for about 3 months in a small dustbin. 3 lb bags are convenient for a batch of bread or buns.

Fresh yeast can be kept for about 10 days in a covered bowl in the refrigerator. If supplies are erratic, it is worth buying 8 oz or 1 lb packages which can be stored in the freezer (divide the yeast into 1 oz cubes and wrap each cube in polythene or foil); frozen yeast will be ready for use after 30 minutes at room temperature.

Dried yeast is convenient to store and use, though it sometimes has a stronger flavour. The maker's specific instructions must be carefully followed. 1 oz of dried yeast is equal to 2 oz fresh yeast if you are following a recipe which does not specify dried yeast. 3 lb flour requires 1 oz dried yeast, and the yeast takes longer to start working than fresh yeast (usually about 15 minutes) before being added to the flour.

Fat and sugar added to the basic mixture give a richer, longer-keeping bread. Salt is an essential in bread and should be dissolved first in a little water, as dry salt affects the growth of the yeast cells.

Storage

Home baked bread is best stored in a refrigerator in a polythene bag. The addition of 1 oz fat to 3 lb flour keeps bread fresh longer.

Bread and buns freeze best when 1 day old. They can be packed in foil or polythene, and should be thawed in wrappings at room temperature. A 1½ lb loaf will take 3 hours to thaw.

Bread may be thawed in a moderate oven, but will then stale very quickly. Richer yeast doughs, such as used for tea breads and savarins, will keep for 3 months in the freezer; yeast pastries which include fat, are best kept for only 1 month.

Uncooked yeast mixtures may be frozen for up to 2 weeks, but proving after freezing takes a long time, and the texture may be heavier. Unbaked dough for freezing should be proved only once, and then either shaped for baking, or kept in bulk if storage in this form is easier.

The surface should be brushed with a little olive oil or unsalted melted butter to prevent toughening of the crust. A little extra sugar should be added to sweet mixtures.

Wrap the dough or shaped bread in freezer-paper or polythene. The dough should be thawed in a moist warm place as quickly as possible to give a light-textured loaf, then shaped and proved again before baking. Shaped bread and rolls should be proved at once in a warm place before baking.

Making the dough

Before work begins, the flour should be sieved and warmed. Warm liquid must be added—1 part boiling water to 7 parts cold tap water gives an approximately correct temperature.

When the yeast is added, it is set working by the addition of water and/ or sugar, then well kneaded into the flour mixture.

Kneading is best done on a floured board, folding the dough over on itself and pushing with a firm, rocking motion until the dough becomes smooth and shiny.

The dough must then prove in a warm place, covered with a damp cloth. A rack over a cooker, or in front of a fire, are suitable warm places, but the dough should not be over direct heat or steam, or in a draught. When the dough has doubled in size, it should be lightly re-kneaded and shaped.

Baking and finishing

Bread is baked in a hot oven 450°F (Gas Mark 8), though sweet light mixtures are cooked at a lower temperature. A dish of water in the oven gives a crisp crust. Bread is ready when it sounds hollow if tapped underneath with the knuckles.

A professional finish can be added. Plain loaves painted with rich milk or cream before baking have a gleaming brown crust; beaten eggs give a dark crust; melted butter or margarine a crisp, crunchy crust. Thick milk and sugar syrup painted on after baking, gives a sweet, sticky finish.

WHITE BREAD

2½ lb white bread flour   ½ oz salt
1 oz fresh yeast   1½ pints warm water
2 oz fat (butter, margarine
or lard)

Put flour in a large warm bowl, make a well in the centre, and sprinkle
salt around the edge. Cream yeast with a little warm water and pour into
the well. Add the rest of the water and the warmed fat and mix well to
a soft putty-like consistency. Leave to prove until double in size. Put
into tins and leave to prove again until bread reaches top of the tins.
Bake at 450°F (Gas Mark 8) for 45 minutes, turning bread once in the
oven. Cool on a wire rack.

WHOLEMEAL BREAD

3 lb wholemeal flour   1½ oz fresh yeast
1 oz salt   1½ pints warm water
1 oz sugar

Take half the flour and make into a batter with all the water. Cream the
yeast with 2 tablespoons of warm water and mix well into the batter.
Cover the basin with a damp cloth and let the batter stand for 15 minutes.
Add the rest of the flour, salt and sugar, and make the dough. Mix well
and knead for 10 minutes. Warm and lightly grease 4 × 1 lb loaf tins, and
divide dough amongst them. Flatten each piece and roll up to fit lengthwise in the tin, pressing down to avoid cracks and folds. Leave for 1 hour
in a warm place until the dough doubles in volume. Bake at 450°F (Gas
Mark 8) for 45 minutes, turning the loaves (moving them through a
right-angle in the oven) half way through cooking time. Turn the loaves
on to a wire tray and cool thoroughly before cutting.

WHOLEWHEAT BREAD

3 lb wholewheat stoneground   2 level tablespoons brown
flour   sugar
2 level teaspoons salt   1 oz dried yeast
2 level teaspoons vegetable   1½ pints warm water
fat or oil

Dissolve 2 teaspoons of the sugar in ⅔ of the water. Sprinkle yeast into
liquid, whisk and disperse with a fork, and leave to stand for 15 minutes
in a warm place until frothy. Dissolve rest of sugar and salt in remaining
water. Add oil, and add to flour. Pour in yeast mixture and mix thoroughly

to a smooth dough. Knead for 5 minutes. Prove in a warm place for about 20 minutes and wait until double in size. Knead again and shape into loaves (this quantity will fill 4×1 lb tins). Prove for 20 minutes. Bake at 450°F (Gas Mark 8) for 35 minutes, and brush tops with oil as soon as loaves come out of oven.

BEGINNER'S BREAD

$1\frac{1}{2}$ lb wholemeal flour
$1\frac{1}{2}$ lb plain flour
4 level teaspoons salt
1 level tablespoon syrup or
brown sugar

$1\frac{3}{4}$ pints lukewarm milk and
water
1 teaspoon honey
2 oz yeast

Put the flour, salt and syrup (or sugar) into a warm basin and leave in a warm place. Whisk the milk and water with the honey and yeast in a jug. Add to the flour, mix with your hands to a stiff dough.

Half fill greased bread tins, press down firmly with damp fingers, cover with a damp cloth, and put to rise in a warm place until the dough has filled the tins. One rising only is necessary because you're using wholemeal flour.

Remove the cloth, brush the tops of the loaves with milk or melted butter, and bake in a hot oven, the first 5 minutes at 450°F (Gas Mark 8), then reduce the heat or move to a lower shelf, and cook for a further 25–30 minutes or until done.

Turn the loaves out of the tins and tap the bottoms. If they sound hollow, the bread is done, if not, put back in oven, out of tins and cook for a further 5 minutes. Cool on a wire rack.

QUICK BREAD

3 lb plain flour
1 level teaspoon sugar
$\frac{1}{4}$ pint boiling milk, mixed
with

$1\frac{1}{4}$ pints cold water
1 teaspoon honey or syrup
2 oz yeast
4 level teaspoons salt

Put 1 lb of flour into a bowl, add the sugar, and leave in a warm place. Mix the boiling milk, the cold water, the honey or syrup together in a jug. Add the yeast and stir thoroughly. Add all this liquid gradually to the warmed flour, mixing with a wooden spoon to a smooth batter. Beat well, cover with a cloth and stand in a warm place again for 15 minutes. The mixture will rise and bubble. This period counts as the first rising.

Sieve the salt with the remaining flour and add to the batter a little at a time, using a spoon first to stir, then your hand, as the batter becomes a dough knead well until the dough feels elastic. Shape into a ball with well-floured hands, put into a well-greased baking tin, cover with a damp cloth and stand again in a warm place until the dough has doubled its size.

Turn the dough onto a floured board, divide into 4 pieces and shape each piece into a roll. Flour and flatten each piece, and roll up like a Swiss roll. Do this 2 to 3 times to each piece. Put each roll into a greased 1 lb bread tin, press down well. Cover with a damp cloth and put in a warm place until the dough rises to the tops of the tins. Brush tops with milk. Bake in a hot oven, 500°F (Gas Mark 9) for 10 minutes, then 400°F (Gas Mark 6). Small loaves 20 minutes or large loaves 30–35 minutes.

JOYCE GARDENER'S AIRING CUPBOARD BREAD

To a 3 lb bag of stoneground wholemeal (plain) flour, I add 2 heaped teaspoons salt and rub in 2 oz lard. I put the flour and bowl in a warm place some hours before making. When I am going bread making I remove the clothes and use the airing cupboard for rising. I think the bread has a better flavour if it does not rise too quickly. I put $\frac{1}{2}$ oz dried yeast (1 oz if you use fresh, but I found it so unreliable) in a cup with a heaped teaspoon sugar (I use brown) and a little warm water and stir, put this in the airing cupboard (saucer on top) then rub in lard into the flour and put back in the cupboard. When the yeast is working well (about 12 minutes) I make a hole in the flour and pour in the yeast and $1\frac{1}{4}$ pints water, warmer than tepid but not too hot. Mix well and gather together, turn onto a board and knead for 5 minutes. I do not flour the board, as I find this quantity of water is enough to make a soft dough without being sticky, also the final loaves stand up better. Then return to bowl and cover with damp cloth and return to cupboard for 1 hour. Then knead for 5 minutes and return to cupboard covering with cloth again, after $\frac{3}{4}$ hour I look at it. If I consider it has doubled its size I knead for 5 minutes and return to cupboard for $\frac{1}{2}$ hour covering with cloth. Then knead for a few minutes, divide and shape into 4 loaves making cuts across the top with a sharp knife and put in the tins and place in the cupboard for 40–45 minutes, covering with cloth. When I have shaped the loaves I turn the oven as high as it will go and then turn it down to 500°F when I put the bread in, 2 loaves on a shelf; after $\frac{1}{4}$ hour I swap the shelves over and turn down to 450°F (Gas Mark 8), and turn off the oven after $\frac{1}{2}$ hour. I give the loaves a few minutes more (usually 5) then remove from oven and place on racks and cool quickly.

JUNE'S BREAD

2 lb strong flour (10-12 oz
wholemeal flour and white)
2 teaspoons salt
1 oz yeast (fresh)
2 teaspoons castor sugar

1 egg (optional)
1 pint (lukewarm) liquid
including egg ($\frac{1}{2}$ milk, $\frac{1}{2}$ water)
1$\frac{1}{2}$ oz lard

Rub in fat to flour and salt. Put Castor sugar with yeast into liquid. Make a well in flour and add yeast and liquid. Mix in. Stand in warm place about $\frac{1}{2}$ an hour or until it is bubbling. Knead for about 7–8 minutes until dough leaves side of bowl (the longer you do it, the better the bread). Stand again until it doubles in size. Knead again and put in tins. Leave to rise and double. Bake rolls at 425°F (Gas Mark 7) for 30 minutes, and loaves for 45 minutes.

EMERGENCY BREAD

Mix 1 lb flour with 1 teaspoon salt and 1 teaspoon bicarbonate of soda. Add $\frac{1}{2}$ pint sour milk and mix to a dough. Grease a loaf tin and place the dough in this, making a shallow trough down the centre so that the bread rises evenly. Bake in a fairly hot oven, 400°F (Gas Mark 6) for about 45 minutes. Let it get cold before cutting.

IRISH GRIDDLE BREAD

8 oz wholemeal flour
8 oz plain flour
1 level dessertspoon sugar
1 level teaspoon bicarbonate
of soda

1 level teaspoon salt
1 dessertspoon dripping
Milk

Mix together flours, and add sugar, soda and salt. Rub in dripping and mix to a batter with milk, to make a dough which is stiff but will roll easily. Roll out in a round 1 inch thick, and cut into 4 sections. Cook on a hot griddle for 10 minutes each side.

BROWN SODA BREAD

1 lb white flour
3 lb brown wholemeal flour
1 tablespoon baking powder
1 teaspoon bicarbonate of soda

1 tablespoon sugar
$\frac{1}{2}$ teaspoon salt
2 oz butter or lard
1$\frac{1}{2}$ pints warm milk

Sift flour, baking powder, bicarbonate of soda, sugar and salt into a large bowl. Rub fat into flour and mix to a stiff dough with warm milk. Knead until smooth and shape into an oblong loaf. Score a cross on the top and bake at 400°F (Gas Mark 6) for 1 hour.

OATMEAL AND WHOLEMEAL BREAD

8 oz wholemeal flour
6 oz medium or coarse
oatmeal
2 teaspoons cream of tartar

(not required if sour milk is
used)
1 teaspoon bicarbonate of soda
1 teaspoon salt
Milk and water to mix

Mix dry ingredients. Add enough milk and water to make stiff dough. Work together as quickly as possible with hands and put in floured tin or form into round loaf. Bake in fairly hot oven.

MALT BREAD

1½ lb white flour (or a mixture
of plain white and wholewheat
flour)
1 oz fresh yeast
¼ teaspoon salt

¼ pint warm water
2 tablespoons black treacle
2 tablespoons extract of malt
2 oz butter
2 oz sultanas

Sieve flour into bowl. Cream yeast with a little water, and dissolve salt in rest of water. Add the yeast and water to the flour, then add treacle, malt, butter and sultanas. Knead to an even texture, prove till double in size, knead again and shape into tins. Prove until the mixture reaches the top of the tins, then bake at 425°F (Gas Mark 7) for 45 minutes, turning the loaves half-way through cooking time. Remove to a wire tray and glaze with milk and sugar syrup.

CURRANT BREAD

1½ lb white flour
4 oz sugar
Pinch of salt
1 oz fresh yeast

4 oz warm butter
½ pint warm milk
8 oz mixed dried fruit
2 oz chopped mixed peel

Mix flour, sugar and salt, and add yeast creamed with a little sugar. Work in warm butter and milk, knead and leave to prove for 1½ hours. Knead in fruit and peel, and shape into loaves or buns to prove for 45 minutes. Bake at 375°F (Gas Mark 5) for 45 minutes, turning after 20 minutes. Small buns will need about 20 minutes cooking time. Remove to a wire tray and glaze with a mixture of milk and sugar.

BAPS

1 lb plain flour
2 oz lard
2 level teaspoons salt
1 level teaspoon sugar

1 oz yeast
½ pint lukewarm milk and
water

Sieve the flour, rub in the lard and sugar. Cream the yeast in half the liquid and dissolve the salt in the rest. Mix into the flour, knead and prove until double in size. Divide into pieces and make into small loaves about 4 inches across. Brush with milk, put on to a greased baking sheet, prove again, and bake at 450°F (Gas Mark 8) for 20 minutes.

MUFFINS

1 egg	1 lb flour
½ pint milk	1 teaspoon salt
1 oz butter or margarine	½ oz fresh yeast

Beat together egg, milk and warm butter. Put flour and salt into a bowl, and put in yeast creamed with a little warm water. Add butter, milk and egg mixture, and knead thoroughly to a soft but not sticky dough. Cover and prove for 1½ hours. Roll out dough to ½ inch thickness on a floured board, and cut out muffins with a large tumbler. Bake on a griddle, turning as soon as the bottoms are browned, or on a baking sheet in a hot oven at 450°F (Gas Mark 8) for 15 minutes, turning half way through cooking.

CORNISH SPLITS

1 lb strong plain flour	1 oz yeast
2 oz fat	½ pint warm milk
1 teaspoon salt	1 teaspoon sugar

Warm milk and add sugar and yeast. Sieve flour and salt. Work in fat finely. Add liquid altogether. Mix and knead. Allow to rise till double in size in a warm place. Knead again till fine in texture. Divide into equal sizes, roll into balls and place on floured baking tray. Allow to rise again. Bake at 375°F (Gas Mark 5) for approximately 15 minutes.

FRUIT BANNOCK

Batter ingredients:	Additional ingredients:
2 oz plain flour	6 oz plain flour
1 oz melted butter or lard	1 oz castor sugar
⅛ pint warm milk	⅛ pint warm milk
¼ oz fresh yeast	1 oz sultanas
	1 oz currants
	½ oz candied peel

Blend batter ingredients together in a mixing bowl and leave for 20–30 minutes until the batter is frothy. Add the additional ingredients and mix well. Knead the dough thoroughly for about 10 minutes on a lightly floured board. Put the dough to rise in a warm place under a damp cloth and leave for 1 hour, until the dough springs back when pressed gently with a floured finger. Knead the dough again and shape into a ball. Flatten with the hands to approximately 8 inches across and ½ inch thick. Put on a greased and floured tray and slash with sharp knife into 8 equal sections. Brush top with milk, cover with a greased paper and leave to rise until the dough feels springy (about 45 minutes). Brush top again with milk, and bake towards the top of a fairly hot oven, 400°F (Gas Mark 6) for 20 minutes. Cool on a wire tray.

BATH BUNS

12 oz plain flour
4 oz butter
¾ oz yeast
⅛ pint milk
2 eggs
½ teaspoon salt

3 oz sugar
Grated rind of 1 lemon
1 oz chopped mixed peel
2 oz sultanas
Sugar crystals or crushed
loaf sugar

Rub the butter into the warm flour. Cream the yeast with a little milk and add with the rest of the milk and the eggs to the flour, stirring in the salt. Knead well and leave to rise until double its size. Knead in sugar, lemon rind, peel and sultanas, and make into 10 rough balls. Leave to prove again for 10 minutes. Brush with egg, sprinkle with crushed loaf sugar or sugar crystals, and bake at 450°F (Gas Mark 8) for 15 minutes.

CHELSEA BUNS

12 oz plain flour
3 oz melted butter
½ oz yeast

1½ gills milk
2 oz castor sugar
2 oz currants

Put the flour in a warm basin, and add 2 oz of the melted butter. Cream the yeast with a pinch of sugar and add to the flour mixture together with the milk. Knead well and leave to rise until double its size. Re-knead to a square shape. Brush with remaining melted butter and sprinkle with the sugar and currants. Roll up like a Swiss roll, and cut into slices 1½ inches thick. Place cut side up on greased baking sheet, leaving room to swell. Leave to prove for 10 minutes. Brush with egg and bake at 450°F (Gas Mark 8) for 15 minutes.

ICED PLAIT

8 oz plain flour
Pinch of salt
½ oz yeast
¾ gill milk
1 oz butter
2 oz sugar

1 egg
3 oz mixed dried fruit
Water icing
Chopped nuts and glacé
cherries

Put the flour and salt into a warm bowl. Cream the yeast with a little sugar, and add to the flour, together with the butter, sugar, warm milk, egg and dried fruit. Mix well, knead thoroughly, and leave in a warm place until double its size. Re-knead, form into a long roll, divide into three and plait together, pressing the ends together firmly. Prove for 15 minutes, then brush with egg and bake at 450°F (Gas Mark 8) for 15 minutes. When cold, coat with white water icing and sprinkle thickly with chopped nuts and glacé cherries.

SALLY LUNNS

12 oz plain flour
½ teaspoon salt
½ oz yeast
1 teaspoon sugar

1½ gills milk
2 oz melted butter
1 egg

Warm the flour and salt. Cream the yeast with the sugar, add warm milk, and stir into the flour with melted butter and egg. Knead well and divide in half. Shape the pieces to fit 2 greased 6 inch round cake tins or soufflé dishes. Leave in a warm place until risen to the top of the tins. Brush with egg and bake at 450°F (Gas Mark 8) for 30 minutes. If the Sally Lunns are to be eaten hot, they should be split in 4 and spread thickly with butter, then the slices replaced and cut into wedges. They should be covered with a damp cloth and reheated in the oven until the butter has melted.

TEA CAKES

8 oz plain flour
Pinch of salt
½ oz butter
½ oz yeast

1 teaspoon sugar
1 egg
¼ pint milk
2 oz sultanas

Warm the flour and salt and rub in the butter. Cream the yeast and sugar and add to the flour, together with the egg, milk and sultanas. Knead well and leave in a warm place until double its size. Knead well again and divide into 3, shaping into rather flat round cakes. Put on greased tins, and prove for 10 minutes. Bake at 450°F (Gas Mark 8) for 12 minutes. Brush over with milk and sugar glaze immediately after removing from oven.

LINCOLNSHIRE PLUM BREAD

12 oz plain flour	*3 oz sultanas*
1 teaspoon baking powder	*3 oz raisins*
¼ level teaspoon nutmeg	*2 oz mixed peel*
Pinch of salt	*2 oz chopped glacé cherries*
4 oz butter	*1 oz yeast*
6 oz castor sugar	*½ pint warm milk*
6 oz currants	

Sieve flour, baking powder, nutmeg and salt into a basin. Rub in butter. Add most of the sugar, keeping a little back and add dried fruit. Cream the yeast with remaining sugar, make a well in dry ingredients, and add yeast and warm milk, mixing well together. Turn mixture into a greased 2 lb loaf tin and bake in a very moderate oven, 325°F (Gas Mark 3) for 2½ hours, covering with thick brown paper after 1½ hours. Turn out on wire rack to cool. Slice and spread with butter.

BARA BRITH WITH YEAST

½ pint milk	*½ level teaspoon salt*
½ oz yeast	*1 level teaspoon mixed spice*
1 egg	*2 oz cooking fat*
1 lb plain flour	*10 oz mixed dried fruit*
2 oz soft brown sugar	*2 oz candied peel (chopped)*

Heat the milk until lukewarm. Dissolve the yeast in 1 tablespoon of the milk. Beat the egg and add to remainder of milk. Sift the flour, brown sugar, salt and spice into a bowl, and rub in the fat. Stir in the dried fruit and peel. Make a well in centre of dry ingredients and pour in egg, milk and yeast. Beat until smooth and beat or knead for a further 5 minutes. Place in a well greased 2 lb loaf tin. Put to rise in warm place until double its bulk. Bake for 15 minutes at 425°F (Gas Mark 7) and for 1 hour at 375°F (Gas Mark 5).

HARVEST CAKES

Make a piece of dough as if for loaf of bread with warm milk. Let it stand till quite light. Then work in a *small* piece of butter, a *very little* sugar and a very few currants. Then make the cakes about as large as a light dumpling. Let them stand again till light. Bake on flat tin.

Mrs Garden, 1847

BARLEY CAKES

3 oz sugar
2 oz butter
2½ oz barley flour
1½ oz plain flour
½ teaspoon baking powder

1 egg
About 1 teaspoon milk
Vanilla or almond essence
Pinch of salt

Cream fat and sugar, add egg and flavouring. Mix flour, barley, baking powder and salt, add to fat and sugar, mixing lightly with sufficient milk to make fairly stiff mixture. Bake in paper cases or small greased tins 20 minutes in moderate oven, 375°F (Gas Mark 5).

DEVONSHIRE YEAST CAKE

1 lb plain flour
6 oz dried fruit
1 oz yeast

2 oz lard
4 oz sugar
Warm water

Warm flour and put into warm bowl. Rub in fat, add fruit and sugar. Make a well and crumble in yeast, sprinkle with a teaspoon sugar, then pour in about a breakfastcup warm water. Mix with hand to a sticky dough and put aside in a warm place to prove for 1 hour. Turn out, knead lightly and make into small dough cakes about the size of a sticky bun or into 2 large, as required. Prove again for 10 minutes and bake at 450°F (Gas Mark 8) to a light brown, about 25 minutes.

Mrs Bidder

SULTANA DOUGH CAKE

1 lb bread dough
3 oz caster sugar
3 oz butter

7 oz sultanas
1 egg

Line 7 inch tin with greaseproof paper. Put butter, sugar and fruit into warm bowl and stand it in a warm place to bring temperature up to that of bread dough, and warm the egg. This should be done immediately after rolling dough and putting it to rise (about 20 minutes). When dough is ready, add it to the mixture in the bowl and with the hands break it into small pieces. Add the egg, then continue working all the mixture together until thoroughly blended. It should then be of a soft consistency and be almost poured into the tin. Cover, and let rise in a warm place for 30 minutes. Bake in middle of oven at 400–420°F (Gas Mark 6–7) for 1–1¼ hours.

Mrs Wesley

WILTSHIRE LARDY CAKE

8 oz flour
¼ teaspoon salt
¼ teaspoon mixed spices
¼ oz yeast
1 teaspoon sugar

¼ pint warm milk
2 oz lard
2 oz sugar
2 oz dried fruit

Warm flour, salt and spice. Cream yeast and sugar together and add to flour, mix with enough warm milk to make a soft dough. Beat well. Cover and stand aside in a warm place till doubled in size. Roll out on well floured board to ¼ inch thickness. Spread on half lard, sugar and fruit. Fold in 3, turn to left (flaky pastry-wise) and roll again. Repeat with rest of lard, etc. Roll out to oblong 1 inch thick. Place in deep tin and leave till well risen. Score top with knife, brush with sugar and water. Cook in hot oven about 30 minutes.

Mrs A. Padgham, Minehead, Somerset

7 Tea Breads, Scones and Rusks

Now for the banquet we press;
Now for the eggs and the ham !
Now for the mustard and cress !
Now for the strawberry jam !
Now for the tea of our host !
Now for the rollicking bun !
Now for the muffin and toast !
Now for the gay Sally Lunn.
                              W. S. Gilbert

Mealtimes have varied considerably over the centuries. In the early eighteenth century, the leisured classes took a late breakfast at 10 or 11 o'clock, followed by a cup of coffee or chocolate around noon. Dinner was eaten in the late afternoon, about 5 or 6 o'clock, and supper very late. This followed an earlier custom of dinner at 11 a.m. and supper at 6 p.m. Towards the end of the century, there was a swing back to this more natural division of the day, and dinner went back to 2 or 3 p.m. and supper to 7 or 8 p.m. At this period, afternoon tea was introduced about 5 o'clock, with thin bread and butter, and toast, much in evidence.

DATE LOAF

Soak overnight 1 packet of dates cut small and covered in boiling water with ½ teaspoon bicarbonate of soda. Rub in 2 oz margarine into ½ lb self-raising flour and add 4 oz soft brown sugar, 1 dessertspoon golden syrup and 1 very small egg. Add date mixture and put in *lined* loaf tin. Bake at 300°F (Gas Mark 2) for approximately 1¾ hours. Cool, slice and butter.

Pat Brown, Keynsham, Somerset

ORANGE LOAF

2 oz butter	*2 tablespoons milk*
6 oz castor sugar	*7 oz plain flour*
1 egg	*2½ teaspoons baking powder*
Grated rind and juice ½ large orange	*½ teaspoon salt*

Cream butter and sugar until light and fluffy. Add beaten egg gradually with orange rind, juice and milk. Sieve flour, baking powder and salt, and fold into creamed mixture. Put mixture into buttered 2 lb loaf tin, and bake at 375°F (Gas Mark 5) for 1 hour. Cool, slice and spread with butter.

HONEY LOAF

4 oz butter	*10½ oz plain flour*
4 oz castor sugar	*3 teaspoons baking powder*
6 tablespoons honey	*1 teaspoon salt*
1 egg	*¼ pint milk*

Cream butter and sugar until light and fluffy, and mix in honey thoroughly. Beat in egg. Sieve flour, baking powder and salt, and stir into creamed mixture alternately with milk. Put into buttered 2 lb loaf tin and bake at 350°F (Gas Mark 4) for 1¼ hours. Cool, slice and spread with butter.

DATE AND WALNUT LOAF

8 oz self-raising flour	*Pinch salt*
1 teaspoon bicarbonate of soda	*½ pint milk*
2 tablespoons golden syrup	*2 oz chopped walnuts*
2 oz dates	

Melt milk and syrup in saucepan with dates, add walnuts and dry ingredients when slightly cool; pour into greased tin and put a few chopped nuts on top. Cook for 25 minutes at 325°F (Gas Mark 3). Keep in a tin for a few days to get moist.

Mrs Saunders, Bedfordshire

MALT BREAD

2 *cups self-raising flour*
2 *tablespoons sugar*
2 *tablespoons fruit*
½ *teaspoon bicarbonate of soda*

2 *tablespoons Ovaltine*
2 *tablespoons golden syrup*
1 *tablespoon chopped nuts*
(optional)

Mix all together with ¼ pint milk into a stiff mixture, and bake in a moderate oven for 1 hour.

Mrs Evelyn Walker, Derby

WALNUT BREAD

This sweet cake-bread is excellent sliced and buttered and is good with honey. Stir together 12 oz self-raising flour, ½ teaspoon salt and 8 oz castor sugar. Add 6 oz chopped walnuts, 2 beaten eggs, 8 fluid oz milk and 2 oz melted butter. Beat well together, leave to stand for 20 minutes, then put into a tin lined with greaseproof paper (about 9 × 5 × 3 inches). Bake at 350°F (Gas Mark 4) for 1 hour 10 minutes.

ETHEL'S HARVO

3 *cups white flour*
1 *cup sugar*
1 *lb golden syrup*
2 *cups (or more) milk*
1 *cup brown flour*

6 *oz lard*
1½ *teaspoons bicarbonate of soda*
Fruit if desired

Melt syrup, rub fat into flours, add other ingredients, mix to soft dough and bake in slow oven. Eat buttered.

Eaten at harvest-time, when families doubled up to help their neighbours with the harvest in return for help with their own. The wives all worked together to produce the grub to fill the many who sat around the large kitchen table.

Mrs Alden, Selby

MALT LOAF

3 *oz malt extract*
2 *oz brown sugar*
1 *oz butter*
8 *oz wholewheat flour*
2 *teaspoons baking powder*

¼ *teaspoon salt*
¼ *pint milk*
2 *oz currants and sultanas*
1 *oz chopped mixed peel*

Warm the malt extract, sugar and butter together till dissolved. Cool a little. Sift dry ingredients into a bowl, and pour in the liquid. Mix well, stir in the fruit and put into a greased and floured loaf tin. Bake at 325°F (Gas Mark 3) for $1\frac{1}{2}$ hours.

SPICE BREAD

10 oz self-raising flour
$\frac{1}{2}$ teaspoon mixed spice
1 teaspoon ginger
6 oz sultanas
2 oz butter

6 oz syrup
6 tablespoons milk
1 egg
4 oz brown sugar

Mix flour with spices and stir in sugar and fruit. Melt butter and syrup together over gentle heat. Stir into dry ingredients, together with an egg beaten up in milk. Mix well, pour into a well-greased loaf tin, and bake for about $1\frac{1}{2}$ hours at 350°F (Gas Mark 4). Turn out as soon as possible after it is cooked. Slice and butter.

GINGER AND WALNUT TEABREAD

8 oz self-raising flour
$\frac{1}{4}$ level teaspoon salt
2 level teaspoons ground ginger
1 level teaspoon baking powder
2 oz butter
2 oz sugar

3 oz walnuts, chopped
1 oz crystallised ginger, finely chopped
1 egg, beaten
$\frac{1}{4}$ pint milk

For topping:
1 teaspoon demerara sugar

Sift together flour, salt, ginger and baking powder. Rub in butter until mixture resembles fine breadcrumbs. Mix in sugar, walnuts and crystallised ginger. Mix most of the beaten egg with the milk and add to flour and butter. Beat thoroughly. (This makes a very sticky dough.) Turn into a greased 1 lb loaf tin. Brush top with remaining beaten egg and sprinkle with demerara sugar. Bake in a moderate oven, 350°F (Gas Mark 4) for 1 hour 5 minutes, until golden brown and sounds hollow when tapped underneath. Serve sliced and spread with butter.

AUSTRALIAN TEA CAKE

4 oz sultanas
4 oz raisins
4 oz brown sugar
Cold tea

1 tablespoon whisky
1 egg
4 oz flour

Soak the fruit overnight in cold tea, put into a basin and add sugar, flour, beaten egg and whisky. Bake for 1½ hours at 300°F (Gas Mark 2). Don't drown the fruit—just cover with cold tea.

Miss Mabel Nokes, Priston Mill Farm, Bath

FARMHOUSE TREACLE LOAF

8 oz *wholemeal flour*	1 oz *chopped nuts*
8 oz *plain flour*	1 *egg, beaten*
4 oz *sugar*	½ *pint milk*
6 oz *black treacle*	1 *level teaspoon bicarbonate*
5 oz *raisins*	*of soda*

Sift the flours together. Mix in sugar, raisins and nuts. Make a well in the centre. Heat the milk and treacle to lukewarm temperature, add the bicarbonate of soda and pour into flour, add beaten egg. Stir well and put into 2 well-greased 1 lb loaf tins. Bake in a moderate oven, 350°F (Gas Mark 4) for 1½ hours. Slice and spread with butter to serve.

As this loaf contains no fat, it is not a good keeper, but is delicious sliced and buttered while still warm.

BARA BRITH

1 lb *self-raising flour*	*Juice and rind of* 1 *lemon*
4 oz *black treacle*	¼ *level teaspoon salt*
4 oz *sugar*	1 *level teaspoon mixed spice*
4 oz *butter, margarine or*	1 *level teaspoon bicarbonate*
cooking fat	*of soda*
½ lb *sultanas*	*Milk to make the beaten egg*
1 *egg*	*up to* ½ *pint*

Rub fat into flour. Add the salt, spice, sugar, grated lemon rind and sultanas. Mix well together, then add the treacle, egg, milk and lemon juice, mixing the bicarbonate of soda with the last tablespoon of milk mixture. Mix well and put in a well-greased 2 lb loaf tin and bake in a moderate oven 325°F (Gas Mark 3) for 2 hours. Turn out and cool on a rack. Slice and butter to serve.

PHILLIDA'S TEA BREAD

12 oz *mixed fruit (including*	10 oz *self-raising flour*
cherries)	1 *egg*
1 *cup tea*	*A little milk*
6 oz *brown sugar*	

Soak fruit in tea overnight. Mix all ingredients together. Bake at 325°F (Gas Mark 3) for 2 hours. Good eaten as cake, or sliced to eat with butter.

Miss P. Walpole, Wolterton Hall, Norfolk

CORNISH FRUIT BREAD

8 oz plain flour	1 egg
2 teaspoons baking powder	½ pint milk
¼ teaspoon salt	1½ oz butter
½ teaspoon cinnamon	4 oz sugar
½ teaspoon nutmeg	3 oz mixed dried fruit
¼ teaspoon ground ginger	2 oz chopped walnuts

Sift flour, baking powder, salt and spices together and stir in the sugar. Beat the egg and most of the milk together and stir into the dry ingredients. Add the nuts, fruit and melted butter. If necessary, add a little more milk to make a fairly sticky dough. Put into a greased and floured loaf tin and bake at 350°F (Gas Mark 4) for 1 hour.

GREAT AUNT HARRIET'S TEA BREAD

4 oz butter	3 tablespoons orange rind
5 oz sugar	and 2 tablespoons juice
10 oz flour	4 oz chopped walnuts
½ teaspoon salt	4 oz chopped raisins
2 eggs	A little more than ¼ pint milk

Cream the butter, add sugar gradually and cream till smooth. Beat in the eggs one at a time then add rind and juice. Sift flour and salt, add to the mixture alternately with the milk ending with flour. Add nuts and raisins. Bake in a 1 lb tin at 350°F (Gas Mark 4) for about 1 hour.

My great aunt Harriet used to serve this in slices, buttered, just like bread, but my family like it as cake too. As far as I can gather, this recipe was used by my great-aunt's grandmother though the original recipe was for three times as much again.

Mrs St Clare, Stroud

STEAMED SULTANA BREAD

1 cup All Bran cereal	1 teaspoon bicarbonate of
1 cup wholemeal flour	soda
2 cups plain white flour	1 tablespoon black treacle
½ teaspoon salt	1½ cups thick sour milk
1 tablespoon sugar	½ cup sultanas

Use a breakfastcup for measuring the ingredients. The bread is best steamed in straight-sided earthenware marmalade jars, but otherwise can be cooked in small bowls or in cylindrical tins. Mix together bran cereal and the two flours with the salt, sugar and bicarbonate of soda. Beat the treacle into the milk and stir into the dry ingredients. Add the sultanas and mix well. Fill jars or tins about $\frac{2}{3}$ full and tie on greaseproof paper. Put into a pan of boiling water, put on a lid and boil steadily for 3 hours, adding more boiling water as necessary. Turn out on to a wire rack and leave until cold. Cut in slices and serve with cheese.

STOVIES

1 oz bacon fat or dripping	$\frac{1}{2}$ pint hot water
2 lb potatoes	Salt and pepper
$\frac{1}{2}$ lb onions	

Melt fat. Slice and fry onions without browning. Add sliced potatoes, hot water and seasonings. Cover and cook very slowly for $1-1\frac{1}{2}$ hours, stirring or shaking occasionally to prevent browning. Serve with mince collops or casseroles.

Mrs Biggar, Kirkcudbrightshire

POTATO SCONES

8 oz cooked potatoes	About 2 oz flour
$\frac{1}{2}$ gill milk	Pinch of salt

Mash or sieve potatoes, add salt; knead enough flour into this as it will take, then add enough milk to make a stiff dough. Roll out very thinly on floured board. Cut into rounds and prick with a fork. Bake on hot girdle for about 5 minutes, turning when half-cooked. Butter, roll up and serve very hot; or fry with bacon.

Mrs Biggar, Kirkcudbrightshire

BROTHER DON'S POTATO CAKE

12 oz self-raising flour	1 egg
4 oz margarine	2 tablespoons milk
4 oz sugar	4 oz raisins
6 oz hot potato, mashed	

Rub the fat into the flour. Add the sugar, raisins and potato. Mix well. Add the egg and 2 tablespoons milk to bind. Cook in a coolish oven, about 350°F (Gas Mark 4), in a sandwich tin, well greased, for about 1 hour. Serve hot with lashings of butter.

My brother Don lives in the New Forest, and once when his wife was ill he had to do the cooking. Now he still bashes out the very first recipe he tried all those years ago. He reckons if he can do it, anyone can! It's a great standby in times of emergency.

IRISHMAN'S MUFFINS

Peel and grate potato to fill a breakfast cup and drain off the liquid which forms. Work in half as much flour, plenty of salt and a dash of pepper. Thin with a little milk till it will drop from a spoon. Heat enough dripping to give a $\frac{1}{4}$ inch in the frying pan and drop in dessertspoons of the mixture. Fry well, turning frequently, till brown both sides. Dip in salt or melted butter.

Mrs Toulson says that long before the days of the modern barbecue a group of schoolchildren would gather at the bottom of their orchard, where her father had built them a square of loosely arranged bricks, about 4 or 5 bricks high, to form their own barbecue. Sticks and wood were the fuel and on this they made their feast.

Mrs Toulson

WALNUT AND HONEY SCONES

1 lb self-raising flour
1 level teaspoon salt
4 oz butter
2 level tablespoons castor sugar

2 oz finely chopped walnuts
2 tablespoons clear honey
10 tablespoons cold milk

Sift flour and salt into a basin and rub in butter. Add sugar and walnuts and mix to a soft but not sticky dough with honey and milk. Turn on to lightly floured board, knead quickly and roll out to $\frac{1}{2}$ inch thickness. Cut into rounds and put on greased baking sheet. Brush tops with beaten egg or milk and bake at 425°F (Gas Mark 7) for 10 minutes.

COTTAGE CHEESE GRIDDLE CAKES

1 tablespoon melted butter
4 oz cottage cheese
2 eggs

2 oz self-raising flour
1 tablespoon milk

Add butter to cottage cheese and gradually whisk in eggs. Stir in flour and milk and mix to a smooth thick batter. Drop spoonsful on to a hot greased griddle or frying-pan and turn several times. Serve freshly baked with crisp hot bacon, honey, jam or jelly. These scones are very light and digestible, and particularly good for those who do not want much starch in their diet.

GOLDEN DROP SCONES

8 oz self-raising flour
½ level teaspoon salt
½ level teaspoon grated
nutmeg
1 level dessertspoon castor
sugar

1 egg
2 level tablespoons black
treacle
Scant ½ pint cold milk

Sift dry ingredients into bowl. Make well in centre, and drop in egg and treacle, then gradually mix to thick batter with the milk, drawing in flour from sides of bowl. Beat with back of wooden spoon till batter is smooth and creamy. Drop dessertspoons on to well greased griddle, thick frying pan or hot plate of an electric cooker. Cook for about 1 minute each side. Serve hot with butter.

DROP SCONES OFTEN CALLED PANSCONES

8 oz self-raising flour
1 dessertspoon golden syrup

1 egg
½ pint milk

Mix to a batter. Grease a hot girdle or hot plate slightly. Drop the batter in spoonsful on to the hot plate. When the scones bubble, turn over with a knife. They should be golden brown on both sides. Cool in a clean towel. Cover them until cold.

Mrs Corrie, Burnside of Auchegool, Kirkcudbrightshire

PITCARTHLY BANNOCK

6 oz flour
1 oz rice flour
4 oz butter
3 oz castor sugar

1 oz almonds
1 oz candied orange or
citron peel

Blanch and chop almonds finely. Shred and chop peel finely. Sieve flour, rice flour and sugar, rub in butter and work all together with the lard. Form into a cake or press into shortbread mould. Prick well, and bake in steady oven until beginning to colour, moderate the heat and allow to crisp off slowly for about 1 hour.

Mrs Biggar, Kirkcudbrightshire

LARGE ROUND SCONE

6 oz sifted white self-raising
flour
2 oz wholewheat stoneground
flour
2 oz margarine

1 level teaspoon baking
powder
A little salt
Sugar to taste
Mix with a little milk

Rub fat into flour, add salt and sugar, mix with a little milk. Put into enamel plate (cutting round into 12 segments). Bake at 400°F (Gas Mark 6) for about 15–20 minutes.

Miss Grace Butler, Southstoke, Somerset

LANCASHIRE SCONES

½ lb self-raising flour
¾ oz butter
3 oz crumbled Lancashire
cheese

A little salt
¼ pint milk

Mix the flour and a pinch of salt. Rub in butter and add cheese. Make into a fairly soft dough by adding about ¼ pint milk. Roll the mixture out ¾ inch thick, and cut in small circles. Bake in a hot oven, 425°F (Gas Mark 7), until brown. Split, spread with butter and eat them hot. Lancashire cheese was often referred to as 'Leigh Toaster' because it is so good when cooked.

WHOLEMEAL SPOON SCONES

10 oz wholemeal flour
6 oz plain flour
1 level teaspoon salt
2 oz granulated sugar
1 level teaspoon bicarbonate
of soda

2 level teaspoons cream of
tartar
2 oz butter
1 tablespoon black treacle
Scant ½ pint milk

Sieve together dry ingredients and stir in sugar. Rub in butter, then mix with treacle and milk to give a heavy dropping consistency. Drop dessert-spoons of mixture on to a baking sheet, dusted with wholemeal flour. Brush lightly with milk and dredge with flour or rolled oats. Bake at 450°F (Gas Mark 8) for 15 minutes.

SCOTTISH TREACLE SCONES

2 oz butter or margarine
8 oz self-raising flour
1 oz castor sugar

2 oz black treacle
1 egg
1 oz currants

Rub the fat into the sifted flour, add the sugar and dried fruit, and mix in the well-beaten egg and the black treacle, adding a little cold milk if necessary to make a soft, but not sticky dough. Roll out to 1 inch thickness and cut into 2 inch rounds with a plain cutter. Well grease a hot girdle, or thick frying pan or electric hotplate. Cook the scones on a gentle heat for about 5 to 7 minutes on each side. Pile between folds of a napkin and serve, split and buttered, while still warm.

MRS BLENKIN'S SCONES

1 lb self-raising flour
6 oz granulated sugar
4 oz margarine
4 oz lard

Currants or sultanas
1 egg
Milk to mix
Beaten egg

Stir together flour and sugar and rub in fat. Add dried fruit to taste, egg and a little milk to mix. Roll out and cut in circles, and brush with beaten egg. Bake at 425°F (Gas Mark 7) for 10 minutes, and at 350°F (Gas Mark 4) for 5 minutes.

When Babs Honey had to travel to Hull one autumn day, she arrived at the station in the evening, having left early from Somerset. Her instructions were to have tea in the big store opposite the station and then to catch the bus to the fire station at Patrington. A lady in the bus queue had been born in Somerset so she guided her till she had to get off at her stop. The lady behind said it was another 3 miles and they got off the bus together. Babs asked if she could be directed to the Parish Hall where she was due in an hour's time. Learning that she was the speaker for the W.I. Group Meeting, her new friend took her home, gave her the freedom of the bathroom, and presented her with a steaming cup of tea by the fire and a plate of scones—so delicious and so light that they melted in the mouth. Here is the recipe from a real Christian soul.

Mrs Blenkin, Patrington, E. Yorks

FRUIT SCONE

8 oz flour
2 medium-sized tablespoons golden syrup
8 oz dried fruit (chopped dates are good, but sultanas, currants, peel etc. can be used)

1 heaped teaspoon bicarbonate of soda
1 heaped teaspoon cream of tartar

Melt syrup in about 1 teacup warm water. Allow to cool. Sieve flour with cream of tartar, add dried fruit. Mix to a soft dough with the syrup and water, adding the bicarbonate in the last of the liquid. Divide mixture into 2 greased sandwich tins. Bake till brown (about 10–15 minutes) at 425°F (Gas Mark 7). When cold, split and butter scone.

YOGHURT DROP SCONES

¼ *pint plain yoghurt*
1 *egg*

2 *level tablespoons plain flour,*
sifted with a pinch of salt
A little lard for frying

Beat the egg. Put the yoghurt into a bowl, add the egg and beat well. Add the sifted flour and salt, and fold into the mixture. Heat a little lard in a frying pan and when a haze rises from it, drop dessertspoons of the mixture into it. Cook until golden brown on underside, then, using a palette knife, turn to cook the other side in the same way. Drain on kitchen paper when cooked and keep hot, until all are cooked. Serve immediately with butter, jam or honey.

SCOTCH PANCAKES

3 *tablespoons plain flour*
1 *teaspoon cream of tartar*
½ *teaspoon bicarbonate of soda*

1 *egg*
1 *dessertspoon syrup*
A little milk

Sieve all dry ingredients then drop egg in centre and beat up. Then add syrup and beat up; if too thick, add a little milk. Cook on hot girdle.

Mrs Dunlop

DERBYSHIRE OATCAKE

½ *lb fine or medium oatmeal*
8 *oz plain flour*
Pinch of salt

1 *oz yeast*
1 *level teaspoon sugar*
½ *pint lukewarm water*

Sift together oatmeal and flour with salt. Cream yeast and sugar and add warm water. Stir into dry ingredients and leave in a warm place for 30 minutes. Heat griddle and grease lightly. Pour on a little batter and cook about 2 minutes. Turn and bake the other side. Serve hot with butter or dripping, or with crisp hot bacon.

NORFOLK GOLDEN RUSKS

8 *oz self-raising flour*
2 *oz fat – lard or margarine*
1 *egg*
1 *heaped teaspoon baking*
powder

Pinch salt – or more as
preferred
A little milk to mix, or milk
and water

114

Sift dry ingredients together. Rub in fat; mix to a soft dough – like a scone dough – with the beaten egg adding a little milk gradually as required. Roll out, cut into rounds about ¾ inch thick. Bake in a very hot oven, 475°F, (Gas Mark 9) about 8 minutes by which time they should be well-risen but *not* coloured.

At the turn of the century, no Norfolk tea-table was complete without a dish of crisp, golden rusks, thickly spread with fresh farmhouse butter.

SUFFOLK RUSKS

8 oz self-raising flour
3 oz butter

1 egg
Milk or water to mix

Rub the fat into the flour. Add the lightly-beaten egg, and work in enough milk or water to give a scone-like mixture. Roll out ¾ inch thick and cut into rounds. Bake at 450°F (Gas Mark 8) for 10 minutes. Split in half at once and put on baking sheets split side uppermost. Bake at 375°F (Gas Mark 5) until golden and crisp. These are delicious with cheese or with butter and jam.

8 Large and Small Cakes

He that will have cake out of the wheat must tarry the grinding.
William Shakespeare

Would'st thou both eat thy cake and have it?
George Herbert

CHERRY CAKE

8 oz *plain flour*
1½ *teaspoons baking powder*
6 oz *butter*
6 oz *castor sugar*
Grated rind of 2 lemons
3 *eggs*
1 *tablespoon milk*
4 oz *glacé cherries*

Sift flour and baking powder. Cream butter and sugar until light and fluffy and work in the eggs one at a time, adding a little flour with each one. Add the lemon rind and fold in the flour and the baking powder, then the milk. Add the cherries which have been lightly coated with flour. Put into greased 7 inch cake tin and bake at 325°F (Gas Mark 3) for 1½ hours. Store in tin or freezer.

KPARIN

6 oz *plain flour*
1 *level teaspoon salt*
1 *level teaspoon ground ginger*
2 *level teaspoons ground cinnamon*
1 *level teaspoon bicarbonate of soda*
10 oz *medium oatmeal*
6 oz *black treacle*
5 oz *butter*
4 oz *soft brown sugar*
¼ *pint milk*
1 *egg*

Sift together flour, salt, spices and soda. Add oatmeal, and toss lightly to mix. Warm treacle, butter, sugar and milk until the butter has melted. Cool slightly, add egg and beat well. Pour into the centre of the dry ingredients and stir rapidly until smooth. Turn into a greased and lined 7 inch square tin. Bake at 350°F (Gas Mark 4) for 1 hour. Store in an airtight tin for 2 weeks before using.

APPLE GINGERBREAD

1 *large cooking apple*
6 *whole cloves*
1 *dessertspoon sugar*
3 *tablespoons water*
6 oz *self-raising flour*
2 *teaspoons ground ginger*
3 oz *sugar*
1 *egg*
4 oz *black treacle*
3 oz *melted butter*

Fudge icing:
1 oz *butter*
2 oz *black treacle*
2 oz *icing sugar*
Pinch of cinnamon

Peel, core and slice apple, and put into a saucepan with cloves, sugar and water. Cook until tender, remove cloves and mash apple with a fork. Leave to cool. Put flour and ginger into a bowl and stir in 3 oz sugar. Add the cooked apple, beaten egg, black treacle and butter and beat well together. Turn into 1½ lb greased loaf tin, and bake at 350°F (Gas Mark 4) for 40 minutes. Cool on a rack.

Make the icing by creaming together butter, treacle and sugar until light and fluffy. Add cinnamon and spread icing on the cake. Decorate with a scattering of chopped nuts or chopped crystallised ginger. Store in a tin, or wrapped in foil in the freezer.

SUGAR AND SPICE CAKE

4 oz *butter*
6 oz *sugar*
2 *eggs*
4 *tablespoons hot water*
10 oz *plain flour*
1 *teaspoon bicarbonate of soda*
8 oz *raspberry jam, apricot jam or marmalade*
1 *teaspoon cinnamon*
½ *teaspoon mixed spice*

Cream butter and sugar until light and fluffy. Add the eggs one at a time, then the water. Fold in sifted dry ingredients alternately with the jam or marmalade and beat thoroughly to blend the ingredients. Put into buttered 8 inch cake tin and bake at 325°F (Gas Mark 3) for 1 hour. Turn out and cool, and if liked, ice with a thin orange icing. Store in a tin or freezer.

MOIST CHOCOLATE CAKE

Cake:
8 oz butter
6 oz soft brown sugar
6 oz black treacle
4 eggs
6 oz self-raising flour
2 oz cocoa

For filling:
Fresh or butter cream,
flavoured as liked with orange
rind, peppermint or rum

For Icing:
Chocolate glacé icing, plain
or topped with slivers of
almonds or chopped walnuts

Cream together butter, sugar and treacle. Gradually beat in blended eggs adding tablespoon of sieved flour with last amount of egg. Sieve together flour and cocoa and fold into creamed mixture. Turn into two greased and bottom-lined 8–9 inch sponge sandwich tins; bake in moderate oven, 350°F (Gas Mark 4) for about 50 minutes. Turn out. When cold sandwich with fresh or butter cream and top with chocolate glacé icing.

EGGLESS CHOCOLATE CAKE

5 oz self-raising flour
1 tablespoon cocoa
1½ oz butter
2 oz sugar
1 tablespoon syrup or treacle

1 teaspoon cinnamon
½ teaspoon bicarbonate of soda
Sufficient milk or milk and
water to make moist
consistency

Cream sugar and butter. Add melted syrup. Stir cocoa, cinnamon, baking soda and pinch of salt into the flour, sift into other ingredients. Add milk until mixture is of moist consistency. Bake in greased tin in fairly hot oven, 375°F (Gas Mark 5). This makes a moist cake.

DUNDEE CAKE

8 oz butter
8 oz sugar
5 eggs
8 oz self-raising flour
½ teaspoon nutmeg

12 oz mixed currants and
sultanas
3 oz ground almonds
3 oz chopped glacé cherries
2 oz chopped candied peel
2 oz split blanched almonds

Cream butter and sugar and add eggs one at a time, each with a sprinkling of flour to avoid curdling. Beat well after each addition. Stir in most of the flour and lastly the fruit lightly coated with the rest of the flour. Turn into a 9 inch cake tin lined with greased paper, smooth the top and arrange almonds on surface. Bake at 325°F (Gas Mark 3) for 2–2½ hours.

MARMALADE CAKE

4 oz butter
4 oz sugar
2 eggs

2 rounded tablespoons
marmalade
8 oz self-raising flour
4 tablespoons milk

Cream butter and sugar and beat in eggs. Mix in marmalade, then add flour and enough milk to give a soft dropping consistency. Put in a greased 7 inch cake tin and bake at 350°F (Gas Mark 4) for 1 hour. For immediate use, this is good topped with whipped cream or orange butter icing, decorated with strips of candied peel.

SULTANA ORANGE CAKE

8 oz self-raising flour
Pinch of salt
4 oz margarine
4 oz castor sugar
2 large eggs

7 oz sultanas
Grated rind of 1 small orange
1 tablespoon strained orange
juice

Sift flour and salt. Cream margarine and sugar until light and fluffy, then add eggs one by one, beating well. Fold in half the flour, then the sultanas and grated rind. Fold in the rest of the flour, and add enough orange juice to give a stiff dropping consistency. Turn into a 6 inch cake tin lined with greased paper, and bake at 350°F (Gas Mark 4) for 1½–1¾ hours. It's good, too, if you substitute lemon juice and lemon rind.

CARAWAY SEED CAKE

6 oz butter
6 oz sugar
3 eggs

8 oz *plain flour*
¼ *teaspoon baking powder*
½ *oz caraway seed*

Cream butter and sugar until very soft, and gradually add beaten eggs.
Gradually add flour and baking powder, and finally the caraway seeds.
Turn into a greased 7 inch cake tin and bake at 350°F (Gas Mark 4) for
1¼–1½ hours.

DRIPPING CAKE

8 oz *mixed dried fruit and*
candied peel
3 oz *clarified beef dripping*
5 oz *brown sugar*
1½ *gills water*
8 oz *wholemeal flour*

1 *teaspoon baking powder*
Pinch of nutmeg
Pinch of cinnamon
Pinch of mixed spice
½ *teaspoon bicarbonate of soda*

Put fruit in a heavy pan with dripping, sugar and water, bring to the boil
and simmer for 10 minutes. Leave to cool, then pour into the rest of the
ingredients which have been sifted together. Blend well but do not beat.
Put into a greased 6 inch cake tin and bake at 350°F (Gas Mark 4) for
1¼–1½ hours.

BOILED FRUIT CAKE

5 oz *butter or margarine*
6 *tablespoons golden syrup*
¼ *pint milk*
4 oz *chopped dates*
8 oz *currants*
4 oz *sultanas*
8 oz *stoned raisins*

4 oz *chopped mixed peel*
8 oz *self-raising flour*
1 *teaspoon mixed spice*
1 *teaspoon nutmeg*
Pinch of salt
2 *eggs*
½ *teaspoon bicarbonate of soda*

Put butter, syrup, milk and fruit into a saucepan and heat slowly until the
fat has melted. Simmer gently for 5 minutes, stirring once or twice, then
cool completely. Sieve together flour, spices and salt, make a well in the
centre, add eggs, but do not stir.

Add soda to the fruit mixture and add to the dry ingredients, mixing
thoroughly and beating well. Pour into a greased and lined 10 inch round
tin and bake at 325°F (Gas Mark 3) for 1¾ hours. This is a moist, fruity
cake which keeps well and is excellent for packed meals. It can be stored
in a tin, or frozen when wrapped in foil or polythene.

CORONATION FRUIT CAKE
A moist cake that improves with keeping

8 oz *plain flour*
Pinch of salt
8 oz *butter*
6 oz *sugar*
1 lb *currants*
6 oz *sultanas (or same
quantity of mixed fruit)*
2–3 oz *blanched chopped
almonds*

2 teaspoons *powdered
cinnamon*
½ teaspoon *each of powdered
cloves and nutmeg*
½ teaspoon *bicarbonate of soda*
4 *eggs*
1 tablespoon *black treacle*

Sieve dry ingredients. Beat butter and sugar to a soft cream, add treacle, beat till well mixed. Add well-beaten eggs one at a time, beating each one well in. Fold in sieved flour mixture alternately with dried fruit and almonds. Put into a 7–8 inch tin well lined with greased paper. Make a hollow in the centre of cake to ensure a flat surface when cooked. Bake 3 hours, in a hot oven to start with, 375°F (Gas Mark 5) for 1 hour, then turn to 300°F (Gas Mark 2) for rest of time.

BROWN PLUM CAKE

10 oz *butter*
6 oz *sugar*
1 lb *mixed cake fruit*
Little candied peel
12 oz *flour*
Pinch of ginger

*A little powdered spice, if
liked*
2 *eggs*
½ teaspoon *bicarbonate of soda*
1 *teacup milk*

Cream fat and sugar, add fruit, peel, spice, flour then well-beaten eggs, and lastly milk with the soda dissolved in it. Bake in paper-lined tin for 3 hours in a slow oven, 300°F (Gas Mark 2).

VICARAGE CAKE

Melt 4 oz fat and put it to cool. When cool, mix the fat in 1 lb self-raising flour (brown is best) and add 6 oz sugar, 3 level teaspoons mixed spices and 4 oz fruit. Into a jug put 2 tablespoons treacle, ½ pint and 3 more tablespoons of milk. Stir to dissolve treacle. Make a hole in dry ingredients, put in the liquid and mix well. Bake in moderate oven 1¼ hours.

OLIVE'S CAKE

4 oz butter
4 oz sugar
2 oz golden syrup
2 eggs
8 oz flour
4–8 oz dried fruit (can be mixed)

2 oz dates
2 oz candied peel
1 dessertspoon marmalade
½ teacup milk
¼ teaspoon bicarbonate of soda

Cream fat, sugar, syrup. Beat eggs, add to creamed mixture alternately with flour. Add fruit and marmalade, lastly bicarbonate of soda dissolved in the milk. Line medium-sized tin with greased paper, put in mixture. Bake 1½–2 hours at 350°F (Gas Mark 4).

BROWN FRUIT CAKE

6 oz plain flour
1 tablespoon syrup
2 oz any fat
2 eggs
4 oz any dried fruit (dates and sultanas are excellent)

1 level teaspoon bicarbonate of soda
½ teaspoon nutmeg
½ teaspoon spice
2 tablespoons milk

Rub fat in flour, beat eggs well, add to mixture, put in treacle, fruit, spices, stir bicarbonate of soda in milk. add to mixture. Grease tin and flour it all over. Put in moderate oven 350°F (Gas Mark 4) for 1 hour. Turn out to cool on wire tray.

LIGHT FRUIT CAKE

4 oz butter
2 oz black treacle
2 oz soft brown sugar
3 eggs
6 oz plain flour
1 level teaspoon baking powder

1 level teaspoon mixed spice
Grated rind of ½ lemon
8 oz seedless raisins
2 oz glacé cherries, sliced
2 oz chopped mixed peel (or use 12 oz mixed dried fruit)
A few blanched almonds

Line 7 inch tin with greased paper. Cream the butter, treacle and sugar until fluffy. Add the eggs one at a time, beating well between each. Add the sifted dry ingredients alternately with the fruit, folding in lightly. Put into cake tin, and sprinkle nuts on top. Bake in a moderate oven, 350°F (Gas Mark 4) for about 1 hour. Allow to cool in the tin before removing.

RICH FRUIT CAKE

8 oz butter
6 oz soft brown sugar
1 teaspoon vanilla essence
1 teaspoon almond essence
Grated rind of 1 orange
4 tablespoons black treacle
4 eggs
10 oz plain flour

4 level teaspoons mixed spice
3 lb mixed fruit (raisins,
sultanas, dates, cherries,
candied peel, all well chopped)
$\frac{1}{4}$ lb ground almonds
(optional)
4 tablespoons brandy, sherry
or orange juice

Grease and line cake tin, 9 inch across, with double thickness of grease-proof paper. Cream butter and sugar until light and fluffy; beat in essence and orange rind. Blend treacle with well beaten eggs and gradually beat into creamed mixture, adding 2 tablespoons sifted flour when half egg mixture is added. Lightly stir in sifted flour and spice. Add fruit and ground almonds and lastly liquid.

Turn into prepared cake tin. Bake in very slow oven, 300°F (Gas Mark 1) for about 4 hours, until a bright skewer comes out clean when inserted into middle of cake. Cook on cake rack, leaving on paper until ready to ice or to serve without frosting.

Double quantity is sufficient for tin 12 inch in diameter and takes $5\frac{1}{2}$–6 hours in very slow oven, 275°F (Gas Mark $\frac{1}{2}$).

Half above quantity is enough for 5 inch or 6 inch cake tin and takes about $2\frac{1}{2}$ hours in slow oven, 325°F (Gas Mark 3).

Good for a wedding or Christmas.

TWO MINUTE CAKE

1 lb self-raising flour
8 oz sugar
Pinch of salt
1–1$\frac{1}{2}$ lb dried fruit

4 eggs
2 small cups milk
8 oz butter

Put all dry ingredients in a bowl and add eggs and milk. Melt the butter until quite runny and pour into the mixture. Beat well for 1 minute, and then pour into a greased lined tin. Bake 300°F (Gas Mark 2) for 3 hours. Add spice for extra flavour.

Mrs Cook, Church Allerton on Mendips, near Wedmore

BASIC RECIPE FRUIT CAKE

8 oz butter
About 4 oz sugar

About 4 oz golden syrup

Mix together sugar and butter and syrup. Add 1 or 2 eggs and milk, 12 oz self-raising flour, mixed fruit and almond essence. Cook 1¼ hours at about 300°F (Gas Mark 2).

DARK CAKE

1 *lb mixed fruit*
½ *lb dark soft sugar*

Enough warm tea to cover
Self-raising flour

Leave for a day to let fruit swell. Stir in as much self-raising flour as liquid will absorb. Well grease a bread tin and cook 1½–2 hours in very low oven (350°F, Gas Mark 4). Test with skewer.

GINGER STICKY-TOPPED CAKE

For topping:
2 oz butter
1 rounded tablespoon golden syrup
1 oz soft brown sugar
1½ oz flaked almonds
1½ oz glacé cherries, halves
1 oz sultanas

For sponge:
4 oz self-raising flour
1 level teaspoon baking powder
2 level teaspoons ground ginger
½ level teaspoon salt
4 oz castor sugar
2 eggs
4 oz butter

To make topping—Melt butter, syrup and brown sugar in a saucepan. Add almonds, glacé cherries and sultanas. Pour into the bottom of a greased 2 lb loaf tin.

To make sponge—Sift flour, baking powder, ginger and salt into a bowl. Add castor sugar, eggs and butter. Beat thoroughly for 2 minutes. Pour into the tin, carefully covering the topping. Place in a moderate oven, 350°F (Gas Mark 4) for 45–50 minutes, until firm to touch. Turn out and cool.

GINGERBREAD

4 oz plain flour
4 oz wholemeal flour
1 level teaspoon mixed spice
2 level teaspoons ground ginger
3 oz sultanas
4 oz margarine

1 gill milk
8 oz golden syrup
1 egg
1 level teaspoon bicarbonate of soda
1½ oz brown sugar

124

Sieve all dry ingredients (except soda) into a bowl. Add sugar and fruit, melt fat and syrup, warm milk and mix in soda; add the egg to dry ingredients, followed by fat and syrup; lastly add soda and milk. Pour mixture into greased tin (8 × 10 inches). Bake at 375°F (Gas Mark 5) for 45 minutes. The gingerbread will be 1 inch thick.

Mrs Joslin, Warwicks

DAMP GINGERBREAD

10 oz flour
6 oz butter
6 oz moist sugar
3 oz almonds
6 oz sultanas
1½ teaspoons ground ginger

1½ teaspoons cinnamon
¼ lb treacle
2 eggs
Warm milk
¾ teaspoon baking soda

Sieve the flour; clean sultanas; blanch and shred the almonds (blanch by steeping few minutes in cup of boiling water) and mix 1 teaspoon flour with the fruit. Cream the butter and sugar, add dry ingredients, treacle, beaten eggs and the baking soda mixed with a little milk. Add more milk if necessary to the whole. Turn into greased tin and bake at 325°F (Gas Mark 3) for 2 hours.

Mrs Biggar, Kirkcudbrightshire

BUTTER MILK CAKE

1 lb plain flour
½ level teaspoon mixed spice
½ level teaspoon ground ginger
½ lb butter
½ lb brown sugar
1 lb mixed fruit (raisins,

sultanas and currants)
½ pint buttermilk or sour milk
1 rounded tablespoon black
treacle
1 rounded teaspoon
bicarbonate of soda

Sieve flour and spices into a large mixing bowl. Rub in butter until mixture looks like breadcrumbs. Add sugar and prepared fruit and mix well. Heat buttermilk and add treacle and bicarbonate of soda. Stir until frothy. Add to the ingredients in the bowl and mix well together. Put into a greased and bottom-lined, round, 8 inch cake tin. Bake in a moderate oven, 350°F (Gas Mark 4), for 2¼–2½ hours, covering the cake with a piece of greaseproof paper after about 1 hour.

SUNDAY APRICOT CAKE

4 eggs	Apricot icing:
Butter	5 oz butter
Castor sugar	5 oz icing sugar
Self-raising flour	8 oz can apricot halves

Weigh the eggs and take their weight in butter, sugar and flour. Cream butter and sugar until light and fluffy. Work in eggs and flour, and pour into 2 8 inch sponge tins. Bake at 375°F (Gas Mark 5) for 25 minutes. Cool on a wire rack. To make the icing, cream the butter and sugar and gradually beat in a little juice from the can of apricots to make a really creamy icing. Spread half the icing on to one of the sponge layers. Cut the other layer in half and prop up on top of the filling with remaining cream. Fill the line between the halves with apricots and sprinkle top with castor sugar. This makes a delicious birthday cake.

Maisie Jones

HONEY CAKE

1 lb thick honey	1 level teaspoon baking
6 oz soft brown sugar	powder
4 eggs	2 oz sultanas
1 teaspoon powdered	2 oz blanched chopped
cinnamon	almonds
1/4 teaspoon mixed spice	2 oz chopped peel
12 oz wholemeal flour	

Grease and line a 9 inch square cake tin with greased greaseproof paper. Melt honey and sugar over gentle heat in large saucepan. Remove from heat and cool slightly, then beat in eggs and spices and stir in the flour and baking powder until well blended. Stir in cleaned sultanas, chopped almonds and chopped peel.

Turn mixture into prepared tin and bake in hot oven, 400°F (Gas Mark 6) for about ¾ hour or until cooked through. Cool in tin, then turn out on wire rack and strip off paper. Store in an airtight tin and cut into squares to serve as required.

LUNCHEON CAKE

8 oz self-raising flour	2 oz chopped peel
1/4 level teaspoon salt	Grated rind 1/2 lemon
4 oz butter or margarine	1 egg
4 oz soft brown sugar	5 tablespoons milk
4 oz sultanas	

Sift flour and salt into bowl. Rub in fat lightly. Stir in sugar, the cleaned dry fruit, chopped peel and lemon rind. Beat egg with milk and stir into mixture. Put mixture into greased and floured medium size loaf tin. Bake in moderate oven, 375°F (Gas Mark 5), for 1¼–1½ hours, or until cooked through. Turn out and cool.

FUNERAL CAKE

8 oz soft brown sugar	2 oz ground almonds
8 oz butter	3 eggs
6 oz sultanas	12 oz self-raising flour
6 oz currants	Nutmeg, lemon or mixed
2 oz raisins	spice
2 oz peel	

Put sugar, butter and fruit into a saucepan with 1 tablespoon water and boil for 3 minutes. Cool and stir in ground almonds, eggs and flour, and selected flavourings. Put into 10 inch greased round tin and bake at 375°F (Gas Mark 5) for 1½ hours, and then at 350°F (Gas Mark 4) for 30 minutes. Cool in tin before turning out. Mrs Davies says this is quick to make (for funerals) and rich and good for cutting. She also said it could be made weeks beforehand (presumably for Christmas and not for a funeral); the recipe came from her great-grandmother and has been in the family for generations. In Wales and bordering counties, dying is not 'kept to yourself'. Indeed everyone shares in it, and it's a drama above all else. 'We buried him decently with 'am and funeral cake', and of course *everyone* turns up, and a good time is had by all—well almost. Certainly in the case of a good old-aged person.

Doris Davies, Hay-on-Wye, Hereford

DUNDEE CAKE

8 oz plain flour	3 oz currants
½ teaspoon baking powder	3 oz raisins
8 oz butter	1 oz candied peel
8 oz sugar	Grated rind and juice of 1
3 oz sultanas	orange
3 eggs	3 oz almonds

Sift flour and baking powder. Cream butter and sugar. Add eggs, then flour, fruit, orange rind and juice. Put mixture in a greased paper-lined 8 inch tin. Blanch and slice almonds, and strew on top. Bake at 325°F (Gas Mark 3) for 2 hours.

Mrs Corrie, Burnside of Auchegool, Kirkcudbrightshire

TROUP CAKE

3 oz butter
1 tablespoon golden syrup
½ oz sugar

3 oz seedless raisins
6 oz plain chocolate
7 oz digestive biscuits

Melt the butter, syrup and sugar with raisins over a low heat. Melt the chocolate over hot water. Crush the biscuits with a rolling pin. Stir the crumbs into the butter mixture, together with a dessertspoon of the melted chocolate. Press the mixture into a shallow tin. Pour on the remaining chocolate. Leave to set and cut into small pieces.

MATTHEW'S CHOCOLATE CAKE

10 oz chocolate (plain)
6 oz butter
3 oz castor sugar

3 oz ground almonds
4 eggs
2 oz plain flour

Melt 6 oz chocolate over hot water. Cream the butter and sugar until light and fluffy and beat in the chocolate, ground almonds and egg yolks. Whip the egg whites stiffly. Fold in the flour and the egg whites, and pour into an 8 inch greased and floured tin. Bake at 350°F (Gas Mark 4) for 40 minutes. Cool on a wire rack and top with the remaining chocolate which has been melted over hot water.

CHOCOLATE TRUFFLE CAKE

4 oz margarine
1 tablespoon sugar
1 tablespoon syrup

2 tablespoons cocoa
8 oz sweet biscuit crumbs
2 oz plain chocolate

Cream the margarine and sugar. Add the syrup and cocoa and mix well. The biscuit crumbs should be very fine (they can be crushed with a rolling pin). Add gradually to the mixture and stir in well. Press down into a greased sandwich tin. Melt the chocolate over hot water and pour over the cake. Leave in a cool place for 5 hours to set. Cut in small pieces as it is rather rich.

FESTIVAL CAKE

1 lb mixed dried fruit
1 breakfastcup soft brown
sugar
1 breakfastcup water
4 oz butter
1 teaspoon bicarbonate of soda

2 teacups self-raising flour
2 large eggs
2 oz nuts (almonds, walnuts)
12 glacé cherries
Squeeze of lemon
A drop of brandy also helps

Simmer together fruit, sugar, water, butter and soda for 5 minutes and leave to get cold. Add flour, beaten eggs, chopped nuts, cherries cut in half, and lemon juice with brandy. Mix well and pour into deep 7 inch tin greased and lined. Bake on middle shelf of oven set at 325°F (Gas Mark 3) for 2 hours. This recipe was given to Mrs Thompson by a very old lady who still makes it regularly. She *has* to, as her husband insists.

Helen Thompson, Newbury, Berks

VICTORIAN GINGER CAKE

8 oz butter	*8 oz crystallised ginger*
8 oz castor sugar	*Juice of 1 small lemon*
3 oz plain flour	*½ teaspoon bicarbonate of soda*
½ teaspoon salt	*1 dessertspoon boiling water*
4 large eggs	

Cream the butter and sugar until very light and fluffy. Sift flour and salt together and sprinkle a little on to the butter mixture. Add the eggs one at a time, adding a little flour at each addition. Cut the ginger into very small pieces and put into a bowl. Add the lemon juice, soda and water and stir well. Add to the cake mixture and stir until blended. Put into a greased and floured deep 7 inch cake tin. Bake at 325°F (Gas Mark 3) for 2 hours.

South Stoke Vicarage, Bath

VICTORIAN LUNCHEON CAKE

½ lb sifted self-raising flour	*3 tablespoons milk*
4 oz beef dripping	*1 rounded teaspoon baking*
4 oz soft brown (pieces) sugar	*powder*
1 egg	*8 oz currants*

Butter and flour the sides and base of a 6–6½ inch diameter, sliding-based cake tin. Cream the dripping thoroughly, add sugar, and cream down again. Sift flour and baking powder together. Add 2 tablespoons flour to dripping mixture, then the egg, and whip again. Continue adding flour gradually with single spoonsful of milk until both ingredients are absorbed. Turn into prepared tin. Flour currants and shake off surplus in a sieve. Turn on top of cake mixture and work in with a table fork, being careful not to let fork touch base. Thus fruit will not sink. Bake on middle shelf of oven, 325°F (Gas Mark 3) for 1 hour 10 minutes to 1 hour 15 minutes.

RAISIN PARKIN

12 oz medium oatmeal
6 oz plain flour
1 oz sugar
1 teaspoon ground ginger
¼ teaspoon salt

4 oz seedless raisins
⅛ pint milk
1 teaspoon bicarbonate of soda
1 lb black treacle
4 oz butter

Grease a meat tin (about 8 × 10 inches) and line the bottom with grease-proof paper. Put oatmeal, flour, sugar, ginger and salt into a bowl with the raisins and mix well together. Warm the milk to blood heat, and add soda. Melt together the treacle and butter. Add milk and treacle mixture to dry ingredients. Beat well and pour into prepared tin. Bake at 350°F (Gas Mark 4) for 45 minutes until firm to the touch. Cool a little and turn on to a cake rack. Keep in a tin for a few days before eating.

GINGER SPONGE WITH MARMALADE

4 oz butter
2 oz soft brown sugar
2 tablespoons warm golden syrup
2 eggs

4 oz self-raising flour
¼ teaspoon baking powder
½ teaspoon ground ginger
Marmalade

Cream butter, sugar and syrup and when light and fluffy, work in beaten eggs. Fold in flour sifted with baking powder and ginger. Put into two greased 7 inch tins. Bake at 400°F (Gas Mark 6) for 25 minutes. Turn out on a wire rack and cool. Sandwich together liberally with marmalade and sprinkle with icing sugar.

GILL'S SYRUP SPONGE CAKE

2 oz butter
2 oz sugar
4 tablespoons golden syrup

1 egg
2 tablespoons milk
4 oz self-raising flour

Melt together the butter, sugar and syrup. Beat together the egg and milk. Add egg mixture and flour alternately to the butter mixture. When well mixed, pour into greased 8 inch sponge tin. Bake at 350°F (Gas Mark 4) for 35 minutes. Cool on a wire rack. Do not split the cake, but top with a thin lemon water icing.

PHILLIDA'S BREAD PUDDING

8 slices bread (toast thickness)
½ pint milk
12 oz mixed dried fruit
2 oz mixed chopped candied
peel
1 apple
3 tablespoons brown sugar

2 tablespoons marmalade
3 tablespoons self-raising
flour
2 eggs
Squeeze of lemon juice
1 teaspoon ground cinnamon
4 oz butter

Soak the bread in the milk until it is really soft. Add dried fruit and peel, lemon juice, grated peeled apple, sugar, marmalade, flour, eggs and cinnamon. Beat very thoroughly together. Melt the butter and pour half into the mixture. Beat and put into a greased meat tin. Pour on remaining butter. Bake at 300°F (Gas Mark 2) for 1½ hours; then at 350°F (Gas Mark 4) for 30 minutes. Leave until cold, sprinkle with icing sugar, and cut in slices. It can also be eaten hot as a pudding with egg custard. A plate of this delicious 'rib-sticker' doesn't last long if it is left in the kitchen as a between-meals snack for hungry workers or sportsmen.

SEED SPONGE CAKE

3 teacups flour
2 teaspoons cream of tartar
4 oz butter

1½ cups sifted sugar
A few caraway seeds
2 eggs

Cream butter and sugar. Add flour, caraway seeds and eggs. Bake at 350°F (Gas Mark 4) for 1 hour.

Lewis' Mother's Cookbook, Mary Horrell, Exeter

ELLEN TREMLETT'S CHOCOLATE CAKE

4 oz chocolate
4 oz butter
4 oz castor sugar

4 oz flour
3 eggs
1 teaspoon baking powder

Grate the chocolate and let it get warm in the oven. Beat the butter to a cream with your hand. Add the flour, sugar and baking powder, then the chocolate. When it is cool, add the yolks of the eggs, and lastly the whites, which have been beaten to a stiff froth. Lightly bake for 1 or 1½ hours in a good oven.

Lewis' Mother's Cookbook, Mary Horrell, Exeter

POWDER CAKE

1 lb plain flour
2 heaped tablespoons baking powder

½ teaspoon salt
Milk to mix

Mix all together and mix to a fairly stiff dough. Roll out ½ inch thick and cut into rounds. Bake at 425°F (Gas Mark 7) for 20 minutes. Serve warm with butter and jam, or fry with bacon.

Mrs Biggar, Kirkcudbrightshire

CHERRY ALMOND CAKE

2 oz ground almonds
6 oz plain flour
6 oz butter
6 oz sugar

2 large eggs
¼ lb cherries
½ teaspoon baking powder
Almond essence

Wash cherries in very hot water, drain and cut into 3, dry in a little of the flour. Cream butter, sugar and eggs. Add ground almonds, flour and baking powder, and lastly cherries. Sprinkle top of cake with little fine sugar and blanched almonds. Cook at 275°F (Gas Mark 1) for 1½ hours. Cake should be pale golden colour, and stores well in freezer.

Pat Brown, Keynsham, Somerset

JOAN'S CAKE

12 oz self-raising flour
8 oz butter
8 oz granulated sugar
3 eggs
1 lb mixed fruit and few chopped cherries

1 oz ground almonds
Almond essence
1 heaped dessertspoon cornflour

Mix cornflour with a little milk and thicken by cooking with 1 breakfastcup water. Cool. Cream fat and sugar; add eggs, cornflour mixture and other ingredients. Bake about 1½ hours at 300°F (Gas Mark 2). Cool in tin, and store. Good to freeze.

Pat Brown, Keynsham, Somerset

SCRIPTURE CAKE

4½ *cups 1 Kings IV 22v.*
(Flour)
1½ *cups Judges V 25v.*
(Butter)
2 *cups Jeremiah VI 20v.*
(Sugar)
2 *cups 1 Samuel XXV 18v.*
(Raisins)
2 *cups Nahum III 12v.*
(Currants – figs to be correct)
1 *cup Numbers XVII 8v.*
(Almonds)

2 *tablespoons 1 Samuel*
XIV 25v. (Honey)
Season to taste 11 Chronicles
IX 9v. (Spice)
6 *cups Jeremiah XVII 11v.*
(6 eggs)
1 *pinch of Leviticus II 13v.*
(Salt)
1 *cup Judges IV 19v. last*
clause (Milk)
3 *teaspoons Amos V 5v.*
(Baking powder)

Follow Solomon's prescription for the making of a good boy, Proverbs
XXIII, 14v. (Beat it well.)

Mrs Harbord, Lincs

HONEY GINGERBREAD

4 *cups plain flour*
2 *heaped teaspoons baking*
powder
2 *teaspoons ginger*
½ *cup each of sultanas and*
halved cherries

A little chopped peel
4 *oz butter*
¾ *cup honey*
2 *eggs*
A little milk

Sieve the dry ingredients and add fruit; melt butter and honey in a pan,
add milk, and when cool add to the dry ingredients together with the
lightly beaten eggs. Mix, put in a prepared tin, and bake in a slow oven
for 1 hour.

CARAWAY ANGEL CAKE

5 *oz plain flour*
4 *oz castor sugar*
2 *oz butter*
1 *gill milk*
2 *egg whites*

1 *teaspoon baking powder*
2 *oz mixed candied peel*
1 *large teaspoon caraway*
seeds

Cream together the butter and sugar, add the milk gradually and when
smooth add the stiffly whisked egg whites. Sieve together the flour, baking

powder, and a pinch of salt. Very carefully fold into the egg fat mixture with the peel and seeds. Put into a well greased 6 inch cake tin. Bake 1¼ hours, 350°F (Gas Mark 4).

QUICK GINGER BREAD

4 oz self-raising flour
¼ teaspoon salt
1 level teaspoon ginger
2 oz brown sugar
1 oz oatmeal

3 oz lard
3 oz syrup
1 teaspoon warm milk
1 beaten egg

Sieve the flour, salt and ginger into a bowl and add the brown sugar and oatmeal. Place the lard and syrup into a saucepan. and melt. Add the milk. Mix this mixture into the dry ingredients and add a beaten egg. Beat thoroughly and pour the mixture into a 7 inch greased loaf tin. Bake for 1–1½ hours in an oven at 325°F (Gas Mark 3).

GLOUCESTER PLUM CAKE

4 oz butter or margarine
3 oz black treacle
2 oz sugar
3 eggs
6 oz plain flour
1 level teaspoon baking powder
1 level teaspoon mixed spice

Grated rind of ½ lemon
12 oz mixed dried fruit, raisins, currants and sultanas
2 oz glacé cherries, halved
2 oz chopped mixed peel
2 oz chopped almonds

Cream the butter, treacle and sugar till light. Add the eggs one at a time, beating well between each. Add fruit and nuts alternately with the sifted dry ingredients, folding in lightly. Put into a prepared 6 inch cake tin and bake in a slow oven, 300°F (Gas Mark 2) for 2½–3 hours. Allow to cool in the tin before removing.

YORKSHIRE PARKIN

8 oz plain flour
½ level teaspoon salt
1–2 level teaspoons ginger
1 level teaspoon bicarbonate of soda
8 oz medium oatmeal or

rolled oats
8 oz black treacle
6 oz lard or cooking fat
4 oz soft brown sugar
1 egg
Approximately ¼ pint milk

Sift together flour, salt, ginger and bicarbonate of soda. Stir in oatmeal or oats. Put treacle, lard and sugar into a pan and dissolve gently over a low heat. Make a well in the centre of the flour mixture, pour in melted ingredients then mix to a soft batter with the egg and milk, adding a little more milk if necessary. Stir briskly, without beating, to combine ingredients. Turn into a well-greased and lined 8 inch square tin, then bake in the centre of a moderate oven, 350°F (Gas Mark 4) for 20 minutes, then lower temperature to 325°F (Gas Mark 3) for 50–60 minutes. When cooked, the parkin should be an even brown and have shrunk away slightly from the sides of the tin. If possible keep in a tin for a week before serving.

APPLE GINGERBREAD WITH FUDGEY ICING

1 large cooking apple
3 oz sugar
4 oz black treacle
3 oz butter or margarine,
melted

6 oz self-raising flour
2 level teaspoons ground
ginger
6 whole cloves
1 egg, beaten

Peel, core and slice the apple and put in saucepan with the cloves, 1 dessertspoon sugar and very little water. Cook until tender, remove the cloves and mash well with a fork. Leave to cool.

Put the sieved dry ingredients into a bowl and add the cooled apple and beaten egg, treacle and melted fat and beat all well together. Turn into a 1½ lb loaf tin and bake in a moderate oven, 350°F (Gas Mark 4) for 40 minutes.

Fudgey Icing:

Cream together 1 oz butter, 1 oz treacle and 2 oz icing sugar. Beat well until light and creamy. Add a little ground cinnamon to taste, if liked. Spread on the cake when it is cool and mark with a fork. Chopped nuts may be scattered over.

GINGER CAKE

6 oz self-raising flour
3 oz margarine
2 oz sugar
2 oz golden syrup
2 oz black treacle

1 egg
1 teaspoon ground ginger
½ teaspoon bicarbonate of soda
¼ pint milk
Pinch of salt

Put fat and syrup and milk into a saucepan and melt. Add dry ingredients, then egg and lastly bicarbonate of soda dissolved in a drop of milk. Line a small meat tin and bake in a moderate oven. Test with skewer or knitting needle.

Self-raising flour was first used successfully in 1846, and was noted in *The Lancet* as an interesting invention. It was produced commercially in the 1880s, but does not seem to have come into general use until the 1920s. Curiously, it is still virtually unknown in many European countries, including France.

GRANDMA'S SUNDAY CAKE

2 eggs (beaten)
4 oz sugar
6 oz butter
10 oz self-raising flour

6 oz currants
2 oz mixed peel
A few cherries

Beat sugar and butter to a cream, add eggs. Stir in currants, peel, cherries, fold in flour. If not moist enough, add a little milk. This recipe has been used for years and is always a winner.

Mrs J. Keel, Chew Stoke, Somerset

FAMILY FRUIT CAKE

8 oz self-raising flour
¼ teaspoon salt
4 oz butter
4 oz soft brown sugar
4 oz sultanas and raisins

2 oz chopped peel
Grated rind of ½ lemon
1 egg
5 tablespoons milk

Sift flour and salt, then rub in butter until mixture looks like fine bread-crumbs. Stir in sugar, dried fruit, peel and grated rind, and mix lightly with egg and milk. Put into greased and lined 6 inch cake tin and bake at 350°F (Gas Mark 4) for 1½ hours. Cool on a wire rack. Do not cut for 24 hours.

CHOCOLATE SPONGE

4 oz margarine
5 oz castor sugar
2 eggs
1 tablespoon milk
4 oz self-raising flour
1 tablespoon cocoa

For the Filling:
6 oz icing sugar
1 oz cocoa
2 oz soft butter
2 dessertspoons hot water

Cream margarine and sugar and work in eggs and milk alternately with sifted cocoa and flour. Blend well and bake in greased 2 inch tin at 360°F (Gas Mark 4) for 30 minutes. Cool on rack and split in half. Cream together icing sugar, cocoa, butter and water until very soft and light and use to fill and top sponge. Mark with a fork and decorate with nuts or chocolate chips.

1898 BRISTOL CAKE

6 oz butter
3 eggs
½ lb sugar
½ pint milk
½ lb flour

½ lb ground rice
2 teaspoons baking powder
1 lb fruit (less will do)
¼ lb peel

Beat butter to cream. Add sugar. Beat eggs separately and add milk, lastly flour and rice and fruit and beat for ¼ hour. Bake about 2 hours in a moderate oven.

Miss Jeffrey, Hambledon, Hants

YORKSHIRE SANDWICH

2 tablespoons ground rice
2 tablespoons flour
1 tablespoon castor sugar
2 heaped tablespoons fats

2 eggs
A little milk
1 teaspoon baking powder

Cream fat and sugar. Beat in eggs, add dry ingredients and milk. Bake in moderate oven for 25 minutes.

CHOCOLATE FUDGE CAKE

4 oz margarine
10 oz sugar
2 eggs

6 oz self-raising flour
2 oz cocoa
Vanilla

Melt margarine in saucepan. Add sugar and beaten eggs. Add flour, cocoa etc. Pour into shallow *lined* tin and bake in moderate oven for 30–40 minutes. Really good—kids love it, but oven must *not* be too hot. Quick and easy.

GRANNY CROSSLAND'S COURTING CAKE

2 cups flour
1 cup sugar

3 oz margarine or lard

Beat 1 egg well and put a tablespoon milk into it. Rub all ingredients into a paste and put on a bake sheet, spread well with jam. Bake in hot oven (not *too* hot). Cut into slices (fingers) in tin.

Made by Granny Crossland who lived till she was 94 (born 1848) at Newton-on-Trent and lived there all her life. She used to make this cake to take on holiday because the family, grandchildren and all, used to rent a house at Skegness or Cromer, taking from their farmhouse some of the food, but the rest was cooked for them by the seaside landlady. Farmer's wife and real martinet, Granny Crossland was still working, keeping her household in order, till she died. These recipes came from Granny Crossland's grand-daughter who lives at Crofthouse Farm, Beckingham, near Doncaster (on borders of Yorks and Lincs). Mrs Muriel Selby says she was newly married (1942) when she went to visit her grandmother for what proved to be the last time. The old lady kept saying that she was looking forward to visiting her to help her (Muriel) get her new house straight! But of course she never got there. However, Mrs Selby still makes these cakes to this day.

Mrs Selby, Doncaster

LINCOLNSHIRE CAKES

2 lb self-raising flour	*½ lb sultanas*
6 oz lard	*½ lb raisins*
6 oz margarine	*4 eggs*
1 oz sugar	*A little milk*
½ lb currants	

Rub in or cream. Cook in slow oven. Cut up into slices in tin.

Mrs Selby, Doncaster

GENOA CAKE

6 oz butter	*¼ lb currants*
6 oz sugar	*¼ lb sultanas*
8 oz self-raising flour	*¼ lb cherries*
3 eggs	

Cream butter and sugar together. Beat well for some time. Add eggs, flour, then fruit. Halve cherries and roll in some of the flour to prevent them sinking to bottom of cake.

Mrs Selby, Doncaster

QUICK ORANGE CAKE

4 oz melted butter
8 oz castor sugar
2 eggs
⅓ pint orange juice
8 oz plain flour
4 teaspoons baking powder

¼ teaspoon salt

Topping:
Rind of 2 oranges
3 tablespoons sugar

Add melted butter to sugar, then the beaten eggs and juice. Blend well, then add flour sifted with baking powder and salt, and beat well. Pour into 10-inch spring-form cake tin. Mix orange rind with sugar and sprinkle on top. Bake at 350°F (Gas Mark 4) for 75 minutes. Open sides of tin, leave cake to cool for a few minutes, then remove carefully to wire rack. If the quick topping is omitted, this can be iced, but the flavour is better with baked-on topping.

WALNUT MOCHA CAKE

4 oz butter
8 oz castor sugar
2 eggs
8 tablespoons milk
6 oz flour
2 teaspoons baking powder
Pinch of salt
2 teaspoons vanilla essence

4 oz walnuts

Icing:
2 oz butter
4 oz icing sugar
1 oz cocoa
Strong black coffee

Cream butter and sugar. Add beaten yolks of eggs and the milk. Sift flour with baking powder and salt and stir gradually into the egg mixture. Add vanilla essence and the walnuts lightly broken up and tossed in flour. Fold in stiffly-beaten egg whites, pour into greased rectangular pan and bake at 350°F (Gas Mark 4) for 40 minutes. Make the icing by creaming together butter, sugar and cocoa, softening the mixture with a little very strong coffee. Cover the cake and decorate with more walnuts if liked.

APPLE CAKE

4 oz margarine
4 oz sugar
2 eggs

5 oz self-raising flour
Enough cream or milk to
make a smooth mixture

This amount will fill 2 8 inch sandwich tins. Before baking, peel, core and slice enough apple to cover all over top of cakes, pressing slices in gently. Sprinkle a couple of tablespoons sugar and cinnamon (already mixed) over each cake. Bake at 400°F (Gas Mark 6) for about 30 minutes. This can be eaten warm as a sweet with cream or cold for tea.

Mrs Lye, Oxon

MARY'S CAKE

4 oz butter or margarine　　*Small amount vanilla essence*
4 oz castor sugar　　*4 oz self-raising flour*
2 eggs

Cream the fat and sugar, and beat in the eggs and essence. Fold in the flour. Use two sponge tins. Bake at 350°F (Gas Mark 4) for 25 minutes. This recipe came from the eleven-year-old deaf-and-dumb daughter of a farmer.

CHERRY AND ALMOND CAKE

6 oz self-raising flour　　*3 large eggs*
6 oz butter　　*Pinch of salt*
6 oz castor sugar　　*Few drops vanilla essence*
4 oz ground almonds　　*A little milk to mix*
8 oz glacé cherries

Cream butter and sugar. Then add all the dry ingredients, flour and ground almonds with the eggs. Then the cherries and sufficient milk to mix to a medium soft consistency. Cook in an 8 inch round tin slow oven, 325°F (Gas Mark 3) for 1½ hours. Allow the cake to cool in the tin 30 minutes before turning it out.

Note Rinse the cherries in warm water, cut in half and well dry; toss them in a little flour from the cake weight before using.

Miss Mabel Nokes, Priston Mill Farm, Bath

DATE CAKE

1 packet chopped dates　　*8 oz flour*
8 oz butter　　*2 oz chopped walnuts*
3 eggs　　*1 teaspoon bicarbonate of soda*
4 oz sugar

Just cover the dates with *hot* water and the baking soda. Leave for an hour. Beat the sugar and butter, add the flour and beaten eggs, lastly the dates and walnuts. Bake in a shallow tin in a moderate oven, 350°F (Gas Mark 4) for 60 minutes.

Miss Mabel Nokes, Priston Mill Farm, Bath

ORANGE SPONGE

The weight of 2 eggs in flour, castor sugar, also butter. Cream the sugar and butter, add the flour. Then add 1 tablespoon warm water. Bake in 2 tins at 350°F (Gas Mark 4) for 30 minutes. Then, when cooling just pour over the juice of the orange leaving a little juice to flavour a butter icing.

Miss Mabel Nokes, Priston Mill Farm, Bath

FRUIT CAKE

4½ oz butter	5 oz raisins
4½ oz soft brown sugar	7 oz currants
1 oz peel	3 oz cherries
6 oz self-raising flour	3 eggs

Cream butter and sugar, add flour and beaten eggs, lastly the fruit. Bake at 325°F (Gas Mark 3) for 1½ hours.

Miss Mabel Nokes, Priston Mill Farm, Bath

ALMOND CAKE

3 oz self-raising flour	4 oz butter
4 oz castor sugar	2 small eggs
2 oz ground almonds	

Cream the butter and sugar. Then add the beaten eggs, also the flour and almonds. Bake in 6 inch tin for 60 minutes at 375°–400°F (Gas Mark 5–6).

Miss Mabel Nokes, Priston Mill Farm, Bath

CORNISH HEAVY CAKE

8 oz plain flour	3 oz currants
2 oz margarine	¼ teaspoon salt
2 oz lard	Peel
2 oz granulated sugar	3 tablespoons water

Sieve flour and salt well. Mix in fat roughly. Add sugar and fruit. Add water to make a fairly stiff dough. Knead out all cracks gently. Shape up and roll out to approximately ½ inch thick, keeping edges smooth. Criss-cross with knife over top. Bake at 375°F (Gas Mark 5) for 25–30 minutes.

CHOCOLATE CAKE

2 *tablespoons butter*   1 *cup sugar*

Cream together and add 1 beaten egg. Mix together 2 tablespoons cocoa,
½ cup boiling water and add to first mixture. Take ½ cup sour milk and mix
in 1 teaspoon bicarbonate of soda. Add to above and fold in 1½ cups flour,
½ teaspoon lemon or vanilla. Bake for 45 minutes.
The icing: Cream 1 tablespoon butter, add 1 tablespoon warm milk,
½ teaspoon vanilla and icing sugar to desired thickness. Spread on top
and sides and sprinkle on coconut.

This cake won first prize of £10 at the 1920 Cardiff Show.

Mary Giles, Marksbury, Somerset

VERY SPECIAL CHOCOLATE SPONGE CAKE

1 *teacup sugar – castor, for*   4 *eggs*
preference   1 *tablespoon drinking*
1 *teacup self-raising flour*   *chocolate (added to the flour)*

Whisk eggs to thick and creamy stage. Add sugar and beat again till
thicker still. Then gently, with a fork, stir in the flour direct from the
sieve. Have ready greased and floured, 2 8 inch tins and put the mixture
evenly into them. Cook for 20 minutes in oven at 350°F (Gas Mark 4).

Icing: ½ *lb icing sugar*
½ *lb butter*   ¼ *lb drinking chocolate*

Beat all together in bowl and spread on top and sides, making pattern
with a fork.

This recipe came from the old cook of Lady Wills of Blagdon, Somerset,
and was taught to Mrs Ball when she was a very young girl.

Mrs J. Ball, Compton Greenfield

KING EDWARD'S GINGERBREAD

½ *lb brown sugar*   1 *oz ground ginger*
½ *lb butter*   1 *teaspoon lemon juice*
¾ *lb treacle*   *Enough soda (bicarbonate) to*
12 *oz flour*   *cover a 6d.*
2 *eggs*

Mix sugar and treacle and put in pan on fire to warm. Beat butter to cream.
Beat eggs and add to butter and beat slowly. Add treacle mixture beating
all the time. Fold in flour into which the ginger and bicarbonate of soda

have been sifted. Bake in slow oven, approximately 325°F (Gas Mark 3) for 60 minutes. This was made at Sandringham for shooting parties given by Edward VII.

From the aunt of Mrs C. Dutnall, Cheam, Surrey
per Mrs A. Padgham, Minehead

KING EDWARD'S LUNCH CAKE

1½ lb self-raising flour
1 lb granulated sugar
½ lb butter

4 eggs
1 teacup milk
2 teacups mixed fruit

Cream butter and sugar. Add eggs with a little flour and beat. Fold in rest of flour and fruit. Bake in moderate oven, 350°F (Gas Mark 4) for 1½–2 hours.

A favourite at shooting picnic lunches at Sandringham.

From the aunt of Mrs C. Dutnall, Cheam, Surrey
per Mrs A. Padgham, Minehead

VICTORIA SANDWICH

2 eggs
2 oz margarine
4 oz sugar

4 oz self-raising flour
1 teaspoon baking powder
1 tablespoon milk

First prepare oven and tins. Remove browning sheet from oven (if one is used) and heat ready to 425°F (Gas Mark 7). Well grease 2 8 inch sandwich tins. Place margarine in oven to just melt, *do not let it boil*. Beat eggs and milk together, add sugar and beat well again (5 minutes with rotary whisk, less with electric beaters). Mix baking powder with flour; fold into mixture using a metal spoon; lastly stir in melted margarine. Now divide mixture into 2 tins and spread evenly. Place in oven one above the other and cook about 12 minutes. Take out upper tin and move under tin up for further 2 minutes.

FIVE GOLDEN RULES

1. Have tins and oven ready. Sponge must not be kept waiting.
2. Always fold in flour—do not beat—beating is already done.
3. *Melt* margarine and add last.
4. To test if sponge is cooked, press lightly with finger. If cooked, it will instantly rise.
5. When taken from oven sprinkle tops with castor sugar, leave 10 minutes before turning out. Spread with jam, sandwich together while still warm.

From Essex came this light-textured, conveniently-made sponge. Try using this recipe if you have had a patch of 'failed sponges' type cake-making—it's guaranteed to restore self-confidence and *the whole operation takes only 30 minutes flat*. It needs beating well.

WALNUT CREAM SANDWICH

2 eggs
Their weight in castor sugar, butter and flour
Grated rind of ½ lemon
½ teaspoon baking powder

½ teaspoon lemon juice
2 tablespoons raspberry jam
2 tablespoons icing sugar
Few walnuts, shelled and skinned

Put butter and sugar into a basin, well beat until it will drop off the spoon, and then add the beaten eggs and a little flour. Mix well, and then add the rest of the flour, the lemon rind and juice. Put in a tin lined with greased paper, and bake for 15 minutes. When cool spread jam on, ice top, and scatter walnuts over.

Mrs F. Webb, Loughton, Essex, 1911

OXFORD GINGER CAKE

4 oz butter
4 oz soft brown sugar
4 oz flour
4–6 oz black treacle

1 egg
1 teaspoon bicarbonate of soda
¼ teacup warm milk
Ginger to taste

Cream butter and sugar, add egg and treacle and mix well, add flour sifted with ginger. Dissolve bicarbonate of soda in warm milk and add last. Bake in slow oven, 325°F (Gas Mark 3) for 1½–2 hours.

I got this black, gooey ginger cake from Oxfordshire W.I. some years ago. It rises right up in the tin while cooking and then sinks in the middle—best looking in a round tin.

Mrs A. Padgham, Minehead, Somerset

DAMP GINGERBREAD

10 oz flour
6 oz butter
6 oz moist sugar
3 oz almonds
6 oz sultanas
1½ teaspoons ground ginger

1½ teaspoons cinnamon
¼ lb treacle
2 eggs
Warm milk
¾ teaspoon baking soda

Sieve the flour; clean sultanas; blanch and shred the almonds (blanch by steeping few minutes in cup of boiling water) and mix 1 teaspoon flour with the fruit. Cream the butter and sugar, add dry ingredients, treacle, beaten eggs and the baking soda mixed with a little milk. Add more milk if necessary to the whole. Turn into greased tin and bake 325°F (Gas Mark 3) for 2 hours.

Mrs Biggar, Kirkcudbrightshire

ICING FOR CAKES

1 heaped teaspoon of gelatine soaked in cold water, add ½ teaspoon of boiling water to dissolve it and make thick with ½ lb sifted sugar.

Lewis' Mother's Cookbook, Mary Horrell, Exeter

LEMON ICING FOR CAKES

Squeeze the juice of a lemon, mix with a tablespoon of water, and boil together. While boiling, pour over ½ lb icing sugar, stir until quite smooth. Spread the cakes while hot, and dry in a warm place.

Lewis' Mother's Cookbook, Mary Horrell, Exeter

CHOCOLATE ICING

1 oz grated chocolate   *½ gill water*
3 oz castor sugar

Put the ingredients into a saucepan and stir over the fire until it thickens. Pour over sandwiches and dry in a cool oven.

Lewis' Mother's Cookbook, Mary Horrell, Exeter

CHOCOLATE MACAROONS

4½ oz ground almonds   *2½ oz melted plain chocolate*
7 oz castor sugar   *Rice paper*
2 egg whites   *Split blanched almonds*

Stir together almonds and sugar. Whip egg whites stiffly and fold into the dry mixture, together with the chocolate. Put in spoonsful on rice paper. Bake at 325°F (Gas Mark 3) for 30 minutes. Top with blanched almonds.

LEMON CHEESE NUGGETS

3 oz lemon cheese (curd)   *½ teaspoon baking powder*
8 oz flour   *2 oz butter*
2 oz castor sugar   *1 egg*

Rub the butter into the flour, add the sugar, baking powder and lemon cheese, with one egg, mix into a stiff dough, place on greased tin in rough heaps. Bake in moderate oven 15 minutes.

Mrs Page 1899

GERTRUDE'S MACAROONS

4 oz ground almonds
8 oz castor sugar
2 teaspoons ground rice

2 large egg whites
Almond essence

Beat egg whites stiff, fold in other ingredients, put 1 teaspoon on rice paper and decorate with half almonds. Bake in cool oven, under 250°F (Gas Mark ½).

Pat Brown, Keynsham, Somerset

WELSH TEACAKES

½ lb self-raising flour
5 oz butter
1 egg
4 oz sugar
3 oz currants

2 oz sultanas
¼ teaspoon ginger
Little grated lemon peel
Milk to mix

Rub fat into flour, add sugar, fruit, peel and ginger, mix with beaten egg and a little milk to a stiff dough. Roll out ¼ inch thick, cut into rounds and bake on a bakestone, turning once. Sprinkle with sugar while still warm.

HOT APPLE MUFFINS

8 oz flour
1 teaspoon baking powder
3 oz lard

1 lb cooking apples
1 small egg
2 oz black treacle

Sift together flour and baking powder and rub in the lard. Peel, core and mince the apples. Beat the egg. Make a well in the flour and stir in the egg, minced apple and treacle. Work well together to a stiff, sticky dough. Add a little more milk if too dry, but on no account should it be too wet, as the apples moisten it in baking. Put on to a greased baking tray and bake in a moderate oven, 350°F (Gas Mark 4) for 30 minutes or till a light golden brown. While still hot cut in rounds and cool on a wire rack. Split open and butter, dusting with castor sugar before serving.

CRUSTY LEMON BUTTER BAKE

6 oz butter	6 oz self-raising flour
6 oz castor sugar	2 eggs

Topping:
Juice of 1 lemon ⎫
4 oz castor sugar ⎭ mix to a paste and stand aside

Cut the butter into pieces stand in the warm until it begins to get soft. Add the sugar, also the beaten eggs, then stir in the flour. Turn into a shallow tin 10×7 inches (greased with butter) smooth the surface and bake at 350°F (Gas Mark 4) for 40 minutes. The surface should be soft, set and golden. Take the cake from the oven and while hot spread over the top the lemon juice and castor sugar. The juice of the lemon will sink and leave the top crispy when cold. (For myself I put 5 oz butter. Also after the cake is cooked. I just prick the top of the cake for the juice to go through.)

Miss Mabel Nokes, Priston Mill Farm, Bath

FOCHABERS GINGERBREAD

8 oz butter	4 oz sultanas
4 oz sugar	1 teaspoon bicarbonate of soda
8 oz black treacle	3 oz ground almonds
½ oz ground ginger	3 oz chopped candied peel
A little ground cloves	½ oz mixed spice
2 eggs	A little cinnamon
1 lb flour	½ pint beer
4 oz currants	

Cream the butter with the sugar. Add the slightly warmed treacle, break in the eggs and beat the mixture well. Mix the flour with all the dry ingredients (except the soda). Dissolve the bicarbonate of soda in the beer and mix everything together thoroughly. Put into a large greased cake tin and bake in a slow oven for 2 hours.

GINGER CAKE

2 teacups flour	2 teaspoons ground ginger
1 teacup golden syrup or treacle	1 teaspoon bicarbonate of soda
	½ teacup hot water
2 oz margarine or cooking fat	Pinch of salt

Mix together flour, ginger and bicarbonate of soda. Warm fat slightly and mix in treacle. Add hot water, mix in flour etc. quickly and bake in a moderate oven, 350°F (Gas Mark 4) for 1 hour. Fruit may be added if desired.

NUTTY GINGERBREAD

2 oz butter	Pinch salt
4 oz golden syrup	Pinch bicarbonate of soda
1 oz granulated sugar	1 egg, beaten
4 oz self-raising flour	6 tablespoons milk
½ level teaspoon ginger	1½ oz walnuts, chopped
½ level teaspoon mixed spice	

Heat butter, syrup and sugar gently until sugar dissolves. Sieve the dry ingredients together into a bowl. Add syrup. Add egg and milk and beat thoroughly. Stir in nuts. Divide mixture between 12 greased, deep patty tins. Bake in a moderate oven, 350°F (Gas Mark 4) for 25–30 minutes. Cool.

CONNIE COOPER'S CUMBRIAN CAKE

Line a Swiss roll tin with pastry.

Filling: Melt 1½ oz butter. Add 9 oz currants, 3 oz soft brown sugar, 1 teaspoon spice, ½ teaspoon cinnamon, ¼ teaspoon mace. Mix. Add filling and cover with pastry. Bake at 375°F (Gas Mark 5) for 45 minutes. Cut in squares.

BUNS FOR AFTERNOON TEA

½ lb flour	1 oz sugar
2 oz butter	1 egg
1 oz coconut	A little milk
½ teaspoon baking powder	

These are very easy to make, and very inexpensive. They are also highly appreciated. Rub the butter amongst the flour, then add the baking powder, sugar, and a pinch of salt, and mix well together. If preferred, currants or raisins may be added. Make into a paste with the egg, which has been beaten up, and a little milk. Knead slightly, and cut into small pieces. Form into buns, and place in a greased baking tin. Bake in a hot oven for 15 minutes. Wait till cool, then serve.

Miss Lily Jamison, Aberdeen, 1911

LEMON SPICE CAKES

4 oz *plain flour*
1 teaspoon *baking powder*
½ teaspoon *ground cinnamon*
¼ teaspoon *ground nutmeg*
4 oz *quick cooking rolled oats*
2 oz *walnuts, finely chopped*
6 oz *butter*
8 oz *soft brown sugar*
½ teaspoon *vanilla essence*
2 *eggs*

3 tablespoons *milk*
Finely grated rind of 1 *lemon*
2 tablespoons *strained lemon juice*

Icing:
6 oz *icing sugar*
2 tablespoons *lemon juice*
Little milk

Sift flour, baking powder, cinnamon and nutmeg. Add rolled oats and chopped nuts. Cream butter with sugar until light. Beat in eggs with lemon juice and rind, a little at a time, mixing well after each addition. Fold in flour mixture with extra milk to make a soft consistency. Spoon into a greased and lined tin 10 × 14 inches and spread top smoothly. Bake at 350°F (Gas Mark 4) for 35 minutes.

Sift icing sugar, mix with lemon juice and little milk. Pour over top of warm cake and spread smoothly. Cut into squares when cold.

BANBURY PUFFS

8 oz *flaky or rough puff pastry*
2 oz *butter or margarine*
1 oz *stale cake crumbs or plain flour*
1 *egg yolk*

2 level tablespoons *black treacle*
4 oz *currants, washed and dried*
1 oz *mixed chopped peel*
½ level teaspoon *mixed spice*

Melt butter in a pan then add cake crumbs or flour. Cook gently, stirring, for 3 minutes. Remove from heat and beat in egg yolk and treacle. Cool mixture then add remaining ingredients.

Roll out pastry thinly and cut into approximately 12 rounds with a 4 inch plain cutter. Divide filling mixture equally between rounds, moisten edges of pastry with water, then draw together so that filling is completely covered. Turn each over – with join underneath – on to a lightly floured board and press with a rolling pin into an oval. Transfer to baking trays, score tops into a diamond pattern (or make 3 diagonal slits in the top of each) then brush with lightly beaten egg white. Dust lightly with castor sugar, then leave in a cool place for 10 minutes. Bake just above centre of a hot oven, at 425°F (Gas Mark 7) for 15 to 20 minutes. Cool on a wire tray.

ALMOND APPLE-CAKES

For Apple Filling:
¾ lb cooking apples
½ oz butter
½ oz soft brown sugar
½ level teaspoon ground cloves

For Almond Sponge:
4 oz self-raising flour

½ level teaspoon salt
2 oz ground almonds
4 oz butter
4 oz sugar
2 eggs, beaten
About 2 teaspoons milk
12 whole blanched almonds
for decoration

To make apple filling: Peel, core and slice apples. Place in a large saucepan together with butter and sugar. Cook very gently until the apples are soft but not completely broken up. Stir in ground cloves and leave mixture to become quite cold.

To make almond sponge: Sift flour and salt together and add ground almonds. Cream butter and sugar until light and fluffy. Gradually add eggs, beating well between each addition. Add 1 tablespoon of the flour mixture with the last addition of egg. Gradually fold in rest of flour and almond mixture. Add enough milk to give dropping consistency. Spoon half the mixture into 12 2-inch paper cake cases.

Make a well in the centre of each and fill with 2 teaspoons of apple mixture. Cover very carefully with remaining sponge mixture and top each with a whole blanched almond. Bake in a moderate oven, 375°F (Gas Mark 5) for 25–30 minutes, until firm to the touch. Remove and cool.

NUTMEG HONEY CAKES

8 oz plain flour
½ level teaspoon salt
4 level teaspoons baking
powder

1 level teaspoon ground
nutmeg
4 tablespoons clear honey,
warmed
1–2 teaspoons milk

Sift together flour, salt, baking powder and nutmeg. Rub in fat until mixture resembles fine breadcrumbs. Gradually add warmed honey, to form a stiff dough. Add extra milk if necessary. Knead lightly. Roll out to ¼ inch thickness and cut out rounds with a 2 inch plain cutter. Re-roll trimmings and cut out more rounds. Place on a greased baking sheet and bake in a hot oven, 425°F (Gas Mark 7) for 15–20 minutes. Remove and cool.

BURWASH DOUGHNUTS

2 oz lard
1 oz sugar
8 oz self-raising flour
½ teaspoon salt

1 egg
Milk
Fat for frying
Castor sugar

Rub the lard and sugar into the flour sieved with salt. Mix with the egg and enough milk to make a soft dough. Roll out ½ inch thick and cut into circles with a floured cutter. Cut out centres with a smaller cutter. Fry a few rings at a time in very hot fat, allowing 2 minutes on each side. Drain on absorbent kitchen paper, cool slightly and roll in castor sugar. Eat while very fresh. The small centres can also be fried and are delicious if cooled slightly, then iced with lemon or chocolate water icing.

CARAMEL CHOCOLATE SQUARES

4 oz butter
2 oz sugar

1 cup flour

Cream butter and sugar and add flour, spread in a Swiss roll tin and bake until brown 400°–425°F (Gas Mark 6–7) for about 20 minutes.

Caramel:
4 oz margarine
2 oz sugar

1 tablespoon syrup
½ tin or small tin condensed milk

Put all in a saucepan and bring to boil, boil for 5 minutes, spread over shortcake. Melt 4 oz chocolate spread over caramel. Cool and cut in squares.

Mrs D. Hurst, East Riding College of Agriculture

1903 ROCK CAKES

1 lb flour
6 oz sugar
2 teaspoons baking powder
Ginger
Nutmeg
Salt

3 oz butter or lard
6 oz currants
1 egg
A little milk
Piece of candied peel

Bake in a rather hot oven for 15 minutes. 24 rock cakes.

Mrs Watson, Salisbury

CHOCOLATE CAKES

6 tablespoons flour
3 tablespoons cocoa
4 tablespoons sugar
1 tablespoon baking powder

¼ lb margarine
1 egg
Milk to mix

Mix sugar, margarine and egg to cream, then add flour, cocoa, baking powder and a little milk. 12–15 little cakes.

Mrs Fordham, 1927

CHOCOLATE MERINGUES

2 egg whites
Pinch of salt
Pinch of cream of tartar

6 oz castor sugar
6 oz plain chocolate or
chocolate chips

Beat egg whites, salt, and cream of tartar until soft peaks form. Add sugar gradually, beating until peaks are stiff. Chop chocolate roughly, or use chocolate chips, and stir into the mixture. Cover baking sheets with plain paper and drop mixture on by rounded teaspoons. Bake at 300°F (Gas Mark 2) for 25 minutes, and cool slightly before removing from paper. Do not fill these meringues with cream. 12 meringues.

CHOCOLATE COOPER

4 oz margarine or butter
1 dessertspoon white sugar
3 dessertspoons drinking
chocolate

1½ tablespoons golden syrup
2 oz mixed dry fruit
½ lb plain biscuits

Put all ingredients except biscuits into a small saucepan, heat ingredients until sugar and syrup have melted. Stir in crushed biscuits and put into a shallow baking tray. Melt 4 oz cooking chocolate and spread over.

Patricia Jones

CHINESE CHEWS

3 oz flour
3 oz margarine or butter
5 oz sugar (brown if liked)

4 oz chopped walnuts
10 oz chopped dates
2 eggs

Cream butter and sugar, and add flour. Add eggs, and fruit, cut fairly large. Spread in a small Swiss roll tin and bake at about 375°–400°F (Gas Mark 5–6) until firm and brown. Sprinkle with castor or icing sugar.

Leave in tin to cool and then cut into fingers before turning out on to a cooling tray. Recipe can be halved if necessary and then cooked in a square tin, sandwich-sized.

Margaret Jeffes

MELTING MOMENTS

5 oz self-raising flour
$\frac{1}{2}$ egg
1$\frac{1}{2}$ oz margarine
$\frac{1}{2}$ teaspoon vanilla essence
3 oz sugar

Beat margarine and sugar, add vanilla, egg and flour. Dip in rolled oats. Flatten top and cook in moderate oven for 15 minutes.

BERKSHIRE ALMOND SPOON-HANDLE CAKES

Rub 3 oz cooking fat (or mixture of fats) into 6 oz self-raising flour. Add 2 oz sugar (castor for preference). Mix 1 tablespoon water with $\frac{1}{2}$–1 teaspoon almond essence and add to dry ingredients. Finish mixing by using fingertips, for kneading. Divide into pieces and roll into balls with hands. Make a circular dent with the handle of a wooden spoon and fill with honey or syrup (*very* little required).

Put mixture into well-greased fancy little tins or in paper baking cases. The latter keep cakes a better shape and look more festive. Bake 15–20 minutes in moderate oven, 375°F (Gas Mark 5). Do not make dent too deep with the spoon handle and take care not to overcook.

YORKSHIRE FAT RASCALS

1 lb flour (self-raising or plain with 1 heaped teaspoon baking powder)
1 oz brown sugar
Pinch of salt
4 oz currants
8 oz butter or margarine
Little milk and water

Mix flour with sugar and salt and rub in butter or margarine. Add currants and mix well to a soft dough with the milk and water. A fairly soft scone-type dough is required. Roll out dough to approximately $\frac{1}{2}$ inch thickness. Cut into 2 inch rounds, dust with castor sugar, then bake for about 20 minutes in a hot oven.

SUSSEX FLEAD CAKES

1 lb flead (or fleck)   Pinch of salt
1½ lb flour   Cold water

Remove all skin and signs of veins from the flead and cut into thin cubes. Sift flour and salt in a basin, add flead and mix to a stiff dough. Place on a floured board. Beat with the end of a rolling pin as hard and quickly as possible, turning over if necessary.

Leave 15 minutes, then repeat beating and rolling. Repeat above twice more—as for flaky pastry. Rest again for 15 minutes then roll out to 1 inch thickness, cut into rounds, bake in hot oven, 450°F (Gas Mark 8) for about 10 minutes.

These really do take quite a lot of energy, but if all goes well should be very light and fluffy. Best eaten warm, I think, with jam or sprinkled with salt according to taste.

My father loves these above everything—and, as a child I can remember buying them at a small baker's in Bexhill (the last place where they could be obtained). My own make were much appreciated by Canadian friends during the war.

Flead is the white fat from a pig—like a kind of flat sheet held together with a flat membrane, which needs pulling off. This 'flead' or 'fleck' is still obtainable from good butchers.

Mrs A. Padgham, Minehead, Somerset

ECCLES CAKES

6 oz flaky or rough puff pastry   ¼ teaspoon allspice
2 oz currants   A little grated nutmeg
1 oz sugar   ½ oz butter
¾ oz peel

Slightly oil butter in saucepan, add currants, chopped peel, sugar, spice. Mix together, Roll out paste, cut into rounds, place in centre 2 teaspoons of mixture. Close up the rounds, flatten with rolling-pin, mark across top of each cake with knife. Brush over with white of egg, sprinkle on castor sugar. Bake in quick oven for 10–15 minutes, 450°F (Gas Mark 8).

SHREWSBURY CAKES

½ lb self-raising flour   ¼ teaspoon cinnamon
4 oz butter   Pinch of nutmeg
4 oz sugar   Pinch of salt
½ egg or 1 yolk

Cream butter and sugar together until soft. Add egg and gradually the flour and cinnamon until stiff, smooth paste is formed. Roll out on floured board till about ¼ inch thick, cut into rounds 4–5 inches wide. Bake slowly 15–20 minutes on flat baking sheet, 300°F (Gas Mark 2).

9 Biscuits

Now stir the fire, and close the shutters fast,
Let fall the curtains, wheel the sofa round,
And, while the bubbling and loud-hissing urn
Throws up a steamy column, and the cups,
That cheer but not inebriate, wait on each,
So let us welcome peaceful evening in.

William Cowper

VANILLA BISCUITS

4 oz plain flour
4 oz flaked oats
4 oz margarine
3 oz granulated sugar
2 level teaspoons golden
syrup

2 level teaspoons baking
powder
2 small teaspoons bicarbonate
of soda
½ teaspoon vanilla
2 teaspoons boiling water

Cream the margarine and sugar. Add all dry ingredients. Dissolve syrup in boiling water and add to mixture to make a firm consistency. (The cooler it gets, the firmer it sets.) Roll out to ⅛ inch thickness. Cut into shapes and bake in a moderate oven for about 15 minutes.

When cool, sandwich together with chocolate butter icing, made the following way: beat together 1 oz margarine or butter, 2 oz icing sugar, chocolate or cocoa to taste. A little milk or hot water facilitates the mixing and 'softens' the consistency.

Mrs Titley, Glos.

BOURBON TYPE BISCUITS

4 oz sugar
4 oz butter
6 oz plain flour
¼ oz baking powder
2 oz coarse semolina
1 beaten egg
1½ dessertspoons cocoa

Filling:
1½ oz margarine
2 oz castor sugar
1 teaspoon coffee essence
1½ dessertspoons cocoa
Few drops vanilla essence

Sift together all dry ingredients *except cocoa*, stirring in lastly the semolina. Bind with sufficient of the egg to make a rolling-out consistency (i.e. dampish but not too wet). Roll out; fold and work in the cocoa powder. *This must not be added before.* Roll out again until ⅛ inch thick, then cut into fingers 3 × 1 inches, making 4 holes down each side of biscuits and then baking in hot oven, 450°F (Gas Mark 8) for 8 minutes. When cold, pair together with the filling.

To make filling: Warm butter, coffee (instant coffee with hot water will do) and sugar together until dissolved. Take off stove and beat well. Add cocoa and vanilla essence and beat well again. It is now ready, but if too stiff beat in a little milk or hot water.

A well-tried and proven recipe which has proved invaluable on a wet day for keeping the family quiet by letting them make these very more-ish biscuits.

POOR MAN'S PETIT FOURS

4 oz flour or semolina
2 oz plain flour
3 oz sugar
3 oz butter

2 teaspoons almond essence
About 4 tablespoons warm
water

Rub fat into dry ingredients. Mix essence with half the water, mix to a pliable dough with that and with the rest of water. Roll out onto floured board to ¼ inch or even less thick, cut into shapes, fancy or plain. Decorate centres with nuts, cherries, or anything you wish, sprinkle with dragées and place on well-greased baking sheets. Bake about 20 minutes, 350°F (Gas Mark 4). This quantity makes 32 small rounds. Get off sheets fairly quickly as they may stick if left too long. Great variety can be made with any colour. A spot of melted chocolate makes a pretty finish, if a few are left unadorned for cooking and the chocolate added afterwards.

Ironically this recipe came, during wartime, from King's Road, Chelsea, and has proved a great standby when almonds are so expensive.

DATE FINGERS

3 oz castor sugar
4 oz rolled oats
8 oz plain flour

5 oz butter (melted)
6 oz chopped dates
$\frac{1}{8}$-$\frac{1}{4}$ pint water

Put sugar, oats and flour in bowl. Add melted butter, mixing to a crumbly mixture. Put dates and water into a pan and cook for a few minutes until soft enough to spread. Put half the biscuit mixture into a Swiss roll tin, cover with date spread, and sprinkle remainder of mixture on top. Press down well. Bake in a moderate oven, 350°F (Gas Mark 4) for 55 minutes. Turn out and cut into 16 biscuits. Cool.

BROWNIES

2 oz lard
6 oz soft brown sugar
1 egg
2 oz melted unsweetened
chocolate

3 oz self-raising flour
$\frac{1}{4}$ teaspoon salt
2 oz chopped hazelnuts or
walnuts
$\frac{1}{4}$ teaspoon vanilla essence

Cream lard and sugar together. Add the egg and continue to beat. Mix in the melted chocolate and fold in the dry ingredients, vanilla and chopped nuts. Pour this mixture into a square baking tin and bake for 40–45 minutes at 350°F (Gas Mark 4). Cut into squares while still warm.

BRANDY SNAPS

2 oz butter
2 oz castor sugar
2 oz black treacle
1 teaspoon lemon juice

2 oz plain flour
1 level teaspoon ground
ginger

Melt butter, sugar, treacle and lemon juice together over gentle heat. Blend in sieved flour and ginger. Put teaspoons of mixture on well-greased baking trays, 5 inches apart. Bake 8–10 minutes in moderate oven, 350°F (Gas Mark 4) until rich brown and well spread. Remove from oven and leave to cool for moment until they are easily lifted. While still warm wrap each one around a wooden spoon handle, working quickly. Allow to become firm before lifting on to wire tray. Store in airtight tin.

CHOCOLATE MACAROONS

2 egg whites
4 oz ground almonds
4 oz castor sugar

3 tablespoons drinking chocolate
Blanched almonds
Rice paper

Whip the egg whites until the peaks are stiff, then fold in almonds, sugar and drinking chocolate. Spoon in small heaps on rice paper placed on baking trays, and put a blanched almond on each. Bake at 350°F (Gas Mark 4) for 20 minutes. If plain macaroons are preferred, mix them in the same way, using 2 egg whites, 6 oz ground almonds and 8 oz castor sugar.

CHOCOLATE CRISP BARS

2 oz self-raising flour
1 oz cornflakes
1 tablespoon cocoa

3 oz coconut
3 oz sugar
3 oz margarine

Grease 7 inch square tin with oil. Crush cornflakes into bowl. Add self-raising flour and cocoa then coconut and sugar. Mix *well*. Melt margarine and add to dry ingredients. Spread evenly in oven, 350°F (Gas Mark 4) for ½ hour. Remove and cool. Cut into 18 bars. Very good for Sunday tea.

KRINKLES

4 oz plain flour
2 oz lard
2 oz sugar
1 level teaspoon baking powder
1 level teaspoon bicarbonate of soda

1 level teaspoon ginger and cinnamon
2 level tablespoons golden syrup (warmed)
Pinch of salt

Rub dry ingredients into flour, add warm syrup, mix well, roll into balls (walnut). Place well apart on baking tray and cook in top oven for approximately 7 minutes, then transfer to bottom oven.

DIGESTIVE BISCUITS

4 oz porridge oats

5 oz self-raising flour

2 oz lard

½ teaspoon bicarbonate of soda

1 oz sugar

1 tablespoon syrup

Pinch salt

Mix together dry ingredients, melt lard, sugar, syrup, bicarbonate of soda in pan, add to dry ingredients. Roll out very thin, cut out and place on greased tray. Bake in moderate oven for 10 minutes till golden brown (transfer to bottom oven if needed).

HONEY WALNUT DROPS

6 oz butter

6 oz castor sugar

1 egg

10 level tablespoons honey

3½ oz walnuts

9 oz plain flour

2 level teaspoons baking powder

Cream butter and sugar until light and fluffy, and add beaten egg, honey and chopped walnuts. Mix flour and baking powder and stir into creamed mixture. Drop small spoonfuls of mixture well apart on greased baking sheets, and bake at 350°F (Gas Mark 4) for 15 minutes. Lift off biscuits while hot, and cool on a wire rack.

HONEY DATE BARS

3 oz butter

6 tablespoons honey

3 eggs

6 oz plain flour

1 teaspoon baking powder

½ teaspoon salt

6 oz chopped dates

4 oz chopped nuts

Blend butter and honey until creamy. Beat eggs in one at a time. Sift in flour, baking powder and salt, and stir in dates and nuts. Spread on a greased rectangular baking sheet (9 × 12 inches) and bake at 350°F (Gas Mark 4) until golden brown, about 30 minutes. Cut into bars. These bars will keep well and are 'chewy' and moist – excellent for the lunch box.

DOROTHY'S FLAPJACKS

3 oz fat (butter or margarine)

4 oz sugar (mixed brown and

white)

5 oz porridge oats

Some golden syrup may be substituted for part of the sugar. Melt the fat and sugar together and work in the oats. Spread in a Swiss roll tin and bake at 350°F (Gas Mark 4) for 20 minutes. Cool in the tin and cut into squares. These are made in vast quantities for every money-raising event in a village in north-west Essex, and always add greatly to the profits.

GIANT CURRANT BISCUITS

4 oz self-raising flour	Grated rind of 1 orange
4 oz fine semolina	4 oz currants
4 oz butter	2 eggs
4 oz castor sugar	1 tablespoon milk

Sift flour and semolina together and work in butter until the mixture is like fine crumbs. Add sugar, orange rind and currants. Stir in beaten eggs and milk to make a stiff light dough. Turn on to a well-floured board and knead lightly. Roll out thinly and cut into large rounds with a biscuit cutter. Place on a greased baking sheet and bake at 375°F (Gas Mark 5) until crisp and golden, about 15 minutes.

CHOCOLATE OAT CRISPS

4 oz butter or margarine or white vegetable fat	1 level teaspoon baking powder
8 oz sugar	½ teaspoon salt
1 egg	3 oz porridge oats
2 oz plain chocolate	1 teaspoon vanilla essence
4 oz plain flour	1 teaspoon almond essence

Cream fat and sugar and add beaten egg. Melt chocolate and blend into mixture. Sift flour, baking powder and salt and stir into creamed mixture. Add oats and essences and mix thoroughly. Drop by teaspoons on buttered baking sheet. Flatten with a fork dipped in cold water. Bake at 350°F (Gas Mark 4) for 10 minutes.

OATMEAL NUT BISCUITS

6 oz butter	4 oz plain flour
6 oz brown sugar	1 level teaspoon salt
4 oz granulated sugar	½ level teaspoon bicarbonate of soda
1 egg	
4 tablespoons water	9 oz porridge oats
1 teaspoon vanilla essence	4 oz walnut kernels

Blend together butter, sugars, egg, water and vanilla until light and fluffy. Add flour sifted with salt and soda. Stir in oats and chopped walnuts.

Drop by teaspoons on greased baking sheets. Bake at 350°F (Gas Mark 4) for 15 minutes.

COFFEE CREAMS

8 oz butter	**Filling:**
4 oz castor sugar	2 oz cocoa
8 oz self-raising flour	1 gill strong coffee
2 oz cocoa	2 oz butter
	Sugar to taste

Cream butter and sugar and work in flour and cocoa to make a stiff mixture. With the hands, form balls the size of a walnut, put out on buttered tins and flatten with a fork dipped in water. Bake at 350°F (Gas Mark 4) for 12 minutes. Lift carefully on to rack and when cool, sandwich together with filling. Make this by cooking cocoa in coffee until the mixture is a thick cream. Beat in butter off the fire, add sugar to taste. Leave until cold before using.

SPICED COFFEE DROPS

8 oz butter	1 level teaspoon bicarbonate
1 lb brown sugar	of soda
2 eggs	1 level teaspoon salt
¼ pint cold strong coffee	1 level teaspoon nutmeg
1 lb plain flour	1 level teaspoon cinnamon
	1 level teaspoon ground cloves

Cream together butter and sugar, beat in eggs and coffee. Work in flour sifted with soda, salt and spices. Put in a cold place for 1 hour, then put in small spoonfuls on a greased baking sheet. Bake at 400°F (Gas Mark 6) for 10 minutes.

NORFOLK SHORTCAKES

8 oz plain flour	1½ oz granulated sugar
½ teaspoon baking powder	1½ oz currants
4 oz butter or lard	½ teacup water

Sieve the flour with the baking powder and rub in 2 oz of the fat. Divide the rest of the fat, also the currants and sugar, into 3 portions. Mix the flour etc. into a pliable paste with the cold water and roll it out into a long strip. Spread this with dabs of fat and sprinkle with sugar and currants. Fold into 3 layers, give the paste a half turn and repeat this process twice more. Roll out about $\frac{1}{4}$ inch thick, cut into rounds or squares and bake in a hot oven for 15 minutes at 400°F (Gas Mark 6) until golden brown. Dredge with castor sugar when cooked.

MRS BALDWIN'S BISCUITS

$\frac{1}{2}$ lb of flour, a teaspoon of baking powder, a teacup of cream and sugar sifted in to your taste made into a paste and rolled out very thin.

Mrs Garden, 1847

BUCKINGHAM BISCUITS

2 cups sugar
$\frac{1}{4}$ cup cocoa
$\frac{1}{4}$ cup milk
4 oz butter

$\frac{1}{2}$ cup peanut butter
2 teaspoons vanilla essence
3 cups porridge oats

Use a breakfast cup to measure the ingredients. Put sugar, cocoa, milk and butter into a saucepan and boil for 1 minute, stirring all the time. Add the peanut butter, essence and oats, and mix very well. Press into greased Swiss roll tin. Bake at 350°F (Gas Mark 4) for 25 minutes. Mark into squares and cut when cold.

Chris Sharples, Milk Officer

OLD SPICE BISCUITS

6 oz plain flour
$\frac{1}{2}$ level teaspoon bicarbonate of soda
$\frac{1}{2}$ level teaspoon ginger
1 level teaspoon mixed spice

1 level teaspoon cinnamon
3 oz butter, margarine or cooking fat
2 oz castor sugar
2 tablespoons black treacle

Sift together dry ingredients. Put fat, sugar and treacle into a pan and melt slowly over a low heat. Remove from heat, stir in sifted dry ingredients and work with finger tips till well blended. Roll mixture into small balls, transfer to greased baking trays—allowing plenty of room between each for spreading—then press flat with a knife or prongs of a fork. Bake in the centre of the oven, at 350°F (Gas Mark 4) for 10–15 minutes. Cool on a wire tray, then store in an airtight container.

SUGAR AND SPICE BISCUITS

10 oz *plain flour*
1 *level teaspoon bicarbonate*
of soda
1 *level teaspoon salt*
1½ *level teaspoons cinnamon*
½ *level teaspoon nutmeg*
6 oz *butter or margarine*

4 oz *granulated sugar*
6 oz *brown sugar*
2 *eggs*
4 *tablespoons milk*
9 oz *porridge oats*
4 oz *chopped stoned raisins*

Sift together flour, soda, salt, cinnamon and nutmeg. Add softened fat, sugars, eggs and milk. Mix until smooth, then stir in oats and raisins. Chill dough, then roll out on floured board ¼ inch thick. Cut in 3 inch rounds with a cutter. Put on greased baking sheets, sprinkle lightly with sugar, and bake at 375°F (Gas Mark 5) for 15 minutes. Remove from baking sheets immediately.

HUNTER NUTS

8 oz *plain flour*
1 *level teaspoon ground ginger*
3 oz *butter*

6 oz *sugar*
1 *small egg*
3 oz *black treacle*

Sift flour and ginger. Rub in butter. Stir in sugar and bind with beaten egg and treacle. Form into small balls about size of marble and place on greased baking sheet, an inch or 2 apart. Bake in slow oven, 325°F (Gas Mark 3) for 30 minutes.

GINGER NUTS

¾ lb *self-raising flour*
½ lb *sugar*
¼ lb *butter*
3 oz *golden syrup*

1 *teaspoon bicarbonate of*
soda
1 *teaspoon ground ginger*
1 *egg*

Melt butter and syrup to liquid in pan (do not boil). Add dry ingredients. Beat egg into mixture. Knead well and roll into balls the size of a walnut. Bake in a moderate oven. Leave plenty of room between each ball on the baking sheet.

Mrs Fred Harper, Holt Castle, Worcs.

GINGER SNAPS

1 lb plain flour
½ lb soft brown sugar
¼ teaspoon salt
1 level teaspoon bicarbonate of soda

2 level teaspoons ground ginger
3 oz lard
2 oz butter
8 oz golden syrup
1 egg

Mix all the dry ingredients. Warm the fats until they melt, then add syrup and beaten egg. Beat well into the dry ingredients, and form dough into a ball. Chill thoroughly, then roll out mixture thinly on a floured board. Cut into shapes and bake at 350°F (Gas Mark 4) for 10 minutes. Cool on a wire tray.

GINGER BISCUITS

10 oz plain flour
4 oz butter or margarine
4 oz sugar
1 tablespoon ground ginger

½ teaspoon bicarbonate of soda
3 tablespoons (6 oz) golden syrup
Yolk of an egg

Beat butter and sugar to a cream, add other ingredients, mix to a dough, roll into small balls and bake in moderate oven about 20 minutes till wrinkled on top. Recipe about 100 years old and very good.

Miss Blackman, Stilton, Huntingdon

LINCOLN GINGER CRUST

Rub together ½ lb flour, 1¼ lb sugar, ¼ lb butter until it looks like breadcrumbs. Add 1 teaspoon ground ginger and 1 teaspoon baking powder. Beat 1 egg, add to mixture, working it with fingers, until sufficiently moist to spread (not runny). Grease flat dripping tin, put in mixture, making level about 1 inch thick. Bake in moderate oven, 375°F (Gas Mark 5) for ½ hour. When cooked cut into small squares. Do not take out of tin until cold.

CORNISH FAIRLINGS

4 oz flour
Pinch of salt
¼ teaspoon ground ginger
¼ teaspoon mixed spice
¼ teaspoon cinnamon

1½ teaspoons bicarbonate of soda
2 oz butter
2 oz castor sugar
2½ level tablespoons syrup

Sift the flour, salt, ground ginger, cinnamon, spice and bicarbonate of soda into a basin. Rub the butter into the dry ingredients. Mix in the sugar. Melt the syrup and stir it into the mixture, to make a soft dough. Roll the mixture between the hands into balls about the size of marbles and place them on greased baking trays with a space between them to allow them to spread. Bake the fairlings at 350°F (Gas Mark 4) for 10 minutes. Take the tray out of the oven and hit it on a solid surface to make the fairlings crack and spread. Then put them back into the oven for another 5 minutes to finish baking.

CRUNCH BISCUITS

2 oz butter
1 teaspoon syrup
1 teaspoon water
1 teacup oats

½ teacup flour
½ teacup sugar
½ teaspoon ginger
½ teaspoon bicarbonate of soda

Melt butter, syrup and water and mix with dry ingredients. Bake about 20–25 minutes in moderate oven, 350°F (Gas Mark 4).

COCONUT CRISPS

4 oz butter
3 oz soft brown sugar
4 oz granulated sugar
1 egg
1 teaspoon vanilla essence
5 oz plain flour

½ teaspoon baking powder
½ teaspoon bicarbonate of soda
½ teaspoon salt
4 oz desiccated coconut
1 oz cornflakes

Cream butter, add brown and granulated sugar, egg and vanilla essence and cream the mixture until light and fluffy. Sift together flour, baking powder, soda and salt and stir into the creamed mixture. Stir in coconut and cornflakes. Chill slightly, then shape into small balls, about ¾ inch diameter. Put about 2½ inches apart on an ungreased baking sheet, and flatten with a damp fork. Bake at 350°F (Gas Mark 4) for 10 minutes. Cool slightly before removing from baking sheet. These are crisp and sweet biscuits, which store very well.

GOOD SHORTBREAD

1 lb plain flour
8 oz ground rice
8 oz castor sugar

8 oz butter
8 oz soft margarine

Rub fats into mixed flour, ground rice and sugar. Roll $\frac{1}{4}$ inch thick, prick and put in refrigerator for 30 minutes. Bake at 350°F (Gas Mark 4) for nearly 30 minutes. It should be *pale* golden. Cool on trays. Good to store in freezer.

Pat Brown, Keynsham, Somerset

AYRSHIRE SHORTBREAD

4 oz plain flour $\frac{1}{2}$ beaten egg
4 oz butter   4 oz castor sugar
4 oz rice flour   2 tablespoons cream

Sieve flour and rice flour and rub in butter, mix in sugar and bind to a stiff consistency with the egg and the cream. Roll out thinly, prick with a fork and cut into shapes. Bake in a steady oven for about 15 minutes until a pale brown colour.

Mrs Biggar, Kirkcudbrightshire

SHORTBREAD BISCUITS

1 lb plain flour   Pinch salt
10 oz butter   2 egg yolks
6 oz sugar

Rub butter in, add sugar. Make well in centre and put in yolks. Knead. Roll to $\frac{1}{4}$ inch thickness. Bake 25 minutes at 350°F (Gas Mark 4).

Mrs Greenwood, Yorks

ALMOND SHORTBREAD

14 oz plain flour   6 oz castor sugar
2 oz ground rice   2 oz chopped mixed peel
2 oz blanched almonds   10 oz butter

Sift flour and ground rice onto a pastry board. Add chopped almond, sugar and peel and mix very well together. Have butter soft all the way through and put in the centre of flour mixture. Gradually knead the dry ingredients into it. Press mixture into two Swiss roll tins, prick all over, and mark into neat squares. Bake at 350°F (Gas Mark 4) for 1 hour.

GRASMERE SHORTBREAD

1 orange or tangerine   8 oz plain flour
10 oz sugar   1 dessertspoon ground ginger
4 oz butter

On the day before making the shortbread, peel an orange or large tangerine. Remove white pith, and cut the peel into fine shreds. Make a syrup with 6 oz sugar and 4 tablespoons water, and in this boil the peel for 2 minutes. Leave the peel to stand in the syrup overnight. Rub the butter into the flour and work in the remaining sugar and the ginger. Add the peel drained of its syrup. Knead until all the ingredients are thoroughly blended. Pack the mixture into an ungreased baking tin to form a compact mass, and flatten evenly with the hands. Bake at 325°F (Gas Mark 3) for 25 minutes. Cut in small squares while still hot, but do not remove from the tin until cold.

OAT BISCUITS

4 oz self-raising flour
4 oz porridge oats
3 oz sugar
2 oz butter

2 oz lard
1 tablespoon golden syrup
1 teaspoon bicarbonate of soda

Mix flour, oats and sugar together. Melt fats and syrup in saucepan and add bicarbonate of soda. Pour on to dry ingredients and form into small balls. Flatten these on a greased baking sheet with a fork. Bake at 375°F (Gas Mark 5) for 10 minutes. Leave in the tin until cold.

NORFOLK GINGERS

4 oz brown sugar
4 oz margarine or butter
2 teaspoons ground ginger
½ teaspoon mixed spice

1 small teaspoon bicarbonate
of soda
8 oz flour – plain is best
About 2 tablespoons milk
1 egg

Sift flour, spices and sugar into a basin and rub in margarine or butter. Dissolve soda in warm milk. Add egg. Beat till blended. Stir into dry ingredients. Knead till smooth. Flour hands lightly. Roll equal-sized small portions of dough into balls. Place well apart on greased baking sheet. Press each ball lightly on top. Bake in a moderate oven, 350°F (Gas Mark 4) for about ½ hour. Leave on baking sheet until they cool, or they will break, then lift with a broad-bladed knife on to a wire tray.

NORFOLK GINGER DROPS

2 oz sugar
1 tablespoon golden syrup
1½ gills boiling water
1 egg
1¼ lb self-raising flour
1 tablespoon ground ginger

2 teaspoons ground cinnamon
2 teaspoons mixed spice
2 tablespoons weak coffee
¼ teaspoon ground cloves
1 teaspoon ground mace
1 teaspoon bicarbonate of soda

Whisk egg and sugar in basin till fluffy. Dissolve syrup in boiling water. Add coffee. Stir in egg and sugar. Beat in carefully to all dry ingredients which have been previously sifted together. Have ready a greased baking sheet and drop mixture from a teaspoon on to it, keeping drops about 1½ inches apart. Bake for about ½ hour, 350°F (Gas Mark 4).

SUFFOLK OATEN WAFERS

6 oz plain flour or 6 oz
self-raising flour and take
only half the baking powder
1 teaspoon baking powder
½ oz sugar

½ teaspoon salt
1½ oz rolled oats (porridge oats)
2 oz margarine
Enough milk to make dough

First mix dry ingredients, then rub in fat with finger tips. Mix to a firm dough with a little milk. Knead lightly on a lightly floured board. Roll out thinly. Cut into rounds. Bake on a greased baking sheet, a little apart, in a moderately hot oven at 425°F (Gas Mark 7) for about ¼ hour or till brown. Cool on a wire rack.

TOFFEE BARS

4 oz butter
3 oz brown sugar
1 egg yolk
2 oz plain flour
2 oz porridge oats

Topping:
3 oz plain chocolate
1 tablespoon butter
Walnuts

Beat together butter, sugar and egg yolk until smooth. Add flour and oats and stir well until smooth. Press mixture in a rectangular tin and bake at 375°F (Gas Mark 5) for 15 minutes. Cool slightly. Melt chocolate and butter over hot water, spread over warm biscuit mixture, and decorate with whole or chopped walnuts. Cut into bars while warm, but leave to cool completely in tin before removing.

GINGER BISCUITS

2 oz self-raising flour
1 oz fat
1 oz sugar

½ teaspoon ginger
½ teaspoon bicarbonate of soda
2 tablespoons melted syrup

Rub in and mix with melted syrup. Put in teaspoons on greased baking sheet and bake at 350°F (Gas Mark 4) for 15 minutes.

GINGERNUT MEN

6 oz plain flour
¼ level teaspoon salt
1 level tablespoon ground ginger
1 level teaspoon mixed spice

2 oz butter
4 oz demerara sugar
3–4 tablespoons syrup, warmed
Glacé cherries

Sift together flour, salt and spices. In a separate bowl cream butter and sugar. Mix in flour and enough syrup to form a stiff dough. Roll out to ½ inch thickness and cut out the men with a biscuit cutter. Place carefully on a greased baking sheet and bake in a moderate oven, 375°F (Gas Mark 5) for 15 minutes. Remove and allow to cool. Cut very small pieces of glacé cherry and use to represent buttons.

10 Sweetmeats

Sain Mihel byd bees, to be brent out of strife:
Saint John bid take honey, with favour of life.
For one sely cottage, set south good and warme:
Take body and goodes, and twise yerely a swarme.

Christmas take hede, if their hives be to light:
Take honey and water, together wel dight.
That mixed with strawes, in a dish in their hives:
They drowne not, they fight not, thou savest their lyves.

Thomas Tusser

PULLED TOFFEE

1½ *lb granulated sugar*
½ *gill vinegar*
½ *oz butter*

1 *teaspoon vanilla essence*
1 *gill water*

Pour the vinegar and water into a clean pan (not too small), add the sugar and boil for 15 minutes. Add the butter in little bits, and boil for another 15 minutes. Have ready a plate, greased with butter, turn out the toffee on it and sprinkle on the vanilla essence. Turn the edges inward (as if folding them) when cool enough to handle, smear the fingers with butter and hang the mixture over the hook. Pull the toffee lengthways, then hang it up again and again for 8 to 10 minutes until it is all white, or streaked with white. Then twist in sticks about ¾ inch thick and before it can set cut into ½ inch and 1 inch lengths with a pair of scissors. Place on greased paper to harden.

TREACLE TOFFEE

10 oz *black treacle or golden*
syrup
¼ *lb brown sugar*
½ *oz butter*
2 *teaspoons vinegar*

½ *small teaspoon bicarbonate*
of soda
6 *drops lemon essence or*
1 *teaspoon lemon juice*

Mix treacle, butter, sugar and vinegar in a saucepan (a large one) and boil without stirring until a few drips will harden and snap if placed in a little cold water.

See that there are no lumps in the bicarbonate of soda when added—dry —to the mixture. Let all boil again for about 8 minutes, pour out on to a greased tin, sprinkle the essence of lemon or lemon juice over. When cool enough to handle, smear a scrap of butter on the hands and roll into small balls. Leave on the greased tin to harden.

YORKSHIRE BUTTER TOFFEE

1 *lb demerara sugar*
3 *oz butter*
1¼ *gills water*

Lemon or vanilla essence
1 *dessertspoon glucose*

Dissolve sugar in water. Add glucose and ⅓ butter and boil to 240°F. Add remainder of butter in thin flakes, one at a time, allowing butter to boil into the toffee quite undisturbed. Boil gently to 285°F. Remove pan to table and add chosen essence. Twist pan once or twice in rotary fashion to mingle the essence, but do not stir. Pour out on to oiled slab between bars, and when sufficiently set cut into 1 inch bars. Wrap in waxed paper and store in airtight tin when cold.

Mrs Bracewell, Northallerton, Yorks

RUSSIAN TOFFEE

1 *lb castor sugar*
½ *gill cream or top of the milk*
¾ *gill water*
1 *dessertspoon glucose*

¼ *lb butter*
¼ *lb honey*
Lemon essence
Carmine

Dissolve sugar, cream and warm slowly. Add glucose, honey and a third of the butter and dissolve. Boil to 240°F stirring all the time. Add the remainder of the butter, cutting it in thin slices so that it may boil quickly through the syrup and so no heat is lost. Add sufficient carmine to just tinge the toffee. Boil slowly and very carefully to 280°F. Add lemon essence to taste. Pour into greased tin or finish in bars. Russian toffee needs very careful cooking to avoid burning. Stir the toffee slowly and gently throughout the process.

Mrs Bracewell, Northallerton, Yorks

BONFIRE TOFFEE

1 lb granulated sugar   *1 tablespoon golden syrup*
2 oz butter   *1 teaspoon lemon juice*
1 large tin condensed milk

Put sugar, butter and syrup into a large heavy pan and stir over a low heat until they have melted together. Bring to the boil, add the milk and lemon juice and boil to 245°F (or until a little dropped in cold water forms a firm ball). Take the pan off the fire and leave to stand until the toffee stops bubbling, then pour into a well-greased tin. Mark into squares when nearly set, but leave until cold and hard before breaking up.

TREACLE TOFFEE

10 oz sugar   *2 oz butter*
2 tablespoons water   *1 dessertspoon vinegar*
2 tablespoons black treacle

Place all ingredients in saucepan. Boil steadily; about 12 minutes or until small amount dropped in cold water forms firm ball, 300°–310°F. Pour into shallow greased tin, about 8 × 8 inches. When beginning to set mark into squares with a knife which has been dipped in oil.

BUTTERSCOTCH (1)

1 lb soft brown sugar   *3 tablespoons treacle*
2 oz butter   *1 teaspoon vinegar*
2 tablespoons water

Put all in pan, boil till a little hardens at once in cold water. Pour in flat greased tin to set.

Mrs L. Booth, Weston-super-Mare

BUTTERSCOTCH (2)

1 lb granulated sugar
¼ pint water
¼ level teaspoon cream of

tartar
3 oz butter
½ teaspoon vanilla essence

Put sugar and water into a large pan, and heat until sugar dissolves. Add cream of tartar and boil to 240°F. (At this stage a little dropped from a teaspoon into cold water will form a hard ball.) Remove from heat, stir in vanilla essence. Pour into a buttered rectangular tin (11 × 7 × 1¼ inches) Cool slightly and mark into squares. When almost cold, turn butterscotch out, and break into pieces.

EXHIBITION TOFFEE

1 lb granulated sugar
8 oz golden syrup
1 tablespoon water

2 tablespoons vinegar
Flavouring

Put sugar, water, vinegar and syrup into a heavy pan, and stir occasionally until it boils, then boil gently without stirring 20 minutes. To ascertain if sufficiently boiled, drop a few drops into a large basin of cold water, and if in a few minutes you find it crisp, withdraw from fire and stir in flavouring to taste, then pour into a well-buttered tin, and before it is quite cold turn on to a cold dish and cut into pieces with a pair of scissors or knife.

Mrs Page, 1899

TOFFY

Take a lb of brown sugar, 3 oz butter, 1 teacup of water, 1 lemon. Boil the sugar, butter and water and half the rind of the lemon together. When sufficiently done (this you will know by dropping a little into cold water when it should be quite crisp) let it stand aside until the boiling has ceased, then stir in the juice of the lemon. Butter a dish and pour in the toffy. It should be a ¼ of an inch thick.

Lewis' Mother's Cookbook, Mary Horrell, Exeter

ALMOND BRITTLE

4 oz sugar
1 teaspoon lemon juice

2 oz flaked almonds

Dissolve sugar and lemon juice over a low heat until it is liquid. Boil until the liquid starts to colour. Add the almonds and mix thoroughly. Put into an oiled tin and press down with a cut lemon brushed with oil. Mark into squares at once. Break when cold.

EVERTON TOFFEE

Dissolve $\frac{1}{2}$ lb sugar, 4 tablespoons water and 1 tablespoon of syrup and 2 oz margarine in a pan, keep stirring. Add $\frac{1}{2}$ teaspoon cream of tartar and boil, don't stir. Add 2 oz margarine, slicing so that it will melt quickly. Lower the temperature and boil till light brown and just past hard ball stage. Pour into tin and set.

TREACLE TOFFEE

Place 3 oz sugar, 3 oz treacle, $\frac{1}{2}$ cupful water and 1 tablespoon vinegar in a pan. Heat until the sugar has dissolved. Boil for 2–3 minutes or until it is at the hard ball stage. Add 2 oz margarine, stirring so that it will melt quickly. Pour into a tin and set.

BUTTERSCOTCH

Put $\frac{1}{2}$ lb demerara sugar, 2 oz butter, 8 tablespoons water and 1 tablespoon vinegar in a pan. Heat until the sugar dissolves. Boil for 2–3 minutes, don't stir, until it is golden brown, quite thick and at the hard ball stage. Pour into tin and set.

SYRUP FUDGE

2 oz butter
4 tablespoons water
2 rounded tablespoons golden syrup

1 lb granulated sugar
8 level tablespoons ($\frac{1}{2}$ large can) sweetened condensed milk

Put all ingredients into a thick-based saucepan, and stir over gentle heat until sugar dissolves. Bring to boil, and boil gently for 10 minutes, without stirring. Remove from heat, and beat well until mixture begins to 'fudge'. Pour into a lightly buttered $7\frac{1}{2} \times 7\frac{1}{2} \times 1$ inch deep square tin. Leave until cold, then cut into squares.

CHOCOLATE FUDGE

Put 1 oz cocoa in a pan with $\frac{1}{4}$ pint milk and 1 oz margarine and $\frac{1}{2}$ lb sugar. Stir over a low heat until the sugar and the cocoa have melted, then simmer, stirring frequently, till the mixture forms a soft ball when placed in cold water. Remove from heat. Add ½ teaspoon of vanilla essence and keep stirring until the mixture thickens. Pour into a tin and set.

W.I. FUDGE

1 lb sugar
½ pint milk
1 oz cocoa

⅛ teaspoon cream of tartar
2 oz butter
½ teaspoon vanilla essence

Dissolve the sugar in the milk over gentle heat. Add the cocoa and cream of tartar and boil until a little of the mixture forms a soft ball in cold water. Remove from heat and add butter and vanilla. Beat until creamy and smooth and pour into a greased tin. Cut into squares when cold. This recipe was demonstrated at a Women's Institute meeting many years ago, and has never been known to fail.

CHOCOLATE FUDGE

2 oz chocolate
½ lb soft brown sugar
1 small tin condensed milk

1 oz butter
½ lb icing sugar

Melt chocolate over hot water, beat in butter, then stir in milk. Add soft brown sugar and stir in. Sieve icing sugar into mixture and knead it well until soft and creamy looking. Press into lightly buttered tray 6 × 4 inches. Leave to set and cut into 1 inch squares.

Mrs Bracewell, Northallerton, Yorks

SHERRY FUDGE

2 tablespoons seedless
raisins
4 oz plain chocolate
2 oz butter

4 tablespoons evaporated milk
12 oz sieved icing sugar
Sherry

Soak the raisins in sherry overnight. Place chocolate and butter in a mixing basin over hot, not boiling water. Stir until melted and smooth. Remove from heat, stir in evaporated milk and drained soaked raisins. Gradually stir in sieved icing sugar until fudge is smooth and thick. Turn into a buttered and waxed paper lined tin. Leave to cool. When set, remove from tin, peel away paper and cut into squares.

MINISTRY CRUMB FUDGE

2 tablespoons syrup
2 oz margarine
2 oz sugar
2 oz cocoa

Few drops vanilla,
peppermint or orange essence
6 oz dried crumbs

Heat the syrup, margarine, sugar and cocoa gently until all is melted.
stir in the required flavouring and then the breadcrumbs (these are best
lightly crisped in the oven). Mix thoroughly and turn into a well-greased
7 inch square tin. Spread evenly and mark lightly into fingers or squares.
Leave for 24 hours and then use as a cake or sweet. The fudge improves
with keeping for a day or two. This recipe comes from one of the many
Ministry of Food leaflets issued during the 1939–45 War, and the few lean
years afterwards. Many of them feature dried milk and dried egg, but
some are still useful when budgets are low and ideas are needed.

GRANNY'S OLD-FASHIONED FUDGE

1 tablespoon golden syrup
1 lb sugar
2 oz butter
¼ pint milk

4 oz chocolate chips
½ teaspoon vanilla essence
1 teaspoon rum

Grease a heavy saucepan. Heat the sugar, milk and syrup, stirring gently
until sugar has dissolved. Add chocolate and stir until melted and mixture
is boiling. Cook to 238°F (or until mixture forms a soft ball when a little
is dropped into cold water). Take off heat, add butter and cool without
stirring. Add vanilla and rum and beat until fudge is thick and loses its
shine. Put into a shallow buttered tin and cut into squares while warm.

FRUIT AND NUT FUDGE

½ pint fresh milk
2 lb granulated sugar
¼ lb butter
½ teaspoon vanilla essence

2 oz raisins or sultanas,
cleaned
2 oz blanched or coarsely
chopped almonds

Soak sugar in the milk for 1 hour, then cook very slowly till sugar dissolves. Add the butter and when melted bring mixture to the boil. (Brush
sides of pan with water to prevent graining from time to time.) Simmer
steadily till a temperature of 238°F is reached, or till a little of the mixture
forms a soft ball when dropped into cold water, (this can take up to 1 hour),
stir frequently, especially when nearing 238°F to prevent burning.
Remove from heat, cool slightly, then beat till fudge is thick and creamy.
Add essence, fruit and nuts and pour quickly into a well greased shallow
tin, smooth with a knife, mark into squares and cut when cool and set.

RUM RAISIN FUDGE

1 *lb granulated sugar*	¼ *pint water*
2 *oz butter*	1 *teaspoon rum*
¼ *pint evaporated milk*	4 *oz seedless raisins*

Put the sugar, butter, milk and water into a large saucepan. Heat gently till the sugar has dissolved and the fat has melted, then bring to the boil. Boil rapidly, stirring until a temperature of 240°F is reached (to the 'soft ball' stage). Remove from heat, add the rum and seedless raisins, beat well until the mixture becomes thick and creamy. As the sugar begins to grain, pour into a greased tin about 6×8 inches. When nearly set, mark into squares with a sharp knife.

SUGAR BALLS

4 *oz plain chocolate*	*finely crushed*
3 *tablespoons single cream*	2 *tablespoons sherry*
16 *sponge finger biscuits,*	2 *oz castor sugar*

Place chocolate in a basin over hot, not boiling, water. Stir until smooth. Remove from heat. Stir in cream and sugar. Add finely crushed sponge finger crumbs and sherry. Blend well. Leave mixture in a cool place overnight to stiffen. Roll heaped teaspoons of the mixture into balls; roll in castor sugar. Store in a screw-topped jar.

CHOCOLATE WALNUTS

Sandwich together 2 walnut halves with melted chocolate. When set, dip the whole walnuts into softened chocolate and place in sweet paper cases to set.

COFFEE WALNUT CREAMS

¼ *lb icing sugar*	1 *teaspoon lightly beaten egg*
1 *level tablespoon double*	*white*
dairy cream	*Walnuts*
1 *teaspoon instant coffee*	

Work sugar, coffee and cream together to a smooth paste, adding egg white as required and more sugar if necessary. Beat until very stiff. Leave for an hour, then roll into small balls and flatten each on greaseproof paper to an oval with a quarter of shelled walnut.

CHOCOLATE TRUFFLES

8 oz *plain chocolate*
1 *heaped tablespoon castor*
sugar

2 oz *butter*
2 *tablespoons rum or cream*
1 *egg yolk*

Melt the chocolate over hot water. Remove from heat and stir in sugar, butter, rum or cream and egg yolk. Beat until thick and cool. Shape into small balls and leave to dry. Roll in cocoa, chocolate vermicelli, hundreds-and-thousands or desiccated coconut.

NO-COOK FONDANTS

4 *tablespoons evaporated milk*
1 *lb icing sugar*

Flavouring and colouring

Put the milk into a bowl, sieve icing sugar and gradually work into the milk. Knead until smooth and shiny, and add flavouring and colouring to make a variety of sweets. To make *peppermint creams*, add a few drops of oil of peppermint, and a little green colouring if liked. For *orange creams* add orange-flower water and orange colouring. For *rose creams* add rose-water and cochineal. Oil of peppermint, orange-flower water and rose-water are all obtainable at any chemist. For *fruit rolls*, knead in 4 oz chopped mixed peel and 1 oz chopped glacé cherries with a little more icing sugar if necessary. Shape into 6 inch logs about 1 inch diameter and chill until firm before cutting each roll into 12 pieces. All the fondants may be shaped by this easy method, or else rolled out and cut with canapé cutters. Top of the sweets may be decorated with nuts, coloured balls, crystallised petals or angelica.

COCONUT KISSES

¼ *lb fondant*
A few drops almond
flavouring
¼ *lb desiccated coconut*
A few drops green vegetable
colouring

A few drops vanilla
flavouring
A few drops raspberry
flavouring
A few drops cochineal

Knead all but one tablespoon of the coconut into the fondant; divide the mixture into 3 parts. Into 1 work a few drops of vanilla; into the second a few drops of almond flavouring and green colouring; into the third a few drops raspberry flavouring and cochineal. Form each batch of mixture into small pointed rolls, using the remaining coconut to help press the soft mixture into shapes.

COCONUT ICE

2 lb lump sugar   *10 oz desiccated coconut*
½ pint water

Put sugar and water in a strong saucepan and stand over a gentle heat until the sugar is dissolved. Bring to the boil and continue boiling rapidly for 10 minutes, stirring all the time. Remove from the heat, stir in coconut and mix well. Pour half the mixture into an oiled rectangular tin (11 × 7 inches). Colour the remainder lightly with cochineal and press on top of the white ice. Mark into 12 bars when partly cool and finish cutting when cold. Wrap in Cellophane.

SPICED NUTS

Almonds and walnuts are good spiced. Mix in a bowl 2 oz castor sugar, 1 level tablespoon cinnamon, a good pinch each of nutmeg and powdered cloves. In another bowl, put a slightly beaten egg white, and dip the nuts in this, a few at a time, rubbing them in the fingers to coat them well with the egg white. Toss the nuts into the bowl of sugar and spice so they are covered completely; put on to buttered baking sheet and bake at 300°F (Gas Mark 2) for 30 minutes.

SUGARED NUTS

In a heavy shallow pan, boil together 8 oz sugar and 4 fluid oz water for 5 minutes. Add 8 oz blanched almonds, hazelnuts or walnuts and continue cooking gently, stirring well, until the liquid begins to look white and slightly sugared. Add 1 teaspoon vanilla essence and ½ teaspoon powdered cinnamon, and leave the pan on one side of the stove for 10 minutes. Put back on a very low heat and stir well until the sugar starts to melt. Pour on to a wire cake rack placed over waxed paper, and separate the nuts to allow them to cool and dry.

SALTED NUTS

Almonds, filberts and walnuts are very good toasted. Blanch and dry the nuts and sprinkle with olive oil. Brown on baking sheets at 400°F (Gas Mark 6) with an occasional stir, and while still hot, sprinkle with salt.

NUT BALLS

Mince finely, or chop in electric blender, 8 oz mixed nuts. Cream 5 oz butter and work in the nuts, 3 level tablespoons castor sugar, 4 oz plain flour and 1 teaspoon of vanilla essence. With the fingers roll the mixture into balls the size of marbles. Bake on lightly buttered tins at 375°F (Gas Mark 5) for 10 minutes, and roll while hot in powdered castor or icing sugar.

CANDY KISSES

6 oz granulated sugar
½ pint water
4 oz butter
4 oz finest semolina
2 oz ground almonds (or

fine cake or biscuit crumbs
or fine coconut)
½ teaspoon each of almond
and vanilla essence

Boil the sugar and water together till thick and syrupy but remove from heat before it changes colour. Melt the butter, stir in semolina and brown lightly; then add ground almonds and essences. Add this mixture to the syrup, stirring over low heat till thick and cook gently for 3 minutes. Leave to cool slightly, then divide into 4 portions and colour to taste with green, yellow and red colourings, but leaving one portion natural. Working fairly quickly so that the mixture keeps warm, form into assorted shapes. Roll some in coconut and decorate others with blanched almonds, walnut halves, hazelnuts, silver dragées and glacé cherries. Transfer to paper cases. Chopped cherries, dates and ginger can be added to the mixture for variety. This recipe is also delicious for stuffing dates and prunes.

CHOCOLATE BRITTLES

2 oz almonds
6 oz castor sugar

4 oz plain chocolate

The almonds need not be blanched. Dissolve 2 oz sugar over low heat until liquid. Add the almonds and boil together until light brown. Pour on to an oiled tin and leave until cold. Crush the mixture to a powder. Melt the chocolate over hot water. Remove from heat and mix with remaining sugar. Stir in the almond powder and form into small balls. Leave to harden and roll in a little cocoa or powdered drinking chocolate.

CRUNCHIE

4 oz syrup
4 oz sugar

1 oz baking powder

Boil sugar and syrup together till melted and thick. Take off gas, stir in baking powder. Pour out in greased tin.

11 Jams, Jellies, Marmalades and Mincemeats

Conserves of barberry, quinces, and such,
with sirops, that easeth the sickly so much.

Thomas Tusser

FOR EXTRA FLAVOUR IN JAMS

The flavour of plum jam, and, indeed, all jams made with stone fruits, is very greatly improved by the addition of a few bitter almonds. During the boiling process about $\frac{1}{2}$ a dozen almonds for every lb of fruit is enough, though more may be used if liked. The almonds need not be removed, but may be left in the jam and eaten with it. The addition of vanilla to stone fruit jam also improves its flavour, but vanilla essence will do instead.

APPLE MARMALADE

Cut as many pippins as you like into thin slices and put into a stone jar inside a pan of boiling water. Add an equal weight of loaf sugar, and cinnamon to taste. Keep water boiling and shake jar frequently but do not stir. When smooth and clear, put into pots and tie down when cold. This is good to eat as an emergency pudding with cream.

Mrs Hill, 1864

APPLE AND BLACKBERRY JAM

2 lb blackberries   ½ pint water
2 lb sour apples (windfalls of   3 lb sugar
any variety)

Pick over and wash the berries, peel, core, and slice the apples. Put the fruit into a pan with the water and cook till tender. Add the sugar, stir until dissolved and bring to the boil. Boil until the jam sets when tested. Bottle and cover.

BLACKBERRY AND APPLE JAM

1½ lb blackberries   ¼-½ pint water
1½ lb apples   3 lb sugar

Prepare fruit, simmer gently with water until soft. Add sugar, cook rapidly until setting point is reached. Pour into warm jars, cover with wax circle and cover.

BLACKBERRY AND APPLE JAM

This traditional country favourite is easily and quickly made, and is of course, very cheap. Peel and slice the required apples and boil in water, (allowing 1 gill for each lb of fruit) till they are pulped. Simmer the blackberries without water until soft and add to the apples. Weigh out 1 lb sugar for each lb fruit used, stir into the mixture till dissolved, then boil fast to setting point, testing after 20 minutes.

CAPE GOOSEBERRY JAM

Allow weight for weight of sugar and fruit; bruise ripest fruit in bottom of pan, boil without sugar for 15 minutes, add remainder of the fruit and sugar and boil for 1 hour.

CHERRY JAM

Cherry jam is a wonderful breakfast treat. To get a good colour and set, boil an equal weight of cherries and sugar for 5 minutes. Remove the fruit and cook the syrup for 12 minutes, add ¼ pint blackcurrant syrup. Add fruit and boil for 13 minutes before potting. The fruit is much better for being stoned first.

CHERRY MARMALADE

3 lb black cherries
½ pint raspberry juice

½ pint redcurrant juice
2 lb sugar

Put cherries, juices and sugar into a preserving pan, and simmer gently until sugar has dissolved. Cook gently, until a firm, clear jelly mingles with the cherries. Remove from heat and press cherries gently with the back of a spoon. Cool, and pot when cold.

DRIED APRICOT JAM

1 lb dried apricots
4 lb sugar
3½ pints boiling water

1 oz bitter almonds
Juice of 1 lemon

Quarter the apricots, pour the boiling water over, leaving them to soak for 24 hours. Then boil for 1 hour. Blanch the almonds and add, also sugar and the juice of lemon and boil again for ½–¾ hour.

DRIED APRICOT JAM

1 lb apricots (or any dried
fruit)
5 breakfastcups boiling water

5 cups sugar
Juice of 2 lemons
Blanched almonds if
required

Wash apricots thoroughly, cut in halves, pour the boiling water on, and let stand overnight. Boil next day until skins are tender, then add sugar and lemon juice and boil 20 minutes. A few blanched almonds added is an improvement.

FRESH APRICOT JAM

Cut fruit in halves and remove stones, put fruit aside for night adding some of the sugar to create a syrup (in total use 1 lb sugar to 1 lb fruit). Next day put on a gentle fire and boil for 1 hour; crack the stones and blanch kernels (in cupful boiling water) and add to jam to give extra flavour. Do not add any water, as it will be quite firm jam. A knob of butter improves all jams as it adds 'gloss' and prevents, to an extent, 'catching' the jam on bottom of pan.

FIG JAM

Cut the stalks off the figs and halve them. Put them into a large basin in layers, with a good sprinkling of sugar over each; let them remain for 12 hours. Next day put them in a preserving pan, boil for a short time, then add remainder of sugar and piece of lemon (or juice of 1 lemon). 12 oz sugar should be allowed for each 1 lb fruit. Boil all together until it jellies.

GOOSEBERRY JAM flavoured with ELDERFLOWER

Cut the gooseberries slightly, add ¼ cup of water. Boil for 15 minutes, add sugar, having allowed 1 lb 2 oz for every 1 lb fruit. Boil for ¾ hour. If the delicate flavour of elderflower is required, tie a bunch of flowers (one good sprigful) by the stem and suspend over side of the pan while fruit alone is boiling. Remove before the sugar is added.

GRAPE (ISABELLA) JAM

Using scissors to 'open' grapes, squeeze pulp out of skins, simmer pulp until tender, press through a colander, add skins, and then add ¾ lb sugar to every 1 lb of pulp and skins. Boil for about 1 hour.

GREEN GOOSEBERRY JAM

Wash, top and tail 6 lb gooseberries, and put in a pan with 2 pints water. Stew gently for about 20 minutes until soft and mushy. Add 8 lb warm sugar, dissolve slowly, and boil rapidly for 20 minutes. Skim and pour into warm dry jars.

GREEN TOMATO JAM

Take 8 lb green tomatoes and 6 lb sugar; tomatoes must be firm and sound with no sign of colour, cut into small pieces, mix sugar with a little water in saucepan, add fruit, boil as for ordinary jam; do not add any other ingredients whatever. This is a delicious jam. [Author's note: I can vouch for this—I had it as a child and have never forgotten it; how thankful I am that the recipe has, at last, come into my hands.]

LEMON AND APPLE MARMALADE

3 lemons   *3 lb cooking apples*
3 pints cold water   *4¾ lb sugar*

Slice the lemons and soak in the water overnight. Cook until tender, then add the peeled and sliced apples. Continue cooking until the apples are tender but not broken. Stir in the sugar until dissolved, then boil rapidly to setting point. Cover when cold.

MARROW JAM

4 lb diced marrow
4 lb sugar
Ground ginger – if liked
1 lb extra sugar

1 pint apple juice (made from windfalls, cores, skins and all, plus as little water as possible)

Overnight, in a big bowl, stand the diced marrow covered with 4 lb sugar. Next morning add 1 pint apple juice, and the 1 lb sugar. Boil until marrow is cooked and slightly transparent (about ½ hour). Test for set in usual way, on a cold plate near window.

This recipe from Devon can be thoroughly recommended—it sets well, is of a very good flavour and above all in a wet season, is a wonderful way of using up a glut of marrows.

MARROW JAM

3 lb marrow
3 lb sugar

Rind and juice of 2 lemons
2 oz root ginger

Dice marrow flesh, cover with sugar, leave 24 hours. Bruise ginger, place in a muslin bag with the fruit and lemons. Cook slowly until sugar is dissolved, boil as before.

MIXED JAM FOR CHILDREN

Take equal quantities of gooseberries, red and black currants, cherries, raspberries and apples, pared, cored and cut up. Stew the cherries, then add the apples and finally the soft fruits. To every lb of fruit add ¾ lb sugar, weighing the fruit after it has been prepared for cooking. Boil altogether for 1 hour, allowing the apples and cherries about ½ hour head-start. Pour into hot jars and cover when cold.

PEACH JAM

Peel and stone the peaches. To 6 lb fruit, add 1 quart (2 pints) water, and boil till very soft and tender (i.e. boil until nearly reduced to 6 lb again), add weight for weight of sugar, boil 1–1½ hours.

PEAR AND GINGER JAM

4 lb hard pears   2 oz preserved ginger
3 lb sugar   2 lemons

Peel and core the pears and put into a bowl in layers with the sugar. Leave overnight, then put into preserving pan with chopped ginger, grated lemon rind and lemon juice. Heat gently until sugar has dissolved, then boil rapidly to setting point.

PEAR HARLEQUIN

3 lb pears   1 orange
1 medium can pineapple $\frac{1}{4}$ pint bottle maraschino
pieces   cherries
Sugar

Cut pears in $\frac{1}{2}$ inch cubes without peeling. Put into a bowl with pine-apple, grated rind and juice of orange. Weigh the mixture and add 12 oz sugar to each lb. Cover and leave overnight. Put in preserving pan and cook gently (about 2 hours) until thick. Cut cherries in half and add with liquid from the bottle. Stir thoroughly and pour into jars. This is delicious with ice cream.

PINEAPPLE AND TOMATO JAM

4 pineapples   2 lb tomatoes

Grate or shred pineapples, skin tomatoes and cut them up fine; boil together for $\frac{1}{4}$ hour, then add cup for cup of sugar; boil $\frac{3}{4}$ hour or until it jellies, add juice of 3 lemons.

PLUM GUMBO

5 lb plums   3 oranges
2 lb seedless raisins   5 lb sugar

Cut plums into small pieces and put into preserving pan. Add chopped raisins and oranges cut in thin crosswise slices. Add warm sugar and bring to boiling point, then simmer until the consistency of marmalade. Cool slightly, stir well and fill jars.

PLUM RUM JAM

$3\frac{1}{2}$ lb plums $3\frac{1}{2}$ lb sugar
8 tablespoons lemon juice   4 tablespoons dark rum

Chop plums finely, and put into preserving pan with lemon juice and sugar. Bring to the boil and boil hard for 3 minutes, stirring constantly. Add rum and simmer for 5 minutes, stirring well. Pour into warm jars and seal.

RASPBERRY JAM

For jam with the whole-fruit flavour of raspberries, pick over 4 lb of the fruit and put into a pan which has been rubbed with butter. Warm an equal quantity of castor sugar, and when the berries start to bubble, beat in the sugar vigorously for 20 minutes, then put into jars; be careful to store this jam in a cool dark place.

RASPBERRY AND RED CURRANT JAM

Put 4 lb raspberries in a preserving pan with 1 pint of red currant juice, and bring slowly to boiling point. Simmer for 30 minutes and weigh the pulp. Add 12 oz of sugar for every 1 lb of pulp, boil, then continue simmering for 20 minutes, or until set.

RHUBARB AND BLACKBERRY JAM

4 lb blackberries   *¾ pint water*
2 lb prepared rhubarb   *Sugar*

Use ripe blackberries for this, and simmer them in the water until tender, then put through a sieve. Cut rhubarb into 1 inch pieces, add to blackberry pulp, and simmer until tender. Measure and add 1 lb warm sugar to each 1 lb of pulp. Stir until dissolved and bring to boiling point. Boil for 10 minutes and test for setting. Pot and cover. This makes an inexpensive jam with a good blackberry flavour. It is very good used for tarts or jam slices with a meringue topping.

RHUBARB AND DATE JAM

To every pound of rhubarb add 1 lb sugar and if liked 2 oz dates. Cut the fruit in pieces about 1 in. in length, place in a basin, cover with sugar, allow to stand overnight. Next day put in preserving pan, add dates (if used) and green ginger (or ground ginger) to flavour, and boil till it thickens.

RHUBARB AND GINGER JAM

4 lb rhubarb
2 teaspoons ground ginger
or 1 oz bruised root ginger in

muslin bag
3 lb sugar
½ teaspoon citric acid

Cut rhubarb into 1 inch lengths, and put into a bowl with sugar in layers. Leave overnight, then put into preserving pan. Add ginger and acid, bring to the boil, and boil rapidly until the jam jellies when tested (about 15 minutes). Remove bag of root ginger, pot and cover at once.

RHUBARB AND ORANGE PRESERVE

4 lb rhubarb
4 lb sugar
Grated rind and juice of

6 oranges
½ teaspoon citric acid

Cut up rhubarb into 1 inch pieces, grate rind from oranges, and squeeze out juice. Put into a bowl with sugar and leave for 12 hours. Put into preserving pan, add citric acid, bring to the boil and boil rapidly to setting point.

RHUBARB AND FIG JAM

2 lb rhubarb
½ lb dried figs

3 lb sugar
Juice of 1 lemon

Cut rhubarb and fig finely, combine with sugar and lemon juice, and leave to stand for 24 hours. Bring to boil, and boil rapidly until a little sets when tested on a cool plate. Leave to stand for 30 minutes before filling jars.

RUDWAY RHUBARB JAM

Wipe the rhubarb and cut as for tarts. Then to every lb fruit add ¾ lb sugar and the peel of ½ lemon cut finely. Stand all together in a large pan all night to draw the juice, then place in preserving pan and cook fast for about an hour. Try it by putting some on a plate and if it is done, fill the pots whilst it is warm. Cover with paper soaked in brandy.

Lewis' Mother's Cookbook, Mary Horrell, Exeter

ROSE-HIP AND APPLE JAM

1 pint rose-hips, really ripe
2 pints boiling water
¾ lb cooking apples (cooked

until soft in ¼ pint water)
2 lb sugar

Wash the rose-hips and put them into 2 pints boiling water. Simmer till soft. Mash with wooden spoon and strain through jelly bag, allowing it to drip overnight. Measure the juice and make it up to $1\frac{1}{2}$ pints with cold water. Cook the apples in water until they are reduced to a thick pulp. Mix juice and pulp and bring to boil. Stir in sugar and when dissolved, boil rapidly until the jam starts.

SWEET ORANGE JAM (1)

2 oranges   10 lb sugar
10 quarts water

Slice oranges very thinly, taking out the pips, cover with the water and leave overnight; boil down one-half (5 quarts) then add sugar, and boil till it will jelly.

SWEET ORANGE JAM (2)

Cut oranges in as thin slices as possible, picking out all the pips; put the cut-up oranges in a basin and add 1 pint water for each orange; put pips in another dish, cover with some of the water. Let these both stand all night, then strain the water off the pips and add it to the oranges, boil till skins are quite soft, let stand another night, then add weight for weight of sugar and boil briskly till it sets. To save mess, remember to *weigh pan* before the operation starts. It is then a simple matter to find weight of fruit before adding appropriate quantity of sugar.

THREE FRUIT JAM

Apples   Sugar
Pears   Lemon rind
Plums   Root ginger

Weigh out equal quantities of apples, pears and plums. Peel, core and slice apples and pears and stone plums and cook gently, allowing $\frac{1}{4}$ pint water to each lb of fruit until soft. Weigh the fruit and add warmed sugar in the proportion of 1 lb to 1 pint of fruit. Add the grated rind of a lemon to each lb of fruit, and suspend crushed root ginger in a muslin bag in the preserving pan. Dissolve sugar over a gentle heat, then bring to boiling point. Test for setting after 10 minutes' boiling, pot and cover. This makes an excellent tart filling, or a sauce for steamed pudding.

TOMATO AND LEMON MARMALADE

Allow 1 or more lemons and 1 lb sugar to each lb of tomatoes. Slice lemons very thinly, then take out pips and boil lemons in sufficient water to cover, until tender (test skins with matchstick). Put sugar into preserving pan with small quantity of water, as for toffee, and boil till it comes to crack degree, then add gradually the sliced tomatoes and lemons so as not to stop the boiling. Boil till it jellies.

TOMATO JAM (1)

Scald the tomatoes in order that they will peel easily; remove skins, weigh the fruit; put in the preserving pan with weight for weight of sugar; keep boiling steadily. When beginning to jelly add powdered orris root to taste; lemon peel or green ginger can be used as well, and pot it when it jellies well. Ground ginger may be used to replace green ginger—orris root, made from fragrant iris roots is now very rare.

TOMATO JAM (2)

12 lb ripe tomatoes
16 lb sugar
4 lb full-sized but quite
green tomatoes
2 pints water

Juice of 3 or 4 lemons
(according to size) or a little
citric acid and a few drops
essence of lemon

Boil altogether from $\frac{1}{2}$–$\frac{3}{4}$ hour briskly and it will jelly nicely. Small tomatoes are best for this.

TOMATO MARMALADE

To each 1 lb ripe tomatoes, peeled and sliced, add the juice of 1$\frac{1}{2}$ lemons and 1 lb sugar; boil for 1$\frac{1}{2}$ hours. This makes a most delicious preserve, not generally known.

APPLE CONSERVE

3 lb cooking apples
Sugar as required

1 lemon

Peel and core apples and cook very gently without water. Rub through a sieve when tender. Place in a saucepan with an equal weight of sugar and the strained juice and grated rind of 1 lemon. Stir over moderate heat till sugar has dissolved, then bring to simmering point. Simmer for 20 minutes to 1 hour, until the conserve sets when tested on a cold plate. Pot and seal.

APPLE GINGER

3 lb crisp eating apples   1¾ pints water
3 lb sugar   1½ oz essence of ginger

It is important to use pure essence of ginger for this, not a synthetic flavouring. This is for those who really love a strong ginger flavour. Peel and core the apples, and cut into neat pieces (as near to the shape of ginger in syrup as possible). Dissolve sugar in water, then bring to a slow rolling boil for 25 minutes. Raise heat and immerse apples, then simmer until fruit is just transparent and yellow but not broken. Remove from heat and stir in ginger essence. Lift apples carefully into jars (use preserving jars or screwtop honey jars), cover with syrup and screw down. Serve like ginger as a pudding, preferably with cream.

APPLE GINGER

4 lb apples   4 lb granulated sugar
3 pts water   2 oz ground ginger

Peel apples and cut in thin slices. Cook water and sugar together to a thick syrup. Add apples and boil until transparent. Stir in ginger, boil for 5 minutes and put into jars. Eat with toast, or use as a tart filling, or as a pudding with cream.

ORANGE CONSERVE

Cut some sweet oranges into 8, remove the centre pith; add a large cup of water to each orange, and let stand all night. Put the pith and seeds into a separate basin and cover with part of the water. In the morning, strain and add the liquid to the oranges. Boil till the skins are soft, about 2 hours, then add ½ lb sugar for each orange and boil for a further hour. Tie down in handsome glass jars or tumblers, especially if being used for Sale of Work or attractive personal present.

PLUM CONSERVE

3 lb stoned plums   4 oz chopped blanched
3 lb sugar   almonds
6 oz stoned raisins

Put the plum stones into a muslin bag, and hang in cooking pan. Put plums, raisins, and a little water if necessary in pan, and simmer until soft. Add sugar, stir until dissolved, and boil rapidly to setting point. Stir in almonds. Pour into warm jars. This is good as a spread, makes a delicious tart filling, or with ice cream.

STRAWBERRY CONSERVE

Strawberries   *Sugar*

Weigh out equal quantities of strawberries and sugar and put in alternate layers in a bowl. Leave for 24 hours, then boil for 5 minutes. On the second day, boil for 5 minutes, and on the third day for 7 minutes. Put into warm jars and seal. The result is whole fruit suspended in thick syrup, delicious with puddings, or served on its own with thick cream.

SOMERSET CONSERVE

9 large hard pears   *1 cup water*
6 tart apples   *Preserving sugar*
1½ lemons   *2 oz stem ginger*

Peel, quarter and core pears. Peel and core apples and cut into slices ½ inch thick. Grate off rinds from lemons. Sprinkle over fruit. Sprinkle with ½ the lemon juice, add remainder of juice to the water. Weigh fruit mixture and for every lb weigh 1 lb sugar. Cut ginger into small pieces. Place sugar and water in a preserving pan. Stir over moderate heat till sugar has dissolved, then bring to boil. Boil steadily until of a syrupy consistency, then add the rest of the ingredients and boil until clear and thick for about 45 minutes. Pack into jars and cover.

WATER HALL QUINCE CONSERVE

2 lb quinces (weighed after   *2¾ pints water*
peeling)   *2¾ pints sugar*

Peel, core and cut quinces into small cubes. Put with 2 pints of the water into a pan and bring to the boil. Add the sugar, remove from heat and stir until the sugar has dissolved. Return to heat and boil gently until the fruit is soft but not broken. Meanwhile, boil the cores and peel of quinces in the rest of the water until all is soft and the liquid reduced to about half. Strain this into the quinces. Boil hard until the jam sets when tested. Cool a little, stir and pour into warm pots. The jam is like jelly with cubes of quince, and is a beautiful jewel-red colour.

Joan Smith

APPLE AND ELDERBERRY JELLY

3 lb cooking apples   *½ cinnamon stick*
2 quart elderberries   *2 pints water*
(weighed off stalks)   *Sugar*
Rind of 1 orange

Wash apples, cut into pieces and put into pan with elderberries. Add water, cover pan, and simmer to a pulp. Leave to drip through jelly bag. Measure juice and allow 1 lb sugar to 1 pint juice. Put into a pan, stir well and put in orange rind and cinnamon tied in muslin. Boil rapidly to setting point, remove orange peel and cinnamon, put into warm jars and cover. This jelly is nice if soft and not too firm, and is an excellent way of using elderberries.

APPLE JELLY

6 lb cooking apples
3 pints water

1 lb sugar to each pint of
juice
Flavourings

Wash and cut up apples and simmer until soft in water. Put through a jelly bag, measure juice and add sugar. Stir over gentle heat until sugar has dissolved. Flavour with strips of lemon rind, boil rapidly to setting, pour into small jars and cover. Apple jelly is particularly delicious if a few rose geranium or lemon balm leaves are trailed in the liquid while cooking, but remove before potting. For herb jelly to serve with meat, use mint (for lamb) or sage (for pork) or bay (for ham). Hang a bunch of appropriate leaves in the jelly while cooking; remove them just before setting point is reached. For mint jelly, then add chopped mint; for sage or bay jelly, add a few whole leaves. Colour lightly with pure green colouring and pot in small jars.

APPLE MINT JELLY

2 lb tart green apples
1 quart cold water
Juice of 1 lemon
A bunch of fresh mint

Sugar as required
A little green vegetable
colouring

Cut apples in slices, but do not core or peel. Place in a preserving pan with the water and lemon juice and several sprigs of mint. Bring quickly to boil. Cook to a soft pulp, mashing occasionally. Pour into a jelly bag and allow to drip overnight. Rinse pan and add juice with sugar, allowing $1\frac{1}{4}$ lb to each pint of juice. Wash a bunch of fresh mint thoroughly, bruise the leaves, then hold the bunch in the syrup for a few minutes while it is cooking. Add a little finely-chopped mint as well if you like. Continue boiling until jelly sets when tested, then stir in a drop or two of green colouring. Skim if necessary. Pot in small jars. Serve with lamb or mutton.

BILBERRY JELLY

Allow 3–4 pints of berries to get a pint of juice. Wash them, remove stalks, put in preserving pan or better still a large stone jar. Bruise them a little, then stand jar in a saucepan with water reaching midway up the jar. Bring to the boil and let them simmer till the juice runs out readily. Strain through a jelly bag, measure juice and allow 1½ lb sugar to a pint. Put both in preserving pan, stir till sugar is dissolved, bring to the boil and boil rather fast for 10 minutes, or until a little will set when tested on a cold plate. This is very good with all kinds of game.

BRAMBLE JELLY

Wash 4 lb blackberries and put into a pan with ¾ pint water. Bring to the boil, and simmer very quickly until the juice has run out of the fruit. Strain and leave the juice to drip. Measure, and return to the pan with 1 lb sugar to each pint of juice. Heat gently till sugar dissolves, then bring to the boil and add juice of 1 lemon. Boil rapidly until setting point is reached, about 20 minutes. Put into warm pots and cover.

DAMSON JELLY

6 lb damsons   *1 lb sugar to each pint juice*
3 pints water

Simmer damsons in water until pulpy. Leave in a jelly bag overnight. For each pint of juice, allow 1 lb sugar, stir sugar until dissolved, then boil rapidly until the jelly sets when tested.

GREEN GOOSEBERRY JELLY

This jelly should be perfectly clear and bright. It can be used as a herb jelly if a few sprigs of herbs are plunged into boiling water, then added just before setting. Sage leaves, mint, rosemary and marjoram are particularly successful by this method.

To every lb of gooseberries, allow ¾ pint cold water. Prepare gooseberries and cook gently in water until the berries are broken. Strain through a jelly bag and measure the juice. Weigh out 1 lb sugar to each lb of juice. Boil juice for 15 minutes, then draw off heat and stir in sugar. Stir over gentle heat until dissolved, then boil for 20 minutes, until it jellies on the spoon. Remove scum from time to time. Pour into jars.

GOOSEBERRY AND ELDERFLOWER JELLY

Allow ¾ pint water to each lb of gooseberries. Simmer until berries are broken, then strain through jelly bag. Allow 1 lb sugar to each pint of juice. Allow warmed sugar to dissolve, then add 12 heads of elderflower tied in a muslin bag. Bring to boiling point, and boil for 15 minutes. Remove muslin bag, and pour jelly into small pots. This jelly has a muscat flavour.

GRAPE JELLY

Pick grapes off stems, put in a preserving pan, bruising some to make a liquid; boil for 15 minutes. Strain through a jelly bag, allow 1 lb sugar to 1 lb juice and boil quickly for 15 to 20 minutes. Jelly must not be made of fruit that is damp or picked during wet weather.

ORANGE AND APPLE JELLY

3 large oranges   *3 large cooking apples*
4 pints water   *Sugar*

Peel oranges very thinly, and discard pith and seeds. Cut up the fruit. Boil peel, fruit and water for 1 hour, then strain liquid. Peel, core and cut up apples and weigh with the strained liquid. Put into a preserving pan, and allow 1 lb sugar to each lb fruit and liquid. Boil until apples are reduced to a pulp, and the mixture will set. Put into small jars and cover.

QUINCE JELLY

Cut up quinces with seeds and skin; cover with cold water and boil till soft, about 3 hours, add juice of 1 lemon. Strain, then add a cupful of sugar to cupful of juice, and boil till it thickens (hard boiling is necessary), about ½ an hour. Skim well. Pour into hot jars and seal.

QUINCE JELLY

Take as many quinces as you like, don't peel or core them, but chop them roughly into a pan and just cover with water. Simmer steadily till very soft. Then hang up in a jelly bag and let drip until the juice is through. For each pint of juice add 1 lb granulated sugar, and boil steadily for about 45 minutes, removing the scum as it rises. When the jelly has jellied (pour a little on a plate to make sure), pour it into small pots. The residue left in the jelly bag makes a good jam for immediate use, if you boil it again with ½ lb sugar to each lb of pulp.

If you have a japonica decorating a wall, use the fruit to make a jelly with an intriguing flavour. Follow the directions for quince jelly.

RASPBERRY AND APPLE JELLY

4 lb raspberries   2 pints water
2 lb cooking apples   Sugar

Cut up apples and put in pan with raspberries and water and cook until tender. Strain through jelly bag and add 1 lb warm brown sugar to each pint of juice. Bring to boiling point and boil for 10 minutes. Test for setting, pot and cover. Early windfalls can be used for this jelly.

RED CURRANT JELLY

Serve with mutton, ham, pork and game.

6 lb red currants will give a good quantity of juice if heated until tender, then strained and added to sugar, allowing 1¼ lb sugar to each pint of juice. The jelly will reach setting point quickly and should not be left long in the pan once it is removed from the stove.

RHUBARB JELLY

Stew some rhubarb in a jar in the oven until the juice runs freely from it. Strain the juice and to every pint add the thin yellow rind of a lemon and the juice of half a lemon and 1 lb preserving sugar. Boil till it jellies.

Lewis' Mother's Cookbook, Mary Horrell, Exeter

ROSE HIP JELLY FOR GAME

Provided birds do not get them, leave the hips to get fully rip and soft. Take off tops, cut them up and put in preserving pan with just enough water to cover. Bring to the boil, reduce heat and simmer to a pulp. Squeeze through a coarse jelly bag or cheese cloth then pass through an ordinary jelly bag. To the liquid obtained allow 1 lb of loaf sugar to every pint of juice. Put in preserving pan, stir till sugar is dissolved, then boil for 20 minutes or until a little will 'jell' when a teaspoon is dropped on a cold plate. This preserve is good with roast or jugged hare, also with turkey.

Queen Victoria always had a preserve made with wild rose hips at Balmoral to accompany game. Try the recipe mixing the dog rose hips with large hips of *Rosa Rugosa* from the garden.

ROWAN JELLY

Gather the berries on a fine day. Wash them in cold water, snip off stalks, put in preserving pan with water to barely cover, bring to simmering point and cook for 2 hours. Strain through a muslin bag, letting it drip until no more juice runs through. Measure juice and for every pint allow 3 large cooking apples. Cut up these without peeling or coring, put in preserving pan, cover barely with water, bring to simmering point and cook gently.

In Scotland, as well as 'Rodden Jelly' with game, the scarlet berries of wild barberries are used for jelly.

SUSSEX CONVENT CRAB APPLE JELLY

Cover Siberian (cherry-type) crab apples in water and cook in a casserole or jar in the oven until soft. Drain off juice and add 12 oz sugar to each pint of juice. Boil together to jelly.

If the fruit is left in the juice while it is being cooked to a jelly, it can be bottled separately and makes a lovely tart filling.

APPLE BUTTER

6 lb windfalls (any variety)
2 pints water
3 pints cider

1 teaspoon ground cloves
1 teaspoon ground cinnamon
¾ lb sugar to each 1 lb pulp

Wash the fruit, remove any damaged parts, and cut into pieces, simmer in water and cider until soft. Rub through a fine sieve. Weigh the pulp, return it to the pan, and simmer until thick. Add the spices and sugar, and boil, stirring frequently, until no surplus liquid remains. Pour into hot jars and seal. If poured into small, wide-mouthed jars, this preserve can be turned out as a stiff mould, and makes a good accompaniment to milk puddings.

APPLE CHEESE

1 lb pulped good white
cooking apples
1 lb white sugar

Juice and rind of 3 lemons
4 well-beaten eggs
4 oz butter

Melt the butter in a pan. Add all other ingredients and cook for at least 30 minutes over slow heat. Makes about 3 lb but does not keep too long.

Pat Brown, Keynsham, Somerset

APPLE AND PLUM BUTTER

3 *lb apples* $\frac{3}{4}$ *lb sugar to each pint of pulp*
1 *lb plums*

Peel and core apples and cut in slices, and cook in very little water until soft. Add stoned plums and cook until soft. Put through a sieve, measure and add sugar. Boil to setting point and put into warm jars. This may be used with bread and butter, of if put into straight-sided jars, it can be turned out, sliced and eaten with cream.

PLUM AND APPLE CHEESE

3 *lb apples*   *Sugar*
1 *lb plums*

Cut up apples and plums without peeling or stoning. Add just enough water to prevent burning, and cook until tender, stirring often. Rub the fruit through a sieve and allow $\frac{3}{4}$ lb sugar to each pint of purée. Cook until mixture thickens and clears. Pour into pots. This may be used as a spread, or if put into jars without shoulders, it can be turned out and served in slices with cream.

APPLE AND PLUM CHEESE

Peel and core apples, and remove stones from plums, and weigh out an equal quantity. Put in thick pan and cook gently without water until soft. Add 1 lb sugar to each 1 lb of pulp, and boil slowly for an hour. Put into shallow baking tins or dishes. Dry out in a low oven temperature until the mixture is the consistency of soft leather. Cut in squares and store in tins with waxed paper between layers.

Miss Hill, 1864

BLACKBERRY AND APPLE CHEESE

This is a smooth version of jam, which can be cut with a knife, and is very useful for all sorts of pudding. Peel, core and quarter 2 lb cooking apples and cook in 1 gill water till tender. Add 2 lb blackberries and simmer till soft. Strain through a fine sieve, and measure the pulp. Add 1 lb sugar to each pint of juice, stir till dissolved, and boil the mixture until it sets when tested on a cold plate. It should be very firm. Put into warm pots and cover.

IVERSON CHERRY CHEESE

2 lb red eating cherries   *1 lb sugar*

Stone the cherries and chop the fruit finely. Crack a few stones and save the kernels. Put into a heavy pan with sugar and add just enough water to prevent burning. Simmer slowly, stirring all the time until a smooth mass of semi-solid consistency is formed. Add a few of the kernels. Pour into small jars and cover.

CRAB CHEESE

Siberian crabs make a pretty preserve. Fruit should not be peeled, but after it has been washed, dried, and stalks removed, is cooked whole in preserving pan with just enough water to prevent burning. When tender, press through sieve. Allow 1 lb sugar to same weight pulp. Boil up and then simmer for 45 minutes.

DAMSON CHEESE

Damsons   *Sugar*

Wash damsons, cover with water and simmer until soft. Put through a sieve and measure the pulp. Allow $\frac{3}{4}$ lb sugar to each pint of fruit pulp. Cook in a thick pan, stirring frequently, for 1 hour, until the pulp is thick enough to hold the impression of a spoon. Put into small straight-sided jars, and cover. When cold, this can be used as a spread, or turned out and cut into slices to serve with cream.

GOOSEBERRY CURD

This is similar to lemon curd, and should be put into small jars, being used within a few weeks. Prepare 3 lb green gooseberries and cook in $\frac{3}{4}$ pint water until tender. Put through a sieve, and then put into a double saucepan with $1\frac{1}{2}$ lb castor sugar, 7 lb butter and 4 beaten eggs. Cook gently, stirring until the mixture thickens.

BATH LEMON CURD

4 oz sugar   *1 egg or 2 egg yolks*
1 oz butter   *Rind and juice of 1 lemon*

Combine all ingredients in a double saucepan. Cook very gently until thick—the mixture must not be allowed to boil. Pour into warm jars and cover with wax circles. Put on covers when cold.

STANDARD LEMON CURD

6 oz butter
4 eggs (8 fluid oz when broken)

4 lemons (8 fluid oz juice)
1 lb sugar

Melt butter in a double saucepan, add lemon juice, sugar and thinly peeled lemon rind, and stir until sugar dissolves. Beat eggs lightly in a basin, cool the fat and sugar mixture slightly, and strain into the eggs, stirring all the time. Return mixture to double saucepan, and cook until it starts to thicken. Yield in saucepan: 2 lb 5 oz. Cool slightly before filling jars to top.

LEMON CURD

Beat up 9 oz butter, 2 lb sugar and the strained juice of 6 lemons. Heat gently till the sugar melts in a double saucepan. Stir 6 lightly beaten eggs into the butter mixture; heat, stirring all the time, till it is as thick as cream. Cook 2 more minutes and bottle in warm jars.

OXFORD MARMALADE

8 Seville oranges
Water

Sugar

Wipe fruit, put it into pan of cold water, boil gently until skins are soft and can be pierced with steel knitting needle. Drain, leave to cool, but retain water.

Divide into quarters, cut right through peel and pulp, shredding the orange coarsely into thick strips. Remove pips. Weigh fruit, and to each lb allow 1 lb sugar and $\frac{1}{2}$ pint of the water in which oranges were boiled. Should the water be objectionably bitter, it may be diluted slightly with fresh water. Let sugar dissolve in the water and boil all together steadily for about 35 minutes, or until marmalade sets when tested. Pour into jars, fasten down while hot.

MISS THOMPSON'S MARMALADE

1 lemon to every 6 oranges. Halve oranges, remove pips, squeeze juice in basin. Slice rind finely. Halve lemons. Squeeze juice into orange juice. Put rinds (not sliced) with orange rind. To every lb of sliced fruit add 3 pints water, soak all pips in $\frac{1}{2}$ pint of this water. Leave 12 hours, boil till tender, adding liquid from pips (after heating and straining it) and pips tied in muslin. Leave pulp 24 hours, remove lemon rinds.

To every lb of boiled pulp add 1¼ lb sugar (warmed in oven). Bring slowly to boil, boil till it jellies (about 50 minutes in all). Add orange and lemon juice, boil a minute or 2. Seal when cold.

MARMALADE

5 Seville oranges
2 lemons
1 large sweet orange

8 lb sugar
6 pints water

Wash fruit and quarter. Extract pulp, put in a muslin bag, tie up. Cut peel very thinly and put into a bowl with bag of pulp and 6 pints water. Leave 24 hours. Place in preserving pan and boil gently 1 hour. Remove bag of pulp and strain off any liquid; add this and 8 lb sugar. Boil quickly 20 minutes and test for setting. Makes 12–13 lb.

Mrs Crimes, Anglesey

RUDWAY ORANGE MARMALADE

3 Seville oranges
1 sweet orange

1 lemon

To every lb of fruit sliced, add 3 pints of cold water, and let it stand 24 hours, then let it boil until chips are tender. Stand another 24 hours, add 1½ lb of loaf sugar to every lb of fruit, as it is, then gently boil until the juice jellies.

Lewis' Mother's Cookbook, Mary Horrell, Exeter

GRAPEFRUIT MARMALADE

1 grapefruit
1 lemon

1 orange

Cut all up finely, removing seeds. Pour over 4 pints of cold water and let it stand for 20 hours or more. Tie pips in a piece of muslin and put in with the fruit. Boil until it is tender, then add 4 lb sugar (remove seed bag first). Stir until dissolved then boil up again until it sets when tested. Makes 6 lb marmalade.

TRADITIONAL SEVILLE MARMALADE

2 lb Seville oranges
1 lemon

4 pints water
4 lb sugar

Wash and cut up oranges and lemon, putting the pips and pith in a muslin bag suspended from the pan. Cover with water and simmer until peel is tender ($1\frac{1}{2}$–2 hours). Stir in sugar and warm gently until dissolved. Bring to the boil and boil rapidly to setting point. Cool for 15 minutes, stir and pour into warm jars.

DARK THICK MARMALADE

2 lb Seville oranges   4 pints water
1 lemon   4 lb sugar

Wash oranges and lemon and cut in halves. Squeeze out juice into a pan, remove pips and put in muslin bag, and cut peel and pulp in coarse shreds. Put peel, pulp, pips and water with juice, and simmer for 2 hours. Remove pips, add sugar, stir until dissolved and cook for about 1 hour until the colour has darkened slightly and the preserve sets firmly when tested. The addition of 1 oz black treacle will make the colour darker.

SWEET ORANGE AND LEMON MARMALADE

4 sweet oranges   5 pints water
5 lemons   4 lb sugar

Cut fruit into thin slices, removing pips and putting them into muslin bag. Put fruit, water and pips into pan and boil gently for $1\frac{1}{2}$ hours. Remove pips, add sugar and stir until dissolved. Boil for 10 minutes, or until setting point is reached.

LEMON MARMALADE

8 large lemons   Sugar
8 pints cold water

Peel lemons very thinly and cut peel into very fine shreds. Put pith and pips into muslin, and cut up the flesh of the lemons. Put fruit, peel and pips into a pan with water and boil until the contents of the pan are reduced by half. Remove pips. Weigh the contents of the pan and add an equal weight of sugar. Bring to the boil, boil for about 20 minutes until setting point is reached, and put into pots.

GRAPEFRUIT AND LEMON MARMALADE

2 large grapefruit   4 pints water
4 lemons   3 lb sugar

Peel the fruit and squeeze out the juice into preserving pan. Put lemon pips into a muslin bag but not the grapefruit pips, which will make the marmalade bitter. Cook the shredded peel in the water until the contents of the pan are reduced by half. Remove muslin bag, add sugar, and stir until dissolved. Boil rapidly for 20 minutes until setting point is reached.

TANGERINE PRESERVE

4 lb tangerines
3 lemons
1½ pints water
4 lb sugar

Slice tangerines and lemons thinly and simmer in water, with the pips in a muslin bag, until the peel is tender. Stir in sugar until dissolved, bring to boil, and boil hard to setting point. This is a delicious marmalade to remind us of that special Christmas scent of tangerines all through the year. It is particularly good with rolls or croissants for breakfast, or used as an ice-cream sauce.

PINEAPPLE MARMALADE

3 sweet oranges
1 lemon
1 large can pineapple chunks
4 lb sugar

Slice oranges and lemon, just cover with water and simmer until tender. Add the juice from the can of pineapple chunks and the finely cut fruit, and simmer until fruit is well blended. Add sugar, stir until dissolved and boil rapidly to setting point. This is a particular favourite with children who do not always care for the traditional marmalade, and is very good served with steamed puddings or with vanilla ice-cream.

CRANBERRY APPLE MARMALADE

1 large orange
½ pint water
1 lb cranberries
4 apples
1½ lb sugar

Slice the orange thinly and simmer in water until very tender. Put through the mincer with cranberries and peeled and cored apples, and return to the liquid with sugar. Cook over low heat until thick (about 25 minutes) stirring frequently. Put into hot jars and cover at once.

APRICOT MARMALADE

1 lb dried apricots
12 oz sugar
6 tablespoons lemon juice
1 tablespoon grated lemon rind
1 tablespoon grated orange rind

This is a thick preserve which is excellent for filling jam tarts or for spreading on slices of almond shortbread. Soak the apricots overnight in just enough cold water to cover them. Cook them in the water, then sieve both fruit and juice. Add sugar, lemon juice and grated rinds, and cook over a good heat for 15 minutes until thick. Put into hot jars.

TANGERINE MARMALADE

2½ lb tangerines
1 grapefruit
1 lemon

5 pints water
¼ oz tartaric acid
3 lb sugar

Peel the tangerines, shred the peel finely and put peel into a muslin bag. Peel the grapefruit and lemon, and put the peel through the mincer. Put into a saucepan with the chopped fruit pulp, the bag of tangerine peel, water and acid. Simmer gently for 2 hours, taking the tangerine peel out after 30 minutes. Wash this peel well, and drain. After 2 hours, strain the fruit pulp in a jelly bag. Put juice into a pan with sugar and heat gently until the sugar dissolves. Add the tangerine peel and boil rapidly to setting point. Skim, allow to cool slightly before potting.

APRICOT AND DATE MARMALADE

1 lb dried apricots
2 pints water
1½ lb dates

8 oz sugar
1 lemon
2 oz blanched almonds

This makes an excellent filling used between two layers of flaky pastry, baked in a hot oven and sprinkled with castor sugar. Soak the apricots overnight in 1 pint water. Add another pint of water, chopped dates, and sugar and the juice of a lemon. Cook slowly until the mixture is soft and thick, stir in chopped almonds and cook for 5 minutes.

MINCEMEAT

2½ lb suet
3½ lb soft brown sugar
3 lb currants
2¼ lb raisins
1½ lb peel
2 teaspoons salt
1 tablespoon mixed spice

2 teaspoons ground nutmeg
2 teaspoons ground cloves
4 lb apples (cooked day before)
½ pint sherry
4 lemons, rind and juice

Aunty Tommy's recipe, Gussage, Dorset

MINCEMEAT

Put into basin 1 scraped and sliced medium-sized carrot, ½ lb peeled, cored and sliced apple, 8–12 oz mixed dried fruit (any kinds), 2 oz hazel or other nuts (optional), teaspoon mixed spice, pinch of salt and 4 oz suet or melted margarine.

Pass all through fine mincer twice. Return to basin and mix well with 3 tablespoons sugar, brown if possible, 1 tablespoon marmalade, 1 tablespoon treacle, 1 tablespoon spirit, sherry or vinegar, ½ teaspoon lemon juice. Put into jars and cover like jam.

MINCEMEAT

½ lb each chopped raisins, sugar, sultanas, suet, apple (chopped), 2 oz candied peel or 1 tablespoon marmalade, 1 teaspoon lemon essence, pinch salt, 5 tablespoons ale or stout. Mix all dry ingredients, add liquids, mix well, put in jars, close down.

MINCEMEAT

½ lb butter
1 lb each currants, sultanas, raisins
4 oz peel
8 oz chopped, skinned almonds

1½ lb brown sugar
2 lb apples (weighed after peeling and coring)
At least 2 wineglasses rum or brandy

Put ingredients (except sugar and currants) through mixer. Mix well, stand overnight, remix and jar. Mrs Waggett says this recipe has been in her mother's family for several generations.

Mrs Waggett, Newcastle Emlyn

GREEN TOMATO MINCEMEAT

3 quarts chopped green tomatoes
1 quart chopped apples
8 oz shredded suet
2½ lb soft brown sugar
1 lb seedless raisins
1¾ gills vinegar

½ lb chopped mixed candied peel
Salt to taste
¾ tablespoon ground cinnamon
¾ tablespoon ground cloves
1 small level tablespoon grated nutmeg

Chop tomatoes very finely; drain off liquid. Place in a preserving pan and add 4 quarts cold water; bring to boil and simmer for an hour. Cover and stand overnight. Next morning drain purée thoroughly; add apples, raisins, suet, vinegar, peel and salt to taste. Simmer for 2 hours. Add spice. Stir for a moment or two till thoroughly blended, then pot and seal. Store in a cool dry cupboard.

12 Pickles, Chutneys and Store Sauces

The squirrel gloats on his accomplished hoard,
The ants have brimmed their garners with ripe grain,
And honey bees have stored
The sweets of Summer in their luscious cells;
The swallows all have winged across the main.

Thomas Hood

INDIAN MIXED PICKLE

2 quarts green tomatoes
1 quart small onions
3 large cucumbers
1 firm medium cauliflower
½ medium head celery
2 large tablespoons salt
1 oz stick cinnamon
1 teaspoon allspice
½ teaspoon powdered ginger
20 cloves
½ teaspoon powdered mace
1 inch root ginger, cut up finely
1 chilli pepper
1 dried red pepper
3 green peppers (optional)
1 quart vinegar
1½ lb sugar (use 1 lb if you do not like a sweetish pickle)

Wash tomatoes, peel onions, cucumber. Remove seeds from cucumber, chop tomatoes, onions, cucumber, celery. Break cauliflower in neat pieces.

Put all in bowl, sprinkle with salt. Cover, stand overnight. Drain well next morning.

Tie spices in muslin bag, add to vinegar in which sugar has been dissolved, cook gently with vegetables in preserving pan 30 minutes. Remove bag, pour pickle into hot jars, cover, leave to mature at least a fortnight.

MILITARY PICKLE

1 *marrow*	7 *chillies*
1 *cauliflower*	1 *oz turmeric powder*
1 *lb beans*	1 *oz ground ginger*
1 *lb onions*	1 *breakfastcup flour*
1 *lb demerara sugar*	

Cut the vegetables up small and cover with salt. Leave to stand overnight, then drain. Put into saucepan, add 2 quarts of vinegar and boil 5 minutes. Mix to a smooth paste the dry ingredients and add while boiling. Boil for a good ½ hour. Stir well to save burning. Take up and bottle when cold.

SWEET MUSTARD PICKLE

1 *marrow, medium size*	½ *oz turmeric*
1 *cauliflower*	¼ *oz ground ginger*
1 *cucumber*	½ *oz ground nutmeg*
1 *lb onions*	10 *oz sugar*
1 *lb young French beans*	2 *oz flour*
2 *oz dry mustard*	2 *pints vinegar*

Chop vegetables into ½–1 inch chunks. Sprinkle with 1 oz salt, cover with water and soak overnight, then drain off water. Mix all dry ingredients with a little of the vinegar to make a smooth paste. Add remainder of the vinegar to the vegetables and simmer in a strong pan until barely tender, approximately 10 minutes. Add some boiling vinegar to the blended ingredients. Return to the pan and boil for 10 minutes stirring all the time and allow to thicken. Pot while hot. Yield: 9 lb.

PICCALILLI

5 *lb cauliflower*	1 *oz turmeric*
1 *lb onions*	1 *oz ground ginger*
Salt	8 *chillies*
3½ *oz mustard*	8 *cloves*
10 *oz lump sugar*	4 *pints vinegar*

Cut vegetables into small pieces and put in a pan. Sprinkle with salt and allow to stand overnight. Mix remaining ingredients. Put vegetables in stewpan, pour on the mixture, boil until tender. When cold it is ready for use. The 6 lb of vegetables can be varied. Marrow or green tomatoes instead of cauliflower.

Lewis' Mother's Cookbook, Mary Horrell, Exeter

CUMBERLAND BEAN PICKLE

6 *lb runner beans*	2 *oz dry mustard*
6 *large onions*	1 *lb sugar*
1 *quart white vinegar*	1 *teaspoon black pepper*
4 *oz plain flour*	1 *teaspoon turmeric powder*

Slice the beans and onions thinly and cook in a little water until tender. Drain thoroughly. Moisten the flour with a little vinegar, then mix together in a saucepan the vinegar, flour, mustard, sugar, pepper and turmeric. Bring to the boil and continue stirring all the time until the mixture is thick. Add beans and onions and continue stirring until the mixture boils again. Put into jars, and cover while hot.

PICKLED BEETROOT

8 *medium size beetroot*	1 *quart malt vinegar*
¼ *oz whole black pepper*	¼ *oz allspice*
1 *horseradish (grated)*	1 *teaspoon salt*

Bake beetroot in oven for 1½–2 hours, when cool skin and slice; place in jars. Boil vinegar, horseradish, salt, pepper and spice together; when cool, pour over beetroot. Store in dry place.

PICKLED CABBAGE

Quarter a large firm red cabbage. Take out the stalk. Slice very thinly. Put on a large flat dish and sprinkle with plenty of salt. Leave overnight. In the morning turn all over to mix the salt. Drain. Fill clean bottles or jars. Sprinkle a quarter of a teaspoon of cayenne pepper on top of each jar. Cover cabbage with cold vinegar. Tie down securely and store. With this method the cabbage can be eaten at the end of 2 or 3 days. Some people make it with spiced vinegar, which is allowed to get cold before putting on the vegetable.

SWEET CUCUMBER PICKLE

3 lb cucumbers
1 dessertspoon powdered
alum
1 quart water

2 lb sugar
1 pint vinegar
2 tablespoons whole clove
2 inch stick of cinnamon

Make a syrup with the sugar, vinegar and spices tied in a muslin by boiling them together for 5 minutes. Meanwhile, peel the cucumbers thinly, cut into quarters lengthways and into 3 inch pieces. Cover with alum dissolved in water, and bring slowly to the boil, then drain and chill cucumber in ice water. When the syrup is ready add the drained cucumbers and simmer for 10 minutes. Leave till next day, then on 3 successive days drain off syrup, boil hard for 1 minute and then pour over cucumbers. On the last day, pack cucumber pieces into jars and fill up with boiling syrup. Cover when cold.

PICKLED EGGS

Add pickled eggs to your usual salad. Pickled eggs are popular down at the local. To make: just hard-boil eggs for 15 minutes, peel off shell, drop eggs in spiced vinegar and leave for 10 days.

PICKLED GHERKINS

Soak the gherkins in brine for 3 days, allowing $\frac{1}{4}$ lb salt to each quart of water. Then drain them. Place the gherkins in jars and pour boiling spiced vinegar over them, cover and leave 24 hours. Drain off the vinegar, boil it and pour over the gherkins as before. Repeat several times, until the gherkins are nicely green. Cork and store in a dark place.

NASTURTIUM SEEDS

These make very good mock capers. Gather the seeds on a dry day when quite young and soft. Wipe clean with a cloth. Put in a dry glass bottle. Cover with the following liquid: to 1 pint vinegar add 1 oz salt and 6 peppercorns. If you have not enough seeds ripe, you can add them from day to day till the bottle is filled. Seal well and resin the corks of the bottles. As they take from 10 to 12 months to get really pickled, they should be made 1 season for use the next.

PICKLED ONIONS

Small button onions
Vinegar to cover
To each quart of vinegar
allow 2 teaspoons of allspice
2 teaspoons peppercorns

Peel onions into clean dry jars, boil vinegar with spices, and when cold pour it over to fill jars completely; cover with parchment paper and store in dry place. Ready in 2 weeks. The pickles will be ready much earlier if the vinegar is used while hot.

IVERSON PICKLED GREEN TOMATOES

2½ lb green tomatoes
8 oz onions
8 oz sugar
1 pint white vinegar

Slice the tomatoes and onions. Sprinkle generously with salt. Leave for 24 hours and drain off salt liquid completely. Make a syrup with the sugar and vinegar and put in tomatoes and onions. Simmer until tender, pour into preserving jars and cover while hot.

VEGETABLE MARROW PICKLE

Prepare a large marrow as for cooking. Cut it in small square pieces, sprinkle with salt and let it remain overnight. Take 1 quart best vinegar, add to it a little pepper, and the marrow. Boil all together until the marrow becomes tender, then add 3 oz mustard mixed with a little cold vinegar and boil all together for 3 minutes.

Lewis' Mother's Cookbook, Mary Horrell, Exeter

MOCK OLIVES

These can be made from not-too-ripe plums. Pour over them a boiling brine made from 2 oz salt in ¾ pint vinegar. Let them stand 12 hours, drain off the brine, boil it up and pour over the drained plums. Bottle when quite cold.

APPLE CHUTNEY

6 lb cooking apples
2 lb onions
2 lb sugar
1 lb golden syrup
½ pint water
1½ oz ground ginger
½ oz ground cinnamon
¼ teaspoon Cayenne
1½ oz salt
1 quart vinegar

Peel and cut up the apples and onions, simmer in water for 20 minutes. Add the salt, spices and half the vinegar, and cook until softened. Add the sugar, syrup and the rest of the vinegar, and simmer until stiff. Pot and cover, using vinegar-proof discs underneath cellophane or screw tops.

MRS HAWKYARD'S APPLE CHUTNEY

5 lb apples
½-1 pint vinegar
1 tablespoon salt
8 oz stoned dates
8 oz raisins or sultanas

1 small tablespoon ground
ginger
8 oz onions
1 lb demerara sugar
6 chillies

Peel and core the apples. Put the salt, ginger, chopped chillies and sugar into a pan with some of the vinegar. Add the apples and minced onions and bring to the boil. Add the chopped dates and whole raisins or sultanas and simmer until thick and brown, adding more vinegar as required (the apples make a lot of juice, and the chutney should not be runny). Put into warm jars, and cover well. The chillies make this a rather hot chutney, as Mrs Hawkyard's son liked very 'hot' spicy food. They can be omitted, but are really a good addition to what can often be a rather bland and boring type of chutney.

NORWICH APPLE CHUTNEY

2½ lb apples, peeled and cored
½ lb onions, peeled
½ lb brown sugar
¼ lb sultanas
½ oz salt
¾ pint vinegar

1 tablespoon pickling spice
½ tablespoon dry mustard
1 teaspoon coriander seeds,
optional
2 pieces root ginger

Mince or chop finely onions and apples. Simmer with half the quantity of vinegar until tender. Add sugar, sultanas, salt, pickling spice, mustard, coriander seeds, ginger and remainder of vinegar. Simmer until thick, about 20 minutes. Remove ginger and turn into heated jars whilst hot and place on glass lids firmly. If ordinary jars are used, a cover should be used to stop the vinegar evaporating, i.e. good corks or a layer of thick waxed, vinegar-proof paper then a metal lid and clip, the clip being removed when the chutney is cold.

APRICOT CHUTNEY

1 lb dried apricots
1 clove garlic
3 peppercorns
4 oz sultanas

8 oz sugar
1 orange
½ pint white vinegar

Soak the apricots overnight, drain off the liquid and put the fruit into a
heavy pan with chopped garlic clove, peppercorns, sultanas, sugar and the
grated rind and juice of the orange. Bring to the boil, add vinegar, and
simmer until the chutney is thick. Put into hot jars and seal at once.

BEETROOT CHUTNEY

2 lb beetroot
2 medium-sized onions
¼ teaspoon ginger
½ lb sugar

1 lb apples
½ teaspoon salt
1 tablespoon lemon juice
1 pint vinegar

Boil beetroot till tender and peel when cold. Cut into small cubes. Peel
onions and apples and cut them up finely. Put them into a pan with sugar
vinegar etc. and boil for ½ hour. Add the beetroot and simmer for a
further 15 minutes. Bottle when cold.

BLACKBERRY CHUTNEY

Wash 6 lb blackberries and put in a pan with 2 lb peeled and chopped
apples, 2 lb chopped onions, 1 oz salt, 2 oz mustard, 2 oz ground ginger,
2 teaspoons powdered mace, 1 teaspoon cayenne pepper, 2 pints vinegar,
and cook gently for 1 hour. Put through a sieve to remove pips, add 2 lb
brown sugar and cook till thick.

CHERRY RELISH

1½ lb black eating cherries
4 oz raisins
4 tablespoons honey

2 teaspoons mixed spice
¼ pint white vinegar
4 tablespoons brown sugar

Remove stones from cherries. Put all the ingredients into a heavy pan
and simmer gently until the sugar has melted. Boil for 5 minutes, then
simmer until thick, stirring all the time. Pour into small screw top jars
and seal tightly. Very good with cold ham, chicken, turkey or duck.

ELDERBERRY CHUTNEY

1½ lb berries
1 onion
2 oz sugar (demerara is best)
½ pint vinegar
½ oz ground ginger
A few cloves

1 teaspoon salt
¼ teaspoon pepper
⅛ teaspoon mace
2 oz stoned raisins, if
obtainable

Pass berries through sieve, chop onion finely, and boil with other ingredients for 10–15 minutes. This makes up a small quantity.

GOOSEBERRY RELISH

Prepare 2 lb gooseberries, and add 12 oz seeded raisins, and 1 lb sliced onions. Put through a mincer and put into a pan with ½ lb brown sugar, 1 teaspoon dry mustard, 1 tablespoon ground ginger, 2 tablespoons salt, ¼ teaspoon cayenne pepper, 1 teaspoon turmeric and 1 pint vinegar. Bring slowly to the boil, then simmer for 45 minutes. Put through a coarse sieve, heat thoroughly, fill bottles and seal.

PEAR CHUTNEY

3½ lb pears
2 oranges
1 teaspoon powdered cloves
1 teaspoon powdered
cinnamon

1 teaspoon powdered allspice
1 lb seedless raisins
1½ lb sugar
½ pint vinegar

Peel, core and chop the pears. Grate the rind of the oranges and squeeze out the juice. Add rind, juice and pears to the spices, raisins, sugar and vinegar, and bring to the boil. Reduce heat and simmer for 2 hours. Pour into warm jars and cover tightly.

PEAR AND QUINCE CHUTNEY

4 lb cooking pears
2 lb quinces
2 lb onions
2 lb green tomatoes
1 lb stoned raisins
1 lb tender celery sticks
3 lb demerara sugar

½ teaspoon Cayenne pepper
½ oz salt
½ teaspoon ground ginger
10 black peppercorns
1 teaspoon grated
horseradish
4 pints vinegar

Peel, quarter and core the pears and quinces. Peel the onions. Put the tomatoes and raisins through a mincer into a deep saucepan. Cover, after stirring, and cook gently until tender, stirring frequently. Meanwhile, mince the celery and add the sugar, pepper, salt and ginger. When fruit is tender, stir in this mixture. Tie the peppercorns and horseradish in a small muslin bag and add to pan with the vinegar. Stir till boiling, then cook slowly, stirring frequently, until the mixture is thick, about 4 hours. Remove muslin bag. When contents are cooked, pot and cover.

PLUM CHUTNEY (1)

2 lb plums weighed after stoning	1 lb soft brown sugar
	1 oz chopped garlic
1 lb carrots	1 oz chillies
1 pint vinegar	1 oz ground ginger
1 lb stoned raisins	1½ oz salt

Stone plums and weigh out 2 lb. Mix with minced carrots and vinegar and simmer until soft. Add other ingredients, and simmer until the mixture is thick. Put into jars and cover tightly.

PLUM CHUTNEY (2)

2 lb any plums (or damsons or pears)	1 tablespoon salt
	1 teaspoon pepper
¼ dried fruit (optional)	1 dessertspoon mixed spice in
¼ lb onions	muslin bag (to be removed
¾ lb sugar	after cooking)
½ pint malt vinegar	1 teaspoon powdered ginger

Chop onions, stone and chop plums. Stew onions in half the vinegar until tender. Add all but sugar and vinegar. Add vinegar slowly, stirring, cook gently. Add sugar when mixture is soft. Boil steadily 10 minutes when chutney will be like thick jam. Pour into hot jars and seal.

PLUM CHUTNEY (3)

2 lb ripe plums	8 oz onions
8 oz apples	½ oz chillies
8 oz brown sugar	1 pint best vinegar
1 lb raisins or sultanas	

Skin and stone the plums. Peel apples and onions and cut in pieces. Cook plums, apples and onions in half the vinegar until tender. Add remaining ingredients and vinegar and boil hard for 10 minutes until brown and thick.

LITTLE WYLLIE'S RHUBARB CHUTNEY

2 lb rhubarb
½ lb onions
1½ lb brown sugar
½ lb sultanas
½ oz mustard seeds
1 teaspoon mixed spice

1 teaspoon pepper
1 teaspoon ground ginger
1 teaspoon salt
¼ teaspoon Cayenne pepper
1 pint vinegar

Cut rhubarb into 1 inch lengths and chop onions finely. Put all ingredients into heavy pan and simmer gently, stirring frequently until mixture is of consistency of jam. Put into pots or preserving jars and cover tightly.

RUNNER BEAN CHUTNEY

2 lb runner beans (after slicing)
1½ lb onions (after chopping)
1 heaped tablespoon cornflour
1 tablespoon turmeric

1 heaped tablespoon dry mustard
1 lb demerara sugar
1 lb soft brown sugar
1½ pints vinegar

Prepare vegetables. Cook sliced beans in well-salted water until tender. Cook chopped onions in ½ pint vinegar. Mix dry ingredients to smooth paste with vinegar. Strain cooked beans, then add to rest of vinegar and cook for 10 minutes. Add sugar and rest of ingredients and boil for a further 15 minutes. Bottle and cover. Keeps well. Very good.

Mrs ap Gwynn, Welshpool

GREEN TOMATO CHUTNEY (1)

2 lb green tomatoes
2 lb sharp apples
1 lb Barbados sugar
¼ lb shallots
1 oz garlic

½ oz salt
¼ oz red pepper
½ lb raisins
Juice of 2 lemons
1 pint vinegar

Chop all the ingredients and mix in spices and flavourings. Add vinegar, and simmer gently for about 3 hours with the lid on until it is thick and pulpy. Put into jars.

GREEN TOMATO CHUTNEY (2)

2½ lb green tomatoes
8 oz brown sugar
2 teaspoons ground ginger
¾ teaspoon Cayenne pepper
6 nicely flavoured cooking

apples
2 medium-sized onions
A little salt
¾ pint vinegar

Slice the tomatoes, apples and onions and boil in vinegar for a little while. Strain, retaining the liquid. Chop the vegetables. Put them back in the saucepan with the vinegar and other ingredients and simmer for 4 or 5 hours. Pour into hot jars and tie down firmly.

Mrs Harding, Sixpenny Handley, Wilts

GREEN TOMATO CHUTNEY (3)

1½ lb green tomatoes
1 lb apples
½ lb sugar
¾ lb sultanas (or less)
¼ lb onions

1 teaspoon salt
1 oz mixed spice
1 pint vinegar
Pinch of dry mustard

Chop these ingredients and cook all slowly together until the colour deepens. About 1½–2 hours. Use enamelled pan or casserole.

GREEN TOMATO SWEET PICKLE

2 lb chopped green tomatoes
¾ lb peeled cored and sliced
apples
½ lb chopped onions
Saltspoon Cayenne pepper
½ pint vinegar

4 oz sultanas or chopped
prunes
¾ lb sugar
1 small teaspoon ground
ginger

Boil all ingredients together till thick and stiff like jam. Pour into small pots. Seal and keep in cool, dry place.

RIPE TOMATO CHUTNEY

1 lb ripe tomatoes
8 oz onions
4 oz sour apples
1 lb stoned raisins
4 oz moist sugar

¼ oz salt
¼ oz ground ginger
Pinch of Cayenne pepper
½ pint vinegar

Skin the tomatoes and peel and core apples. Chop the tomatoes, onions, apples and raisins. Mix all ingredients and boil to a mash. This will take an hour or more. Put into small jars and close.

Mrs Harding, Sixpenny Handley, Wilts

SPICED TOMATO RELISH

1 *lb tomatoes*	*pepper*
1 *green pepper*	1 *level teaspoon Cayenne*
1 *lb onions*	*pepper*
1 *lb apples*	1 *level tablespoon mixed*
3 *cloves garlic*	*mustard*
¾ *lb white sugar*	½ *teaspoon mixed spice*
1 *level tablespoon salt*	½ *pint distilled vinegar*
1 *level tablespoon paprika*	6 *oz tin tomato purée*

Dip tomatoes in boiling water for 1 minute, remove skins and cut up. Remove pips from pepper and cut up with onions and apples. Chop garlic finely. Put in pan with vinegar and simmer until tender and thick, about 30 minutes. Add other ingredients, boil for 3 minutes. Pot while hot.

TOMATO CHUTNEY

2 *lb green tomatoes*	1 *tablespoon mustard*
1 *lb apples*	1 *teaspoon pepper*
½ *lb onions*	½ *oz salt*
½ *lb raisins*	1 *teaspoon ground cinnamon*
½ *lb demerara sugar*	*A little more than a pint of*
	vinegar

Chop up the apples and tomatoes or pass through a mincer and then boil all the ingredients together until it sets.

SWEETCORN RELISH

18 *ears corn*	1 *lb sugar*
1 *small cabbage*	4 *oz plain flour*
1 *head celery*	2 *oz salt*
4 *medium onions*	½ *teaspoon dry mustard*
2 *green peppers*	¼ *teaspoon Cayenne pepper*
4 *pints vinegar*	½ *teaspoon turmeric powder*

Cut corn from cob. Chop cabbage and celery, slice onions and chop peppers. Put into saucepan with half the vinegar. Mix remaining ingredients with the rest of the vinegar, combine mixtures, bring to boiling point and simmer for 40 minutes. Put into jars and cover at once.

VEGETABLE MARROW PRESERVE

Peel and take out the seeds, cut in slices $\frac{1}{4}$ inch thick, weigh the pulp, put equal quantities of sugar. If 8 lb, $\frac{1}{4}$ lb bruised ginger (put into a muslin bag), the juice of 4 lemons. If required hot, add $\frac{1}{2}$ teaspoon of cayenne pepper, boil 2 hours.

Lewis' Mother's Cookbook, Mary Horrell, Exeter

BATH CHUTNEY

2 *lb apples or tomatoes*
$\frac{1}{2}$ *lb onion*
$\frac{1}{4}$ *lb dates or dried fruit*
$\frac{1}{2}$ *oz salt*
$\frac{1}{2}$ *lb brown sugar*

$\frac{3}{4}$ *pint vinegar*
2 *pieces root ginger*
1 *teaspoon coriander*
1 *dessertspoon pickling spice*

Prepare fruit and onions (weigh after preparation) mince or chop. Cook gently until soft adding a little vinegar if inclined to stick. Put spices in vinegar, infuse, strain. Add vinegar, salt and sugar to fruit. Cook until thick. Pour into hot jars and cover.

SOMERSET CHUTNEY

Peel 3 lb cooking apples and cut them up. Put them in a saucepan with 2 sliced onions, 1 lb brown sugar, $\frac{1}{2}$ lb seedless raisins or sultanas, $\frac{1}{4}$ lb currants, a dessertspoon ground ginger and 2 of mustard seed, $\frac{1}{2}$ pint vinegar and a tablespoon of salt. Stir all well together and bring to the boil. The mixture should boil gently for an hour or until the chutney is a nice brown colour.

Mrs Huxtable, Bath

CHUTNEY IN THE RAW

1 *lb stoned dates*
1 *lb sultanas*
1 *lb apples*
1 *lb onions*

Salt and pepper
1 *teaspoon curry powder*
1 *lb brown sugar*
1 *pint vinegar*

Mince the first 4 ingredients and stir in sugar and vinegar. Add 1 teaspoon salt, a sprinkling of pepper, curry and a small piece of root ginger in muslin. Stir mixture occasionally. Leave 24 hours. Remove ginger and bottle.

UNCOOKED CHUTNEY

1 *lb sultanas or raisins or*
dates
1½ *lb sugar*
2 *wineglasses of white wine*
vinegar

3 *teaspoons mixed spice*
1½ *lb apples, peeled and cored*
½ *lb onions*
3 *oz salt*

Mince the apples and onion and raisins or dates—the sultanas, if used, can be added whole. Add all other ingredients, mix well and pot. Keeps well and is best after several weeks.

SPICED APPLES (1)

2 *lb apples*
½ *oz whole cloves*
½ *oz stick cinnamon*
½ *oz whole allspice*

1 *pint white vinegar*
2 *lb sugar*
½ *teaspoon salt*

Put sugar, vinegar and salt into a saucepan, with the spices tied in a muslin bag. Bring to the boil and add the peeled, cored and sliced apples. Cook gently until the apples are tender, then take out the fruit, drain carefully and pack into warm jars. Boil the syrup until it thickens, take out the spice bag, pour over the apples and seal tightly.

SPICED APPLES (2)

2 *lb small apples (firm)*
2 *lb sugar*

1 *pint spiced vinegar*

Dissolve the sugar in the spiced vinegar. Prick the apples or cut in halves and simmer in the syrup until just tender, but do not let them break. Pack carefully into jars. Reduce the syrup by half, by gentle simmering, then pour it over the fruit while hot.

SPICED APRICOTS

1 *lb dried apricots*
½ *oz whole cloves*
½ *inch cinnamon stick*

½ *oz whole allspice*
1½ *pints white vinegar*
1¼ *lb sugar*

Soak the apricots in cold water overnight. Put the spices in a muslin bag and bring to the boil with the vinegar. Add the drained apricots and simmer for 5 minutes. Spoon the apricots into warm jars. Add the sugar to the vinegar, bring to the boil and continue boiling for 5 minutes until the mixture is syrupy. Remove the spice bag, pour the syrup over the fruit, and seal tightly. This is a good preserve to eat with ham or pork.

SPICED BLACKBERRIES (1)

This is an unusual use for blackberries, but extremely good with cold meats and poultry. Make some spiced vinegar by simmering gently together ½ pint cider or wine vinegar with ¼ oz each of allspice, coriander seed and cardamons, ½ stick cinnamon and 1 bay leaf. When the vinegar has reached boiling point, remove from heat, and leave to infuse for 2 or 3 hours. Remove the spices, and dissolve 1 lb sugar in vinegar. Add 2½ lb clean, ripe blackberries and 2 rose geranium leaves if possible. Simmer gently for 5 minutes till the fruit is tender. Lift out fruit, drain and put into warm jars. Boil the vinegar till syrupy, pour over the blackberries and seal firmly while hot.

SPICED BLACKBERRIES (2)

3 lb blackberries
1 lb sugar
½ pint vinegar

½ teaspoon each cinnamon
and ground cloves

Vinegar, sugar and spices are cooked together and the blackberries have cooked separately and are then added just before boiling point. Contents of pan are then allowed to simmer for 15 minutes. Bottle and seal down while very hot.

SPICED CRAB APPLES

4 lb crab apples (should be
uniform, ripe; avoid bruised
ones)
Whole cloves
¾ oz stick cinnamon

¼ oz ginger root
1 tablespoon allspice (whole)
½ pint best vinegar
¼ cup water
1½ lb sugar

Wash crab apples, leave stems on. Stick 2 or 3 cloves in each. Make syrup of vinegar, water, sugar, spices (tied in cheesecloth). Heat to boiling point, boil 5 minutes. Add fruit, cook gently until tender. Lift out whole, and seal down put carefully in jars. Boil syrup until thick, pour over. Seal.

SWEET SPICED DAMSONS

4 lb large damsons
1 pint vinegar

1½ lb sugar
1 oz mixed pickling spice

Prick damsons with a large needle. Put vinegar, sugar and spice in a pan and heat until the sugar has dissolved. Add the damsons, cook until soft but not broken, and then lift carefully into jars. Reduce the vinegar to a syrup by boiling, remove spices and pour over fruit. Cover tightly. Good with poultry or cold meat, particularly goose.

PICKLED DATES

Large dates   10 *whole cloves*
White vinegar   2 *inch cinnamon stick*
12 *peppercorns*   1 *level teaspoon salt*

Choose very succulent dates, and stone enough to fill the jars you want to use. Measure out enough white vinegar to cover them. For each pint use the quantity of spices indicated above. Put the spices in a muslin bag in a saucepan, add the vinegar and bring to the boil. Discard the spice bag and pour the hot vinegar over the dates in their jars. Leave to cool, cover tightly and leave for at least a month before using. Serve with all cold meats.

SPICED GOOSEBERRIES

Cook together 2 lb gooseberries with 8 oz brown sugar and 1 pint white wine vinegar. When the berries are tender, stir in 1 tablespoon dry mustard and 2 whole crushed garlic heads, 12 oz raisins and $\frac{1}{2}$ oz cayenne pepper. Add another pint of cold white wine vinegar, stir well and put into preserving jars, storing for at least 6 months before using.

PICKLED PLUMS

Sugar and vinegar are required. Place jars of plums in a moderate oven to heat through. Then cover the fruit with boiling syrup and seal at once. To make the syrup, dissolve sugar in spiced vinegar at the rate of 1 lb sugar to 1 pint vinegar. Boil 10 minutes. Keep the pickled plums 1 month before using.

PICKLED MELON

4 *lb melon*   1 *pint vinegar*
2 *oz salt*   8 *cloves*
1 *pint water*   1 *inch cinnamon stick*
1 *lb sugar*

Peel the melon and cut the flesh in $\frac{1}{2}$ inch cubes. Soak overnight in brine made from the salt and water. Drain and cover with fresh water. Bring to the boil, and simmer until tender and clear. Dissolve the sugar in vinegar with the spices and boil for 20 minutes until syrupy. Strain the syrup and bring it to the boil. Add the drained melon and boil for 10 minutes. Pour into preserving jars and seal at once. Excellent with ham or chicken.

SPICED ORANGE RINGS

6 firm oranges
$\frac{3}{4}$ pint vinegar
12 oz sugar

2 teaspoons cloves
3 inch cinnamon stick

Wipe the oranges and slice across in $\frac{1}{4}$ inch rounds. Put into a pan with water to cover and simmer for 45 minutes until fruit is tender. Put the vinegar, sugar and spices into the pan and bring to boil. Simmer and add rings a few at a time. Cook gently until the rind becomes clear and put fruit into hot preserving jars. Boil syrup until it starts to thicken and pour it over the fruit to cover completely. Add a few of the cloves and seal at once. Particularly good with ham and poultry.

PICKLED PEACHES

$3\frac{1}{2}$ lb peaches
$1\frac{3}{4}$ lb sugar
1 pint white malt vinegar

1 oz cloves
1 oz allspice
1 oz cinnamon

Wash the peaches. Dissolve the sugar in the vinegar, and add the spices tied in a muslin bag. Put in the fruit and simmer until tender but not soft. Drain fruit and pack into jars within one inch of the top. Boil the vinegar mixture until syrup, and pour on to the fruit, covering it completely. Seal at once. These are particularly delicious with cold ham and cold duck.

PICKLED PEARS

4 lb cooking pears
2 lb sugar
$\frac{3}{4}$ oz whole cloves
$\frac{3}{4}$ oz whole allspice

$\frac{3}{4}$ oz root ginger
$\frac{3}{4}$ oz stick cinnamon
1 pint vinegar
Rind $\frac{1}{2}$ lemon

Peel and core pears and cut into quarters. Dissolve sugar in vinegar. Crush spices and tie in a muslin bag and hang in the cooking pan. Simmer fruit in vinegar until tender. Drain off liquid and pack pears in preserving jars. Boil liquid gently until slightly thick, and fill each jar to cover fruit. Cover tightly, and keep for several months. These are very good with cold meat, poultry and ham.

SPICED PEARS

2 lb cooking pears
½ lb sugar
½ pint white vinegar
A piece of lemon rind

Small pieces root ginger and cinnamon stick
2 teaspoons whole allspice
Whole cloves

Peel and core pears and cut in half. Dissolve sugar in vinegar, and tie lemon rind and spices in a muslin bag. Stick a clove into each piece of pear, and then simmer pears in the syrup until they are tender and begin to look transparent. Pack them into clean hot jars, boil the syrup until it thickens slightly, and pour over pears. Seal tightly.

SPICED PLUMS

2½ lb firm plums
1 pint vinegar
1½ lb sugar
1 inch cinnamon stick

1 teaspoon cloves
Blade of mace
10 allspice berries

Prick the plums with a needle. Boil the vinegar, sugar and spices and pour over the plums. Leave overnight. Drain off the syrup and boil it for 10 minutes. Pour over the fruit again and leave for 12 hours. Bring to the boil with the plums. Remove the spices and put the plums into hot preserving jars. Boil up the syrup and pour over the plums, and screw on tops immediately. Delicious with all cold meat and poultry.

SPICED PICKLED PLUMS

1 pint white vinegar
1 oz cinnamon stick
¾ oz mixed pickling spice

¼ oz allspice berries
2 lb sugar
Victoria plums

Boil together vinegar, cinnamon stick, pickling spice, allspice, and sugar until the liquid is thick and syrupy. Wipe and halve plums, and remove stones. Prick well and put into jars. Pour over the cool syrup. Next day, strain off the syrup, reboil, cool and pour over fruit again. When cold, cover and store for at least 3 months before using. Good with poultry or cold meat.

SPICED PRUNES

1 lb large firm prunes
Cold tea
1 pint vinegar
1 lb sugar

1 inch cinnamon stick
1 teaspoon whole cloves
10 allspice berries
Blade of mace

Soak the prunes overnight in cold tea, and then simmer them in the tea until plump. Boil the vinegar and sugar with the spices. Add prunes and cooking liquid and cook for 5 minutes. Lift the prunes out with a slotted spoon, and pack them into preserving jars, or screwtop honey jars. Boil up the syrup, pour over the prunes, and seal at once. These are delicious with all kinds of cold meat, particularly pork.

TOMATO SAUCE (1)

4 lb ripe tomatoes
4 large onions
1 lb demerara sugar
1 oz salt

2 oz peppercorns
½ oz cloves
2 teaspoons Cayenne pepper
1 pint vinegar

Slice tomatoes and onions and mix with other ingredients. Simmer gently for 2 hours, stirring occasionally. Rub through a fine sieve, leaving nothing but spice, seeds and skin in strainer. Bring to the boil and boil for 5 minutes. Bottle when cold. This sauce will keep any length of time and improve by doing so.

Mrs Harding, Sixpenny Handley, Wilts

TOMATO SAUCE (2)

Put 4 lb ripe tomatoes in a pan with about ½ pint water. Boil until soft. Then rub through a sieve and put into a clean pan with a little cayenne, also 1 oz bruised ginger, 3 cloves, 1 teaspoon peppercorns and a blade of mace, all tied in a muslin bag. Boil all with the lid off till the sauce is thick as cream. When cold, bottle. Tie down securely.

TOMATAS KETCHUP

Have ripe Tomata. Bake, pour away the liquor that runs from them. to every pound put a pint of vinegar ½ oz Salt ½ oz White pepper ½ oz Shallot a teaspoonfull Cayenne. Boil it all together ½ an hour then press them thro a cullender when cold weigh it to every lb add the juice of 3 lemons, boil it up once cold bottle it.

Joseph Webb's book, 1823

PLUM SAUCE (1)

4 lb plums or damsons
½ lb onions
1 pint vinegar
1 oz salt

½ oz each of ginger, allspice, nutmeg and mustard
8 oz sugar

Cut up plums and onions and cook with vinegar, salt and spices for 30 minutes. Sieve, stir in sugar and bring to the boil. Simmer for 1 hour, stirring occasionally, and bottle while still warm. This is a good way of using up windfalls, or a mixture of odd plums and damsons which are not good enough for table sauce.

PLUM SAUCE (2)

2 lb cooking plums
½ lb sugar
1 pint vinegar
1 heaped teaspoon salt

¼ oz bruised ginger
8 cloves
½ teaspoon Cayenne pepper

Boil for 30 minutes, sieve and bottle.

STORE SAUCE

For a cheap, tasty sauce, Hampshire housewives save spiced vinegar for the pickle jars. Onions, mixed pickles, gherkins, walnuts can all be turned to account. When a quart or thereabouts is available, chop up 1 onion, 3 apples, 3 tomatoes. Bring these ingredients to boil in the vinegar and simmer till contents of pan are a thin purée. Sieve and bottle.

THIN SAUCE

This goes well with grills and fish. To 1 pint vinegar allow 1 tablespoon sugar, ½ teaspoon treacle, 1 dessertspoon flour, 1 teaspoon each mustard and salt, 3 oz pickling spice. Bring vinegar and spices to boil. Mix remainder of ingredients to smooth paste with a little of the vinegar (cold) and then boil all ingredients for 20 minutes. Strain and bottle.

TARRAGON VINEGAR

Pick leaves as soon as the flower-buds appear on the plant, but before they begin to open. Pack a jar full of leaves and fill with white wine vinegar. Cover, and leave to infuse for at least 2 weeks. Strain, and pour into bottles. Put a branch of tarragon in each bottle. Basil, burnet, marjoram, mint and mixed herbs may be used.

GARLIC VINEGAR

Crush 8 cloves of garlic with salt. Bring 1 pint of vinegar to boiling point, and pour over. Put in jars, cool, cover, and strain after 2 or 3 weeks. Bottle.

SPICED VINEGAR

Crush or ground 1 oz each of mixed allspice, celery seed, mustard seed, cloves, black pepper and 1 oz of whole ginger, 2 or 3 dried chillies, 6 cloves of garlic. Sugar (¾ lb) may be added for improvement though not essential. Heat all together to boiling point in 1 gallon of vinegar, and simmer for 10 minutes. After 3 or 4 weeks strain and bottle.

GOOSEBERRY VINEGAR

Having Bruised some ripe Goosebury add 3 Quarts of Water that has been Boild and coold to 1 Quart of Fruit and let it stand a day then strain it through a Flannel Bag. put 1 lb of Course Sugar to Gallon of Liquor. Stir it well together and let it stand for serverall months till it be fit for use it will Improve by Keeping and is good for Pickling.

Joseph Webb's book, 1823

RASPBERRY VINEGAR

To each lb of ripe fruit allow 1 pint of good vinegar. Pick over the raspberries, cover them with vinegar and allow to stand for 4 days. Strain through a nylon sieve, not pressing the fruit. To each pint of strained vinegar add 4–5 oz sugar. Simmer gently for 10 minutes and bottle.

JELLIED BEETROOT

Small boiled beetroot   *1 pint vinegar*
1 raspberry jelly

Boil the beetroot carefully to avoid 'bleeding'. When cool enough to handle, cut up and place in screwtop jars. Melt jelly in boiling vinegar and pour over the beetroot. Store in the dark, covering inside of screwtops with waxed paper, and making sure the beetroot is completely covered with vinegar and jelly.

13 Bottling and Preserving

What wondrous life is this I lead !
Ripe apples drop about my head;
The luscious clusters of the vine
Upon my mouth do crush their wine;
The nectarine and luscious peach
Into my hands themselves do reach;
Stumbling on melons, as I pass,
Ensnared with flowers, I fall on grass.

Andrew Marvell

BOTTLING: GRANDMA'S WAY

Here are four methods of preserving fruit in ordinary jam jars.

1. Using pig's bladder drawn tightly over jars.
2. Melted mutton fat (this hardens like cement).
3. Layers of paper painted with flour paste.
4. Paper covers dipped in candle-wax melted down from ends.

Here is the old-fashioned way of sterilising the fruit:
Choose ripe, but firm fruit. Warm jars upside down in oven on newspaper.

Remove one at a time, fill with fruit, and replace in oven for about an hour, covering each jar with a patty-pan to prevent the top fruits getting scorched.

The fruit will shrink, so using one jar as a filler, shake fruit from this 1 into each of the others to bring level of fruit up to rim of jar. Now, 1 jar at a time, fill jars just to overflowing (stand on newspaper) with boiling syrup made from water and sugar—a quart of water to 8 oz sugar if you can spare it.

You can use just water, but you'll find that fruit bottled with even a slightly sweetened syrup takes far less sugar when needed for cooking.

Using one of the four methods above, cover the jars immediately. Tie bladder firmly down with string, or if you use melted mutton fat pour this on to the fruit and cover with greaseproof or brown paper.

If you use the flour and water paste method paint a circle of greaseproof with paste to lap over the jar rim to 1 inch below. Paint again with paste, then cover with a circle of newspaper. Finally, cover with a last circle of plain brown paper and tie down firmly with string.

Store your jars on open shelves in a cool, dry place, *and take great care not to tip them.*

PRESERVING: OVEN METHOD

1. Wash and drain the jars and lids.
2. Pack tightly with the prepared fruit to the top of the jar.
3. Place in a very slow oven on a piece of cardboard or several thicknesses of paper. The jars should be covered with the lids, to prevent the fruit from charring.
4. Leave in the oven about $\frac{3}{4}$ to 1 hour until the fruit appears cooked and has shrunk a little. Whole tomatoes take $1\frac{1}{2}$ hours. This method is not recommended for sliced tomatoes.
5. Remove the jars one at a time, place them on a mat or folded newspaper and cover the fruit with boiling water. Tomatoes require salted boiling water; use 1 teaspoon salt to 1 quart water and a little sugar, $\frac{1}{4}$ oz, may be added to the brine if desired.
6. Seal immediately with rubber ring, lid and clip or screw-band. As the jars cool, the screw-bands will need further tightening.
7. Test next day. Remove the screw-band or clip; if the seal is perfect it should be possible to lift the jar by the lid. If the lid comes off, the seal is imperfect and the fruit should be eaten within a few days or re-sterilised. Store in a cool, dark place. Remove screw-band or clip which may rust if left on the jar. Grease and store them for future use.

TOMATOES IN THEIR OWN JUICE

Follow oven method. Press the tomatoes, cut in halves, well down in the jar, sprinkling salt on each layer, 1 teaspoon of salt to 2 lb tomatoes, but add no liquid. A teaspoon of sugar to 2 lb tomatoes improves the flavour. Cover with lid and leave in the oven 1–1½ hours until the juice in the jar simmers. Remove one at a time and seal immediately.

The Oven Method is not as satisfactory for Apples, Pears and Quinces, as Preserving in a Deep Pan.

PRESERVING IN A DEEP PAN

1. Wash and drain the jars and lids.
2. Pack the jars tightly with the prepared fruit. Apples and pears should be peeled with a stainless knife and put immediately into brine; use 1 teaspoon of salt to 1 pint of water and pack into the jars after rinsing.

   Shake soft, juicy fruits down; for hard fruits the handle of a wooden spoon is useful for arranging the fruit in layers and for packing tightly. Pack the fruit almost to the top of the jar.
3. Cover the fruit with cold water, filling the jars to overflowing. Add no water to tomatoes in own juice.
4. When the screw-band is used it should be given a half-turn back to allow for expansion.
5. Put some straw, newspaper, or cloth in the bottom of a deep pan or steriliser; place in the jars and completely cover with cold water. A large fish kettle, bucket or any container which is deep enough can be used. The jars should not touch each other or the sides of the container.
6. Bring the water slowly to simmering point. This should take 1½ hours, then maintain at this temperature for 15 minutes. Pears and tomatoes require 30 minutes.
7. Remove the jars one at a time from the steriliser; place on a wooden table or board and tighten the screw-bands. As the jars cool, the screw-band will need further tightening.
8. Test the next day. Remove the screw-band; if the seal is perfect it should be possible to lift the jar by the lid. If the lid comes off, the seal is imperfect and the fruit should be eaten within a few days or re-sterilised. Store in a cool, dark place. Remove the screw-band which may rust if left on the jar. Grease and store them for future use.

PULPING

This is a simple way of bottling stewed fruit, whether soft or hard. Windfall apples or bruised plums can be bottled by this method if all the bruised parts are removed first. Apples and pears should be peeled with a stainless knife and put immediately into brine; use 1 teaspoon salt to 1 pint water.

1. Stew the fruit in a little water until thoroughly pulped, only enough water is needed to prevent the pan from burning. About 30 minutes' stewing is needed for soft fruit longer for hard-textured fruit. Tomatoes should be stewed with seasoning; use $\frac{1}{2}$ teaspoon salt to 1 lb tomatoes, and about $\frac{1}{2}$ teaspoon of sugar.

2. Pour at once into hot, clean jars.

3. Seal immediately and when screw-band is used, give a half-turn back to allow for expansion.

4. Place the jars in a pan of hot water on a false bottom of straw, newspaper or cloth, bring to the boil and boil 5 minutes. Tomatoes should remain in the boiling water 15 minutes. The jars should be completely covered with water.

5. Remove, then tighten screw-band. As the jars cool, the screw-bands will need further tightening.

6. Test next day. Remove screw-band; if the seal is perfect it should be possible to lift the jar by the lid. If the lid comes off, the seal is imperfect, and the fruit should be eaten within a few days or re-sterilised. Store in a cool, dark place. Remove the screw-band which may rust if left on the jar. Grease and store them for future use.

USING CAMPDEN TABLETS

This method is suitable for most stone and soft fruits, provided the fruit is sound and not over-ripe.

Fruits not recommended to be preserved by this method are: Blackberries, cherries, pears, dessert apples, blackcurrants, gooseberries and tomatoes.

1. Dissolve the tablets in cold or tepid water, allowing 1 tablet to each $\frac{1}{2}$ pint water.

2. Pack the fruit in the jars, do not pack too tightly.

3. Pour in the solution until the fruit is entirely covered. At least $\frac{1}{2}$ pint of solution must be used for each lb of fruit and sometimes more is necessary.

4. Seal at once with screw-band. If metal covers are used, the metal must be protected by 2 or 3 layers of paper fitted into the lid or by smearing the inside of the lid with vaseline.

5. This method does not produce a vacuum, so it is not possible to test after sealing.

The fruit can be used for stewing, in puddings, pies, or for jam making. The fruit should be poured into an open pan and heated until there is no further smell of sulphur. If difficulty is experienced in getting rid of sulphur fumes in the case of plums, remove stones first. Do not throw away the liquid as this contains some of the fruit juices, sugar and protective substances.

N.B. Vegetables should not be bottled by any of these methods

PULPED TOMATOES

1 lb tomatoes
2 teaspoons sugar
1 small teaspoon salt

1 dessertspoon vinegar
Dash of pepper

Melt in saucepan a small piece of cooking fat (not margarine). Skin tomatoes by immersing in boiling water; they then peel easily. Put in saucepan, cook until soft pulp; keep stirring, add sugar, salt, pepper and lastly vinegar. Bring to boil, boil 2 minutes. Place pulp in previously heated jars, fill right up to top and close down quickly with vacuum closures.

Now sterilise by placing jars in saucepan with newspaper in bottom of pan, just covering bottom to avoid a possible crack. Cover jars entirely with cold water and put lid on. Bring slowly to boil, then boil exactly 10 minutes.

PEASANTS' RUNNER BEANS

Fill a stone jar $\frac{4}{5}$ full with stringed beans. You may string and slice them if they are coarse or put in whole. Fill with brine made as follows: bring to boil a sufficient amount of water to cover beans. This will depend on size of jar. For every quart of water allow $6\frac{1}{2}$ oz of brick salt. As soon as it has come to boil, withdraw from heat, allow to cool, then pour over beans packed in jar. See that brine completely covers the beans. Cover well with several thicknesses of brown paper. Tie with string and keep in dark place. To cook beans, wash well in cold water and cook like fresh ones.

TO BOTTLE APPLES AND PEARS

Peel, core and slice the fruit. To prevent discoloration, put the peeled fruit into cold salted water (2 oz salt to 1 gallon), during preparation. Rinse quickly before packing into clean warm jars. Fill up with syrup (6 oz sugar to 1 pint water), fit rubber rings which you have previously soaked in cold water for 15 minutes. Fit screw bands, loosen by one *half turn*, then sterilise. To sterilise, put the bottles into a pan of cold water, bring slowly to simmering point and maintain at this 15–20 minutes. Take out and tighten screw band, test next day for seal.

Apple pulp may also be put into preserving jars, which are then put into a pan of cold water, brought slowly to simmering point maintained for 25 minutes. Apple slices may be preserved in the same way in a syrup of 6 oz sugar to 1 pint water. Pears are always better bottled in syrup, and the best varieties to bottle are good dessert pears which are fully ripe.

GINGER APPLES

Pare, quarter, core and cut enough apples into small squares to give 1 quart. Grate the rind from 1 lemon. Bring 2 cups water to boil. Add 2 cups brown sugar. Stir till sugar has dissolved, then add the juice of the lemon and bring again to boil. Boil until clear for about 5 minutes. Add the lemon rind, 6 pieces of ginger root and apple squares. Stir carefully till boiling, then boil for 2 hours, or longer, if necessary, until the mixture is thick and brown. Pour into sterilised jars and cover.

PRESERVED APPLES

Weigh equal quantities of good brown sugar and of apples. Peel, core and mince them small. Boil the sugar, allowing to every 3 lbs 1 pint of water. Skim it well and boil it pretty thick, then add the apples, the grated peel of 1 or 2 lemons or pieces of white ginger, boil till the apples fall and look clear and yellow.

Lewis' Mother's Cookbook, Mary Horrell, Exeter

BLACKBERRY AND APPLE PURÉE

Blackberries   *Sugar*
Apples

Wash blackberries and put over a low heat to extract juice. Strain the juice and measure liquid. Peel and core apples and cut into slices, and allow 4 lb apples to each pint of blackberry juice. Cook to a pulp, then add 12 oz sugar. Boil together, then put quickly into hot preserving jars and seal down. This purée is very useful for pies and puddings.

SPICED CRAB APPLES

4 lb sugar   *4 lb crab apples*
6 cups water   *¾ teaspoon whole cloves*
2 tablespoons lemon juice   *¾ stick cinnamon*

Place the sugar, water and lemon juice in a preserving pan. Stir over low heat till sugar has dissolved, then heat till boiling. Wash apples, cut into

234

quarters, remove stems and cores. Add to syrup with spices tied in a small muslin bag. Stir occasionally till boiling, then stir till clear and tender. Remove spices, pour apples and syrup into clean hot jars and seal.

TO BOTTLE GOOSEBERRYS

To every Bottle of Goosberys put Six ounces of Loaf Sugar in powder. Tie a Bladder over the mouth of the Bottle and put them in cold water over the fire in the usual way till the Sugar is melted. Then take them out and put them they will not require a Cork.
Damsons done the same way are Beautifull

Joseph Webb's book, 1823

GINGER PEARS

8 lb pears   *4 oz stem ginger*
4 lb preserving sugar   *4 medium-sized lemons*

Pare, quarter and core pears and remove the stems. Cut quarters into small slices, add sugar, chopped ginger and the strained juice of the lemons. Cut lemon rind into long thin strips, add to fruit and mix. Cover and stand in a cool place overnight. Stir over moderate heat till sugar has dissolved, then bring quickly to boil. Cook very slowly for 3 hours till clear and thick. Pour into jars and cover.

BRANDIED PEARS

6 lb hard windfall pears   *4½ lb granulated sugar*
3 lemons   *About 4 inch cinnamon stick*
8 cloves   *6 tablespoons brandy*

Peel the pears, quarter them and take out the cores. Grate the rind off the lemons and squeeze out the juice. Layer the pears, sugar and lemon rind in a large bowl and sprinkle the lemon juice over the top. Cover the bowl and leave overnight.

Transfer the pears to a large casserole, covering them with the juice which has formed during the night. Add cinnamon and cloves. Cover with a lid and bake in a slow oven, 275°F (Gas Mark 1) for 6 hours until the pears are tender and are a golden amber colour.

Leave the casserole to cool, then stir in the brandy. Remove the cinnamon stick and cloves, and transfer the pears to jars, screwing them down for storing.

STEWED PEARS

Peel the pears and put them into cold water. To every lb of pears, add ½ lb of sugar, add cinnamon and cloves. To a dozen lb of pears add the rind of 3 lemons and sufficient water to keep them from burning. Stew them gently until quite soft. When done, add the juice of the lemons and 3 or 4 glasses of port wine. Tie them down tightly and they will keep for years.

Lewis' Mother's Cookbook, Mary Horrell, Exeter

SQUIFFY PRUNES

Cover the best prunes available with a port-type wine and seal down. After some weeks they are excellent. They make an ideal dessert after a good meal, if handed round in a dish with cocktail sticks to spear them. The liquid becomes really good and can be drunk as a dessert wine.

PRESERVED QUINCES

5 lb quinces　　　　　　　　*3 lb sugar*
4 cups cold water

Peel, quarter and core quinces dropping each quarter into cold water to prevent discoloration. Cook the peelings and cores in boiling water to cover for 15 minutes, then strain off the liquid. Add quinces to liquid and cook slowly till tender. Remove quinces to a basin with a perforated spoon so that liquid can run back into pan. Add 3 lb sugar. Stir till dissolved, then bring quickly to boil. Add quince quarters, cook until clear, turn into heated jars and cover.

STEWED RASPBERRIES

Dreary, but if you want to bottle them for winter puddings, try mixing equal quantities of raspberries, currants and gooseberries in the jars—the flavour is excellent.

FRUIT MEDLEY

Use a few late strawberries or raspberries, 1 odd peach, a couple of Victoria plums. Keep in the refrigerator a preserving jar ⅔ full of cheap brandy. Add the fruit as you wish and use fruit and brandy together to enliven a fruit salad or pudding. It will keep for weeks.

EVERLASTING RUMPOT

1 bottle light or dark rum
Granulated sugar
Strawberries, cherries,

apricots, raspberries, plums,
redcurrants, peaches, grapes,
melon

The fruit should be sound, whole and ripe. The rumpot should not be overloaded with fruit and it is best to preserve a little at a time, using only the choicest fruits. Citrus fruits, apples, bananas and pears should not be used. Gently wipe the fruit, and do not peel or stone (except for melon which should be peeled, seeded and cut into large chunks). Put fruit into a large stone crock with its own weight of sugar, and cover with rum. Cover crock tightly with waxed paper and a lid and keep in a cool place. Continue adding fruit to the rumpot throughout the season. The fruit and syrup may be used in small quantities as required:

a) eat fruit as it is, or with cream or yoghurt;
b) add to fresh fruit salad with oranges, apples, nuts;
c) remove top of a melon, pierce flesh with a knitting needle, and fill 'case' with fruit and syrup. Serve chilled;
d) drain fruit, put into pastry case and top with whipped cream.

FRUIT SYRUPS

Make fruit syrups to use as a basis for winter fruit drinks, to serve as sauces for puddings, or to flavour mousses and ices. The usual problem is with sterilising and storage, since bottles tend to burst. The best ones to use are the lever-stoppered type with a china cap and rubber washer; second choice is the traditional sauce bottle with screw cap. Syrups should be stored in a cool dark place, or colours will fade, though a little vegetable colouring may be used for a more attractive appearance.

Latest answer to the storage problem is to use the freezer. Make the syrup in the usual way, cool, and pour into containers, leaving room for expansion, then freeze. Even better is to pour the syrup into ice-cube trays, freeze, then wrap each cube in foil, and put them together in labelled transparent bags. Each cube will be enough for 1 portion, to dilute with water.

Mixed fruit syrups

Syrups can be made from raspberries, strawberries, elderberries, blackberries, loganberries, and blackcurrants, or a mixture of fruit. Use clean ripe fruit, and avoid washing if possible. Add a little water to the fruit (about $\frac{1}{4}$ pint to 3 lb raspberries or strawberries, but $\frac{1}{2}$ pint to the same amount of blackcurrants). Cook gently for about an hour, crushing the fruit at intervals. Drain through a jellybag overnight, then measure and add ¾ lb sugar to each pint of juice. Stir until dissolved. Strain and pour into bottles, or into freezing containers. Make sure the bottles are securely topped and tied down.

Stand the bottles in a steriliser and fill with cold water to cover. Heat slowly so that the water reaches 175°F (simmering point) in an hour. Continue at this temperature for 30 minutes, remove bottles, cool, label and store.

Muscat Syrup

A delectable syrup, to make when gooseberries and elderflowers coincide, can be used for flavouring fruit cups with its scented muscat flavour. Use 3 lb gooseberries with 1 pint water cooked till soft, then add 2¾ lb sugar and bring to the boil. Infuse 8 elderflower heads for 10 minutes, strain through muslin, bottle and sterilise. The gooseberries can be used for a purée or fool.

RASPBERRY SYRUP FOR WINTER DRINKS

Squeeze fresh raspberries through double muslin, and add to every pint of juice a syrup made from 1 pint water and 1 lb sugar. Boil the mixture, then simmer for an hour, and when cold bottle and cork down, or put into preserving jars, and sterilise; this makes a delicious drink with water or soda water, or can be used to flavour winter puddings, or to use on sponge puddings.

FRUIT CORDIALS

These can be made from many fruits and form the basis of summer drinks or winter cures. The most suitable fruits are blackberries, blackcurrants, loganberries, raspberries and strawberries. This is the basic method. Put the fruit into a large earthenware basin and break it up with a wooden spoon, no water need be added, except to blackberries and blackcurrants. For these, add just enough water to start the flow of juice. Put the basin of fruit over a pan of hot water on the stove. Keep the water in the bottom pan on the boil, crush the fruit occasionally. When all the juice has been extracted put the fruit into a double muslin bag and leave to strain overnight.

Add ¾ lb sugar to each pint of juice and stir till thoroughly dissolved. Strain again into clean bottles, filling to within 1 inch of the top of the bottle. Cork securely, using new corks each year. Secure the corks with string, then sterilise. Put the bottles into a pan of cold water. The water must reach to within an inch of the top of the bottles. Bring the water to the boil and simmer for 20 minutes. Dip the corks in melted paraffin wax, and store the bottles in a cool dark place.

CHERRY BRANDY

Well worth the trouble and expense. To each lb of Morella cherries allow 4 oz sugar-candy, $\frac{1}{4}$ oz shredded bitter almonds and $\frac{1}{2}$ inch cinnamon stick. Prick the cherries all over and pack into jars with other ingredients. Fill the jars to the top with brandy. After 6 months, or better still a year, drain off liquid. Use cherries for puddings.

14 Storing and Drying

Season of mists and mellow fruitfulness,
Close bosom-friend of the maturing sun;
Conspiring with him how to load and bless
With fruit the vines that round the thatch-eaves run;
To bend with apples the moss'd cottage trees,
And fill all fruit with ripeness to the core;
To swell the gourd, and plump the hazel shells
With a sweet kernel.

John Keats

Let lay them dark as wind may come not near
And do fair straw upon them, crates them under
Or in heaps them save, a little space asonder,
And these heaps must ye now and now divide
Yet hath a third for them a fresh devise
Only their little feet to close in clay
And on a floor bestroon with chaff to lay
And others dip their little feet in pitch all warme
And so in order lay them on the table.

'Preserving Apples', Palladius

STORING VEGETABLES

Beetroot   Cover with straw, or put into a trench like potatoes, or into box covered with sand in a shed.

Carrots   Lift by mid-November and store in a cool shed in boxes raised above ground level.

Parsnips   Leave in ground, or store under a straw cover in a cool place.

Potatoes   Store in bags indoors. If you have a lot of potatoes, put them into a 3-foot wide trench, about 6 inches deep. Pile in the potatoes in a triangular heap about 3 feet high. Cover with straw and earth, leaving a little straw at the top so that moisture escapes.

Turnips   Put turnips into a trench like potatoes, or put into a big heap covered with straw or sand.

STORING FRUIT

Apples and Pears   As a general rule it is the apples which ripen latest which store best. An apple is ripe when it falls easily into the hand if lifted gently on its stalk. Do not put into store immediately after picking. Let the apples cool and sweat in an airy place before storing. The store should be dark, cool and very slightly moist.

Keep separate different varieties with varying keeping qualities. Store in trays in a frostproof shed, cellar or attic. Greengrocers' boxes, which can be stacked with space between, make useful trays. Special eating apples can be wrapped individually in sheets of newspaper and stored in boxes. Pears tend to ripen suddenly. Inspect fruit regularly and remove unsound fruit.

Marrows and Pumpkins   Store in a cool dry place away from frost.

Quinces   Store on shelves and trays like apples.

Another Way with Marrows. Vegetable marrows may be kept for months by cutting them when they are ripe, but not old, and leaving on plenty of stalk, and if the end of the stalk can be sealed with wax so much the better, though this is not absolutely necessary. Then tie a piece of tape, or something that will not cut the skin, round each end of the marrow, and loop the 2 together so that it can be hung up in a dry, cool place.

A STOCKINGFUL OF ONIONS

Leave outside to dry for a week or 2. Remove the tops and any loose skin and soil, pop them into an old nylon stocking and knot the top when it is full.

KEEPING GRAPES

Cut the bunches with a long stalk and a piece of stem, and stand them in tall jars in a cool larder with the grapes themselves supported if necessary. Put charcoal in the water and leave undisturbed. Keep for 6 weeks.

TO STORE FRESH LEMONS

Choose perfect fruit and pack it in layers in a wooden box with a lid. Separate lemons from each other and from the box by a good layer of silver sand. If the box is stored in a cool, dry place the lemons will keep for about 3 months.

STORING NUTS

Take off any outer husks—scrub walnuts and almonds—and leave to dry in a warm place.Chestnuts and walnuts can be packed in a crock with salt or dry sand between each layer. Small nuts can be packed in jars with a layer of cooking salt over the top and stored in a cool, dark place. Nuts to be used for cooking can be shelled, dried on a baking shelf in a cool oven, and packed into clean, glass jars.

FREEZING NUTS

Nuts kept in the freezer will be moist and fresh. They can be frozen whole, chopped, slivered or buttered and toasted, but they should not be salted. Small containers, foil or polythene bags can be used for packing, and nuts will keep for a year (4 months if buttered and toasted). To use, thaw at room temperature in wrappings for 3 hours.

DRYING FRUIT AND VEGETABLES

Drying is the oldest method of preservation. Suitable for drying are apples, dessert pears, grapes, sweet plums, peas, beans, onions, leeks and mushrooms. They can be dried in the oven, a warm cupboard or a rack over the stove, in a constant gentle heat with a current of air to carry away moisture (this is best obtained by leaving cupboard or oven door slightly open). Heat may be used after a baking session. Food should be spread on oven racks or wire cake trays spread with muslin, which should be scaled before use, or it may scorch during drying. The ideal heat for drying is between 120°F–150°F as the fruit or vegetables should be dried, not cooked or scorched.

APPLE RINGS AND PEARS

This is a useful way to keep apples if the freezer is full, or there is not the time or equipment for bottling. Pears can be dried, but the juicy varieties are rather difficult to handle.

Apples should be ripe but not over-ripe. Using a silver or stainless steel knife, peel and core the apples and cut into rings about $\frac{1}{4}$ inch thick. Put into a basin of salt water immediately ($\frac{1}{2}$ oz salt to 1 quart water) and leave for 10 minutes. The rings should be threaded on a stick which can rest on the runners of an oven, and the rings should not touch each other. Dry at 150°F, for some hours. Apples should be like dry chamois leather, moist and pliable. Cool in the air before packing tightly in paper bags, or in dry jars or tins. Store in a dry, dark place.

It is best to soak fruit for 24 hours before cooking, and to use the soaking water for cooking, flavoured with a little lemon or vanilla, a clove or a piece of ginger.

DRIED GRAPES

Use fresh, fully ripe fruit, to be dried whole. Spread out in a single layer, and test by squeezing. When they are dried, no moisture will appear; a lb of fresh fruit will give about 4 oz dried.

DRIED PLUMS

You can dry plums, too. They must be ripe. Halve and stone them. Stretch muslin on sticks to replace open shelves, and dry plums on these. Dry slowly, as for apples. Plums can also be dried whole.

DRIED BEANS

Leave haricot beans on the plants until dry and withered. Pull up plants and hang in an airy shed. Shell the peas and store as for seed. Young French and runner beans may be sliced, blanched for 5 minutes, drained, and dried in a thin layer.

DRIED MUSHROOMS

These dry very readily. Cut the stalks off short and peel. Lay them on the oven racks and when they are dried quite stiff, store them away. When preparing them for use soak them in water and simmer them in a little stock.

DRIED ONIONS AND LEEKS

These well repay drying, as so often they do not keep, so that when onions are showing signs of growing out or rotting, you know quite well it will not be long before they will all be gone. Peel them and take away any bad parts, and slice them on to muslin on oven racks. Leeks may be cut in strips lengthwise if preferred. Keep them moving about occasionally to help the drying, and when they are quite crisp take them out, and after a little while store them away.

DRIED PEAS

Leave marrowfat varieties on the plants until dry and withered. Pull up plants and hang in an airy shed. Shell the peas and store as for seed. For young, sugary peas, blanch them for 5 minutes, drain them and shake off excess moisture. Spread out in a thin layer and dry very carefully, without scorching.

15 Candied Fruit and Crystallised Flowers

*Here you have that which in itself is good
Made better by the storing of it.*

Fuller

CANDIED FRUIT

Try this with cherries, oranges, pears, pineapple and stone fruits. Canned fruits are very good, and easy to process.

Good quality fresh fruit should be gently cooked in water until just tender before processing. Canned fruit should be drained from its syrup. Fresh fruit should be processed with a syrup made from $\frac{1}{2}$ pint water and 6 oz sugar to each lb fruit. When using canned fruit, allow 1 lb fruit to $\frac{1}{2}$ pint liquid from the canning syrup and any necessary water.

Heat the syrup and use it to cover the fruit completely, keeping the fruit submerged with a saucer over the liquid if necessary. Leave to stand for 24 hours. Drain off the syrup, add 2 oz sugar and dissolve. Boil and pour over the fruit. Repeat this process twice more, adding 2 oz sugar each time. On the fifth day, add 3 oz sugar, and boil fruit for 4 minutes. Leave for 2 days. Repeat the process and leave the fruit to soak for 4 days. Drain off the syrup and put the fruit on a wire rack (such as a cake rack) to drain and finish off in a very cool oven or a warm airing cupboard for about 3 days. Store in boxes with waxed paper in a cool, dark dry place.

QUICK ORANGE PEEL

Peel of 3 oranges   *1 teaspoon water*
1 teacup loaf sugar   *Granulated sugar*

Cut peel in sections, cover with water, boil until white pith can be scraped off with spoon. Make syrup of loaf sugar and water. Cook peel in this until transparent, when it will have absorbed nearly all the syrup. Lift with fork, roll in granulated sugar. Leave on wire tray until cool and dry. Store in airtight glass jar.

ORANGE POWDER

Remove as much pith from orange rind as you can, wash rind, dry slowly in cool oven. When quite crisp, break up in pieces and roll out until very fine. Put through a sieve. Store in tin in dry place. Delicious for cakes and puddings, and a little goes a long way. It does not lose its strength by keeping.

ORANGE PEEL SYRUP

Cut off as much pith as possible from orange peel. Put peel through a mincer or grate on grater. Place a layer of grated peel in a clean screw-top jar. Sprinkle a tablespoon of sugar on peel. Put in layers of peel and sugar till jar is filled. Screw down top tightly and leave for several weeks. Shake every few days. This will make a delicious syrup and flavouring for cakes, puddings and sauces. It sweetens as well as flavours.

ORANGE PEEL PRESERVE

The orange peel can be used to flavour cakes or puddings, but the longer it is kept the richer it becomes. One jar saved for a year matured a rich brown in colour and was as delicious as sweetmeat.

Wipe skins, chop finely or mince. Cover bottom of small jar with layer about ½ inch thick, sprinkle with teaspoon sugar. Fill jar with layers. Fix top, shake well. During first week shake daily (this is important), and if jar is well sealed stand occasionally upside down, as top layers lose moisture. As the preserve sinks down, more peel and sugar can be added. If peel is very dry, add a little more sugar and a very small quantity of water. Use and replenish at any time.

KITTY FURZE'S WAY TO DRY ORANGE PEEL AND PRESERVE

Cut up peel and cover with cold water, 1 tablespoon salt. Soak overnight (or longer if you wish to collect over a day or 2). Drain, cover again with cold water, bring to boil for $\frac{1}{2}$ hour, cover with hot water, boil until tender ($\frac{3}{4}$ hour). Drain and measure and to each cup of peel add $\frac{3}{4}$ cup of sugar, return to saucepan with sugar and water and simmer until sugar is nearly gone. Store in jars covering with syrup.

Lewis' Mother's Cookbook, Mary Horrell, Exeter

CANDIED APRICOTS

4 lb just-ripe apricots   *1 pint water*
4 lb sugar

Cut the skin carefully at the top of each apricot and squeeze out the stones. Make a syrup with sugar and water and when it starts to thicken, add the apricots and bring to the boil. Remove from heat, then bring to the boil again. Do this 3 more times, then pour fruit and syrup into a bowl and leave overnight. On the next day heat the syrup and fruit and boil for 1 minute. Drain the fruit and put into a bowl. Boil the syrup and pour over the fruit. Leave overnight. Repeat this process twice more until the apricots are saturated and the syrup has been absorbed. Place apricots on a rack covered with paper and dry in the sun or in an open oven, turning the fruit occasionally. When dry, store in a tin or wooden box.

CANDIED CHERRIES

2 lb firm black cherries   *1 pint water*
2 lb sugar

The cherries should be weighed after stoning. Dissolve the sugar in the water over a low heat without boiling. When the syrup is clear, put in the cherries. Simmer very gently until the cherries are almost transparent. Drain the fruit and put on flat trays. Dry thoroughly in the sun or in a very cool oven with the door slightly open. Dust with icing sugar containing a pinch of bicarbonate of soda and store in a box with waxed paper layers.

SUGARED FRUITS

Use perfect fruits, ripe but not soft. Wash, cut each in half, stone. Prepare syrup by combining $\frac{1}{2}$ cup golden syrup, 2 cups sugar, 1 cup water. Bring to boil, stirring only until sugar is dissolved. Cook to 290°F or until syrup becomes brittle when dropped in cold water. Lower the prepared fruit pieces into syrup. Cook 5 minutes. Remove from heat, carefully skim out fruits, allowing to dry and cool on greaseproof paper.

CANDIED MARROW

2 lb ripe marrow flesh
2 lb sugar
1 oz root ginger

10 Cayenne pods
2 lemons

Cut the marrow into neat cubes. Cover with water and leave for 12 hours. Strain and mix with sugar and leave for 12 hours. Tie bruised root ginger, cayenne pods and the grated rind of the lemons into a muslin bag. Heat the marrow with the sugar and lemon juice until the sugar has dissolved. Put in the muslin bag, and simmer until the marrow is clear and the syrup is thick. Pour into a covered bowl and leave for 7 days. Strain off the syrup and put marrow on waxed paper on a wire rack in a warm place to dry. Roll cubes in castor sugar containing a pinch of bicarbonate of soda and cream of tartar.

CRYSTALLISED FLOWERS

Primroses, violets, polyanthus, roses, carnation petals, forget-me-nots, mimosa, cowslips, sweet peas, fruit blossoms are suitable for crystallising. Flowers which come from bulbs should not be eaten.

The flowers should be crystallised in a solution of gum Arabic crystals and rose or orange flower water. Allow 3 teaspoons crystals to 3 tablespoons rose water, and leave in a screwtop jar for 2 or 3 days, shaking sometimes, until the mixture is a sticky glue. A small soft paint brush is needed to paint the flowers. Large flowers should be taken apart and the petals reassembled when needed. The petals must be completely coated, or bare spots will shrivel and not keep. A little vegetable colouring may be added to the solution, but this must be very delicate to remain natural. When the flowers have been sugared, they should be dried for about 24 hours until crisp and dry. They are best stored in the dark.

CRYSTALLISED ANGELICA

Select young stems and stalks of angelica in April. Cut into 4 or 5 inch lengths and place in a glass or crockery vessel, pour over them a boiling solution of 1 pint water and ¼ lb salt. Cover and leave for 24 hours. Lift out, drain on a wire drainer, peel and wash in cold water.

Make a syrup of 1½ lb sugar and 1½ pints water and boil for 10 minutes.

Place the angelica in the boiling syrup for 20 minutes; lift out and drain for 4 days on a wire drainer.

Reboil again for 20 minutes in the same syrup. Allow to cool in the syrup, lift out and drain for 3 or 4 days.

Strew well with sugar and store in airtight jars.

CANDIED COWSLIPS

10 oz yellow cowslip 'pips'   *8 oz sugar*

This recipe was first used in 1700. The flowers should be gathered when the dew is off, and only the yellow blossoms should be used. Dissolve the sugar in as little hot water as possible which will absorb the sugar (about 4 fluid ozs). Bring to the boil and cook until the syrup starts to candy. Take off the heat and shake in the flowers gradually. Stir until the flowers become dry and sugary. Store in jars sealed with sticky tape.

CRYSTALLISED MINT LEAVES

Fresh mint leaves   *Granulated sugar*
Egg white

Use fresh green mint and well-shaped leaves. Beat egg white stiffly and coat both sides of the leaves. Coat with sugar and put on a wire rack covered with wax paper. Stand on the rack of a cooker until dry. Store in a tin between layers of waxed paper.

16 Food for Festivals

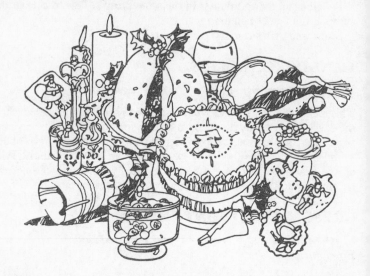

Turkeys, geese, game, poultry, brawn, great joints of meat, sucking pigs, long wreaths of sausages, mince pies, plum-puddings, barrels of oysters, red hot chestnuts, cherry-cheeked apples, juicy oranges, luscious pears, immense twelfth-cakes, and seething bowls of punch, that made the chamber dim with their delicious steam.

'A Christmas Carol' Charles Dickens

'Twas at the public feast and public day,
Quite full, right dull, guests hot and dishes cold;
Great plenty, much formality, small cheer,
And everybody out of their own sphere.

Byron

New Year in Wales

An old lady called Mrs Birkett told Maisie Jones how they had celebrated New Year's Day in Pembrokeshire. She was born in 1872, one of nine children, and her mother was a widow. They used to go to the houses and farms of any standing to collect a sort of bun, in pillow cases, one for each member of the poor family. This was called Pice Calennig and could only be collected between 6 a.m. and noon on New Year's Day. Most of the buns were pretty dry old stuff, but some kinder folk made better buns to give away. A rockbun perhaps, as Mrs Birkett said some of them you could throw against the wall and they wouldn't break, but perhaps this was just childish talk. You had to be up early, as all poor families were entitled to the New Year Buns.

When a baby was christened in the old days, rum butter was made to celebrate the christening, and a bowl of it was hidden, often on top of the grandfather clock. The young folk of the village used to come and hunt till they found it, then they ran back to the village pub, the good lady of the inn used to spread it on bread and butter and hand it around for all to share. When all the rum butter had been used up, the empty bowl was passed round for a collection then returned as a start in life for the baby. We were talking about this old custom the other day at our 'over-sixties gathering', one old lady said when her daughter was christened she got 18 shillings, quite a sum in those days. A friend tells me this custom still continues in a few villages on the fell sides.

Mrs M. Baxter, Carlisle

CUMBERLAND RUM BUTTER

4 oz butter   *8 oz soft brown sugar*
¼ teaspoon grated nutmeg   *½ gill rum*

Cream the butter and work in the nutmeg. Gradually work in the sugar, adding a few drops of rum at a time until it is finished. When the mixture is smooth and creamy, put into small pots and cover.

Cakes were very often made for religious festivals and many of our best-known recipes originated during Lent and the Easter festival. We all know Hot Cross Buns, but Sally Lunns were Good Friday buns too. Shrewsbury Cakes and Tansy Cakes, Johnny Cakes, Popovers, Pikelets and delicious mincemeat and pastry confections called variously Cumberland Cakes, Banbury Cakes, Eccles Cakes and Hawkshead Cakes. Doughnuts were a speciality of Shrove Tuesday, made with jam or fruit, plain or heavily spiced.

The Simnel cake, now associated with Easter, was presented on Mothering Sunday, to be eaten at Easter. The early Mothering Sunday cake was made with figs, the fruit representing 'fruitfulness in offspring' and Fig Cakes dedicated to Palm Sunday are still sometimes made.

EASTER CAKES

Rub 8 oz butter into 12 oz plain flour. Add 5 oz castor sugar, 3 oz currants, $\frac{1}{2}$ teaspoon cream of tartar, $\frac{1}{4}$ teaspoon bicarbonate of soda, and a pinch of salt. Mix well together, then beat in 1 egg and mix the dough with a knife. Form into a ball and roll out $\frac{1}{8}$ inch thick on a flowered board. Cut out with a fluted cutter, and put on a greased and floured baking sheet. Bake at 350°F (Gas Mark 4) for 15 minutes, put on a wire tray to cool and sprinkle with castor sugar. These cakes should be watched carefully as they should be only delicately brown.

SHREWSBURY CAKES

These are richer than the Easter Cakes and very good. Rose water gives a very delicate flavour and may be obtained from any chemist.

Rub together 8 oz plain flour, 8 oz castor sugar, 8 oz butter, $\frac{1}{4}$ oz caraway seeds and a pinch of nutmeg. Beat together 2 small eggs with 3 dessert-spoons sherry, 3 dessertspoons rose water, and mix with the flour a little at a time, blending carefully. Roll out thinly, cut into shapes and put on greased and floured baking sheets. Prick lightly with a fork and bake at 350°F (Gas Mark 4) for 15 minutes, without allowing them to colour.

SEDGEMOOR EASTER CAKE

Rub 4 oz butter into 8 oz plain flour. Add 4 oz castor sugar, 4 oz currants, $\frac{1}{2}$ teaspoon each of mixed spice and ground cinnamon. Beat an egg with 2 tablespoons brandy and mix with the dry ingredients. Roll out $\frac{1}{2}$ inch thick, cut in rounds and bake at 350°F (Gas Mark 4) for 20 minutes.

BANBURY CAKES

Roll out some puff pastry $\frac{1}{8}$ inch thick and cut in 6 inch rounds (use a small plate as a guide). Beat 2 oz sugar and 1 oz butter to a cream, then add 1 oz fine white breadcrumbs, 4 oz currants, 2 oz mixed peel, 1 oz biscuit crumbs (2 oz ground almonds may be used instead of the bread and biscuit crumbs), $\frac{1}{2}$ egg, and a pinch of allspice. Put a spoonful of the mixture on each round of pastry. Damp half-way round each circle and draw the edges up over the filling, putting the damp edge uppermost on the other edge. Press lightly together and form into an oval shape. Turn over, flatten slightly with the hand and reshape into an oval. Brush with milk and sprinkle thickly with castor sugar. Bake at 450°F (Gas Mark 8) for 25 minutes.

PALM SUNDAY FIG CAKE

Chop 6 oz dried figs roughly and stew in just enough water to cover until tender, then leave to cool. Mix together 6 oz plain flour, $\frac{1}{2}$ teaspoon baking powder, a pinch of salt and $2\frac{1}{2}$ oz castor sugar. Rub in $2\frac{1}{2}$ oz butter and mix to a batter with the cooled figs and water. Pour into greased and floured tin and bake at 375°F (Gas Mark 5) for 45 minutes. If liked, butter icing can be used to cover the top of this cake, but it is very good eaten plain.

SIMNEL CAKE (1)

This traditional cake has a layer of almond paste on top and in the centre, but is not iced. The cake may be decorated with eggs, chickens or flowers and a wide ribbon. Prepared almond paste is easily bought and very convenient to use for this recipe. Buy two $\frac{1}{2}$ lb packets and use one for the centre and one for the top. Before the cake is made, the almond paste should be rolled into two rounds the exact size of the cake tin.

Cream together 8 oz butter and 8 oz granulated sugar till light and fluffy. Sift together 12 oz plain flour with 1 teaspoon cinnamon, 2 teaspoons baking powder and a pinch of grated nutmeg. Slowly beat 4 eggs into the creamed mixture, blending in a little of the flour mixture at the same time. When thoroughly blended, add the rest of the flour together with $1\frac{1}{2}$ lb chopped dried fruit (currants, sultanas and raisins) and 4 oz chopped candied peel. The mixture should be stiff but may be softened a little with 2 tablespoons milk. Put half the mixture into an 8 inch tin which has been buttered and lined with buttered greaseproof paper. Cover with a round of almond paste and top with the rest of the cake mixture. Bake at 325°F (Gas Mark 3) for $2\frac{1}{2}$ hours. Cool in the tin. Remove from the tin and paint the top with 2 tablespoons thin jam. Put on the second round of almond paste. Brush the paste with egg-white, sprinkle with castor sugar and put under a hot grill for a few minutes to give a granulated crystalline surface. Decorate to taste.

SIMNEL CAKE (2)

Marzipan:
1 lb ground almonds
1 lb icing sugar
½ teaspoon almond essence
1 tablespoon lemon juice
4 egg yolks

Cake:
6 oz butter
6 oz demerara sugar

3 eggs
8 oz self-raising flour
1 level teaspoon nutmeg
1 level teaspoon cinnamon
1 level teaspoon mixed spice
Pinch of salt
1 lb currants
8 oz sultanas
4 oz mixed peel
Milk to mix

Mix the marzipan ingredients to a stiff paste and knead well; divide into 3 and roll out 2 of the pieces into circles 8 inch diameter. Put aside with remaining mazipan. To make the cake, cream butter and sugar together until light and fluffy, beat in the eggs one at a time. Sieve flour, spices and salt together and add to the mixture; finally add dried fruit. If the mixture is a little stiff, add enough milk to give a dropping consistency. Put half into a greased and lined 8 inch cake tin, then put in 1 circle of marzipan and cover with remaining cake mixture. Bake at 300°F (Gas Mark 2) for 3½ hours. Allow to cool. Brush top of cake with a little warm jam, and put on second circle of marzipan, pressing down well. Make 12 small balls from the remaining marzipan and arrange these around the edge. Brush lightly with a little egg and put the cake into a hot oven or under the grill for a few seconds to glaze lightly. Fill the centre with a little white glacé icing and decorate.

HOT CROSS BUNS

8 oz plain flour
Pinch of salt
¼ teaspoon mixed spice
¼ pint milk
½ oz yeast

2 oz butter
1½ oz castor sugar
1 egg
3 oz currants
½ oz finely chopped peel

Sieve the flour, salt and spice in a mixing bowl. Warm milk to blood heat. Add yeast and butter, stir until dissolved, mix in sugar and beaten egg. Pour on to the flour, and beat with hand until smooth. Turn on to a floured board, work in the currants and peel, and knead well. Put in a buttered bowl, sprinkle with flour, cover with a clean cloth, and put in a warm place to rise for 1½ hours or until mixture has doubled its bulk. Knock down with hand and leave to rise as before for 30 minutes. Knead the dough and shape into 8 rounds. Put on 2 greased baking sheets and on each bun put a paste cross made with flour and water dough. Prove in a warm place until nearly twice the size (about 15 minutes). Bake at 425°F (Gas Mark 7) for 15 minutes. While still hot, brush with a glaze made by boiling 1 tablespoon sugar in 1 tablespoon mik

EASTER BISCUITS

3 oz butter
3 oz castor sugar
1 egg yolk
Pinch of mixed spice
6 oz plain flour
2 oz currants

½ oz candied chopped peel
Milk to mix

Glaze:
1 egg white
Castor sugar

Cream butter and sugar until light and fluffy. Add egg yolk and work in spice and flour. Add fruit and peel and enough milk to give a stiff dough. Roll out thinly on a floured board and cut into shapes with cutter. Put on to greased baking sheets and bake in a fairly hot oven, 400°F (Gas Mark 6) for 15 minutes. After 10 minutes, brush with egg white and sprinkle with castor sugar.

GRANDMA BOY'S EASTER CAKES

1 lb flour
3 oz currants
3 egg yolks
Pinch of salt

6 oz butter or margarine (or half of each)
6 oz castor sugar
Vanilla or almond flavouring

Beat butter and sugar, and add egg yolks. Sieve flour and salt together and add to mixture. Lastly add the currants. Roll out and cut into rounds. Bake in moderate oven for 15 minutes.

Mary Giles

AUNT TOMMY'S EASTER CAKES

8 oz butter
1 lb plain flour
4 oz sugar
2 oz currants

3 egg yolks
1 egg white
5 drops lemon essence
1 tablespoon brandy

Rub butter into flour and work in sugar. Add all other ingredients and mix thoroughly to a firm dough. Roll out thinly and cut in large rounds (using the top of a tumbler). Bake at 350°F (Gas Mark 4) for 15 minutes. Cool on a wire tray and sprinkle with castor sugar.

EASTER CAKE

8 *large white egg whites*
1 *teaspoon cream of tartar*
10 *oz castor sugar*
4 *oz plain flour*
¼ *teaspoon salt*
½ *teaspoon almond essence*
1 *teaspoon vanilla essence*

Filling and Icing:
Apricot jam
2 *egg yolks*
2 *tablespoons butter*
1 *tablespoon grated orange peel*
1 *lb icing sugar*
3 *tablespoons orange juice*

Beat egg whites and salt until foamy, add cream of tartar and beat until stiff but still moist. Mix sugar and flour together lightly, and fold carefully into the beaten egg whites, 2 tablespoons at a time, with flavouring using a spatula and folding gently over and over until the mixture is even. Put into a 10 inch ungreased round tin and bake at 300°F (Gas Mark 2) for 1 hour. Invert the tin on a wire tray and leave the cake in the tin for about an hour until cold.

Leave until the next day, then split cake very carefully into layers, putting them together with apricot jam. To make the icing, combine softened butter, egg yolks, orange peel and orange juice, and gradually beat in the icing sugar, until the mixture is smooth and easy to spread. Spread thickly on top and sides of cake.

EASTER BUN RING

1 *lb strong flour*
1 *teaspoon salt*
3 *oz butter or margarine*
1 *oz fresh yeast*
8 *fluid oz tepid milk*
4 *oz castor sugar*
2 *oz walnuts (chopped)*

8 *oz stoned dates (chopped)*

Decoration:
4 *oz icing sugar (for glacé icing)*
Walnut halves
Glacé cherries

Cream yeast with the tepid milk. Sift flour and salt together. Rub in 2 oz of the butter. Melt the remaining 1 oz. Add sugar to flour. Beat egg, and add with the yeast liquid to flour. Knead well for 10 minutes. Cover and put to rise until doubled in size. Turn out risen dough on to floured board and 'knock back'. Roll out into a rectangle 18 × 18 inches. Brush with melted butter and sprinkle with nut and date mixture. Roll up tightly along long side. Form the roll into a circle on a baking sheet, seal the ends together well. With a sharp knife make 10 slashes halfway through dough at intervals all round. Leave to rise for ½ hour until well risen. Bake the bun ring for 25–30 minutes at 425°F (Gas Mark 7). Decorate with glacé icing, walnut and cherry halves.

CUMBERLAND EASTER CAKE

4 oz lard
3 oz demerara sugar
1 tablespoon golden syrup
¼ teaspoon bicarbonate of soda
1 dessertspoon milk
¼ teaspoon cinnamon

½ teaspoon ginger
7 oz self-raising flour
Grated rind of 1 lemon
1 egg
8 oz almond paste
Water icing

Melt the lard, sugar and syrup in a saucepan. Dissolve the bicarbonate of soda in milk and stir into the syrup mixture. Add the sifted dry ingredients, beat well, then stir in lemon rind and well-beaten egg. Bake in a greased and lined 7 inch cake tin at 325°F (Gas Mark 3) for 1 hour. Knead the almond paste until soft, then cover the top of the cake and the sides with a very thin layer. Mark the top and sides with a fork design, and ice a lattice pattern on top and sides with pale green water icing, using a large writing nozzle.

WILTSHIRE FIRMITY or FRUMENTY

1 pint prepared wheat
1 quart milk
1 oz flour
A little cold milk
4 eggs (beaten)

4 oz sugar (I use demerara)
Grated nutmeg or cinnamon
or flavouring to taste
4 oz raisins
4 oz currants

Cook the prepared wheat and milk in a double saucepan for 1 hour. Mix the flour with the cold milk and add—allow to boil for 5 minutes. Remove from heat and stir in the eggs well beaten with the sugar, return to heat and stir till thickness of custard. *Do not allow to boil.* Then add fruit which should have been previously cooked in a little water till tender. Usually served cold but very good hot on a winter morning.

To prepare wheat: put several handfuls into double saucepan; cover with plenty of water and cook gently until soft—then strain.

Used on Mothering Sunday. When we lived in Calne, we were able to take along a basin to Maslen's Café in Church Street on the Saturday before Mothering Sunday and get ready-prepared wheat. I think this custom must have been carried on for some long time—though I don't know if it is still.

Mrs Padgham, Minehead, Somerset

Note: Frumenty is common to many parts of Britain. In some areas it was a Christmas dish. A Firmity tea was served at the end of harvest in Suffolk.

HARVEST BREAD

Harvest bread is easy to make, and you do not have to be a splendid cook or a gifted artist to get effective results. The dough is a simple one, only proved once, and making the design is no more complicated than using plasticine.

Basic Dough:
3 *lb plain bread flour*
3 *level dessertspoons salt*
1 *oz fresh yeast (or ½ oz dried yeast)*

1½ *pints warm water*
A little beaten egg
A few drops gravy browning
Currants

Sift flour and salt. Mix warm water with yeast, pour into dry ingredients and work well together with the hands to make an elastic dough (if using dried yeast, leave it to stand in water for 15 minutes before adding to flour). Knead well until smooth, then prove the dough in a warm place until double in bulk, which will take about 1 to 1½ hours. The dough can then be formed into shape and baked immediately. It will lose its crisp outline if left to rise again.

For a large design, it is best to model the dough directly on to baking trays, upside down, so that the finished loaf will slide off easily. For a large piece of bread, model it on 2 baking sheets laid side by side, and placed on the oven rack on a table before beginning to form the shape.

Loaves and Fishes

Take half the dough, form into an oval shape, and roll about 1 inch thick, then place on baking sheet. Take half the remaining dough, form small flat fishes and tiny cottage loaves. Arrange on the base, and brush the whole design with beaten egg. Bake just above the centre of a hot oven, 425°F (Gas Mark 7) until it is set and golden brown (about 20 minutes) then lower the heat to 325°F (Gas Mark 3) for 20 minutes.

Wheatsheaf and Mouse

Take about 8 oz dough and form into a sausage shape about 12 inches long. Place on centre of baking trays and flatten the sausage slightly—this is the base on which the design will be modelled. Using 12 oz dough, form into a crescent shape and put it curving round the top of the stalk, flattening this shape too. Using about half the remainder of the dough, roll with the hands small sticks of dough a little thinner than a pencil and about 12 inches long, and lay each one along the basic stalk shape to cover it. Make a plait with 3 of these sticks. Cut a little v-shape out of the sides of the stalks, fairly high up, and bind the stalks with the plait, tucking the ends well under the sheaf.

Reserve about 2 oz dough for the mouse. With remaining dough, make small sausage shapes of dough, weighing about 1 oz each, and lay them round the top of the crescent, like the rays of the sun, and cover the crescent. Brush the whole sheaf with beaten egg. Clip each pair with a pair of scissors—these form the ears of corn.

Knead a little gravy browning into the dough for the mouse, and take off a tiny piece for the tail. Mould the dough into a pear-shape, then model the head and nose, and lift up small flaps for the ears. Make a thin tail and curl it round the mouse, and put in currant eyes. Bake as for loaves and fishes.

HARVEST BETSY CAKE

8 oz barley flour
8 oz plain flour
1½ teaspoons baking powder
½ teaspoon salt
4 oz butter

4 oz castor sugar
1 dessertspoon golden syrup
½ pint milk
8 oz sultanas

Sift the two kinds of flour together with baking powder and salt. Cream butter and sugar, and add syrup. Add the flour mixture and the milk alternately, then fold in the sultanas. Put into a buttered 7 inch cake tin, and bake at 350°F (Gas Mark 4) for 1½ hours.

SOMERSET HARVEST SUPPER (for 100 people)

PICKLED BEEF

40 lb brisket of beef (minus
high percentage of fat)
or a 30 lb silverside of beef
2 gallons water

2 lb salt
12 oz brown sugar
1½ oz saltpetre

Boil the brine ingredients for 10 minutes. Pour into earthenware crock and leave until cold. Remove bones from brisket if used. Place brisket or silverside in cold brine; leave in cold place for 10 days, turning every day. Wash meat well to remove excess salt. Place in pan of cold water; add 3 onions, 3 bayleaves, 6 cloves, 12 peppercorns. Bring to the boil and remove scum. Simmer—allow 20 minutes per lb. Leave in water until cold. Place on board or tin and press well. Some areas prefer to have beef or ham, in this case use half quantities of beef and serve a similar quantity of cooked ham.

APPLE FLAN

Pastry:
6 lb flour
1½ lb lard
1½ lb butter or margarine
1 lb castor sugar
½ pint (only) cold water

Filling:
12 lb cooking apples

2 lb sugar
2 pints cider
5 lb eating apples

Glaze:
2 lb apricot jam
2 pints cider
3 oz arrowroot

Rub fats into flour. Mix sugar with water. Add to form paste. Divide into 12 portions, and line 12×9 inch flan rings. Chill well. Peel and stew cooking apples in sugar and cider to form thick purée—cool. Pour into pastry cases. Peel and slice eating apples—toss in lemon juice. Arrange on top of purée. Sprinkle with sugar. Bake in moderate oven for 30-40 minutes. Boil cider and jam. Add blended arrowroot, cook until clear. Pour over fruit. Serve cold with whipped cream.

SOMERSET HARVEST CIDER CUP

3 gallons cider
3 pints sherry
3 pints port
½ bottle rum

½ bottle gin
7 bottles orange squash
7 bottles lemon squash
Ice cubes for hot day

Pour into large baby's bath or several plastic buckets. Add sliced red apple and sprigs of fresh mint. Stir and taste. Add sugar if necessary and taste again. Decant into large jugs each with apple and mint.

PUMPKIN PIE FOR HALLOWEEN

Short pastry
1 lb pumpkin flesh
6 oz brown sugar
¼ teaspoon powdered cloves
1¼ teaspoons powdered cinnamon

1¼ teaspoons powdered ginger
½ teaspoon salt
2 eggs
½ pint milk
1 tablespoon grated orange rind

Line a flan ring or pie plate with short pastry and bake at 400°F (Gas Mark 6) until just beginning to colour. Dice the pumpkin flesh, steam until soft and put through a sieve. Leave to cool, then stir in sugar, spices, salt, beaten eggs, milk and orange rind. Pour into flan case and bake at 400°F (Gas Mark 6) for 30 minutes.

PARKIN FOR GUY FAWKES

1 lb fine oatmeal
½ lb plain flour
¼ lb brown sugar
2 teaspoons ground ginger

1 teaspoon baking powder
2 lb black treacle
3 oz melted butter

This is a rich dark gingerbread which should be soft and sticky, and is very good eaten with a piece of cheese. Keep it for a week to mellow before eating, if possible in an old-fashioned bread crock. Mix all the dry ingredients together, make a well in the centre and pour in the treacle and melted butter. Beat thoroughly and bake in a buttered rectangular tin at 325°F (Gas Mark 3) for 1½ hours.

CHRISTMAS EVE WIGS

3 oz butter
8 oz self-raising flour
1 oz castor sugar
1 oz chopped mixed peel

2 teaspoons caraway seeds
1 egg
A little milk

Rub butter into flour, add sugar, peel and caraway seeds. Mix to a soft dough with egg and a little milk. Put into greased patty-pans and bake at 425°F (Gas Mark 7) for 20 minutes. Eat with mulled elderberry wine, or dip in ale.

BERKSHIRE ROAST SUCKLING PIG

These may be obtained nearly all the year round, but they should not be older than 4 weeks and they should be cooked immediately after they are killed. They make a very rich dish. Make at least 1½–2 lb good stuffing, stuff the pig and sew up the slit, using thin string or strong thread. It should be trussed in the same manner as a hare, with its forelegs skewered back to its hind legs, which have been brought forward. Brush all over with salad oil and if possible allow to stand in the oil for ½ hour or so, turning the pig round so that all parts have a chance to soak and soften a little. Put into a hot oven and baste continually until it is done. It will take about 2¾ hours to bake.

Remove it from the oven, dish onto a carving dish, pop a nice rosy apple into its mouth and pour over it some nice thick gravy. Make this with a little of the fat left in the roasting tin; sprinkle plain flour in to make a nice soft 'roux' with the fat, add a little lemon juice, some beef stock, cayenne pepper, nutmeg and extra water or vegetable water if necessary. Serve with apple sauce.

SUGAR AND SPICE BAKED HAM

1 *gammon, 10–14 lb*
8 *oz moist brown sugar*
1 *tablespoon mixed spice*
1 *tablespoon ground ginger* } mixed together
½ *oz whole cloves*

Well soak the gammon in cold water, drain and wipe dry. Rub the spice and ginger into the cut surface and into several incisions through the skin. Wrap in flour and water paste or aluminium foil and bake in oven for 20 minutes per lb, 350°F (Gas Mark 4). Remove from foil and strip off skin and rub over the hot fat with brown sugar and score with a knife into squares and insert cloves into each square. Return to oven 375°F (Gas Mark 5) for a further 30 minutes to glaze. Serve hot or cold.

BAKED HAM

1 *ham (about 10 lb)*   ½ *lb dripping*
2 *lb plain flour*

Soak ham in cold water for about 24 hours. Make a paste with flour and water, roll out thin, then cover all over the ham, placing in a baking dish, put dripping over the paste. Bake in a moderate oven 4 hours, when it should be done. Take off paste, skin the ham, sprinkle with breadcrumbs and cayenne pepper, and ornament with cloves.

EASY CHRISTMAS PUDDING

8 *oz self-raising flour*
8 *oz fresh white breadcrumbs*
8 *oz chopped beef suet*
8 *oz currants*
12 *oz sultanas*
12 *oz stoned raisins*
8 *oz brown sugar*
6 *eggs*
Grated rind and juice of
1 *orange*
Grated rind and juice of
1 *lemon*

1 *teaspoon salt*
1 *teaspoon mixed spice*
½ *pint old ale or* 1 *wineglass brandy*
4 *oz chopped mixed candied peel*
4 *oz chopped glacé cherries*
1 *small grated carrot*
1 *small grated apple*
6 *oz chopped blanched almonds*

Mix together flour, breadcrumbs, suet, dried fruit and sugar, then gradually work in all other ingredients. The mixture should be stiff but not dry, and a little milk may be added. The mixture makes 4 medium-sized puddings. Put into basins, leaving a 2 inch space above the surface of the puddings. Cover with greased paper and foil or pudding cloths, and tie tightly. Boil gently for 8 hours, adding boiling water to the saucepan from time to time. Cool completely and replace paper and cloth with clean ones for storage. Store in a cool dry place. Boil for 3 hours before serving.

SANDRINGHAM CHRISTMAS PUDDING

A receipt given to Hon. Albert Petre, a friend of the Royal Family.

1 *lb eggs*	1 *lb sultanas*
1 *lb plain flour*	1 *lb demerara sugar*
1 *lb white breadcrumbs*	¼ *lb mixed peel*
1 *lb suet*	½ *oz salt*
1 *lb currants*	1 *dessertspoon mixed spice*
1 *lb raisins*	1 *wineglass brandy*

Beat eggs and mix all ingredients except brandy thoroughly *with hands* then stir in brandy. Cover with thick cloth and leave for 12 hours. Put into buttered basins, cover with 3 layers of greaseproof paper within bowls and completely cover with floured and buttered cloth. Boil 21 hours and a further 3 hours day of eating having, of course, removed damp cloth after first boiling, also top layer of paper and replaced with clean pudding cloth.

Mrs Padgham, Minehead, Somerset

CHRISTMAS PUDDING

½ *lb suet*	1 *tablespoon marmalade or*
½ *lb self-raising flour*	*grated orange peel*
½ *lb breadcrumbs*	1 *tablespoon black treacle or*
1 *lb mixed fruit (sultanas,*	*brown sugar*
chopped prunes, dates etc.)	4 *eggs*
1 *teaspoon mixed spice*	1 *pint brown ale or stout*
½ *teaspoon salt*	

Mix all dry ingredients thoroughly. Add treacle, egg and lastly ale or stout. Put into well-greased basins, cover with greased paper, steam for 5 hours. These were always served at an officers' convalescent hospital in the last war.

Miss Henry, Heathfield, Sussex

CHRISTMAS PUDDING WITHOUT SUET

This is dark and rich

4 oz each flour, breadcrumbs,
grated carrot, apple, sugar,
margarine
8 oz mixed fruit
½ teaspoon each ground ginger
cinnamon, grated nutmeg,
salt

1 tablespoon marmalade
2 dried eggs
1 teacup milk and ale mixed

Peel and grate apples and carrots, grate or cut up margarine, prepare
dried fruits. Add all dry ingredients, let stand overnight. Next day stir
well, add marmalade, blend with beaten eggs and milk mixture. Put
into greased basins, tie down, steam 4 hours.

Mrs P. Macneill, Burwash

FESTIVE PLUM PUDDING

4 oz plain flour
1 level teaspoon each salt,
mixed spice, ground ginger
and ground cinnamon
½ level teaspoon grated nutmeg
4 oz fresh white breadcrumbs
8 oz shredded suet
4 oz soft brown sugar
4 oz each dried apricots,
prunes and dates
4 oz each currants and
sultanas

1 large banana, chopped
1 cooking apple, peeled, cored
and chopped
1 oz mixed peel
2 oz shredded almonds
Juice and grated rind of
1 lemon and 1 orange
½ teaspoon vanilla essence
4 oz black treacle
4 eggs

Sift flour, salt and spices, stir in breadcrumbs, suet and sugar. Chop
apricots, prunes and dates and add to flour mixture, together with remaining fruit, peel and almonds and rind of lemon and orange. Beat lemon and
orange juice, vanilla essence, treacle and eggs well together and add to
other ingredients. Mix to moist consistency. Turn mixture into well-
greased 2½–3 pint sized pudding basin, cover with greased greaseproof
paper or aluminium foil and steam steadily for 5 hours. Steam further
2 hours before serving.

A RICH PUDDING

2 lb each of currants, sultanas, raisins
2 lb breadcrumbs
2 lb flour
2 lb demerara sugar
¾ lb mixed peel
1 lb minced apples

2 lb beef suet
8 eggs
1 tablespoon mixed spice
1 teaspoon nutmeg
Salt
Brandy or milk

Prepare the fruit. Sieve the flour and spices into a bowl, add the bread-crumbs, the fruit, the minced apple and sugar. Add the suet and mix well with the beaten eggs and the brandy or milk. If you like a really dark pudding, dilute a spoonful of gravy browning with a little warm water and add this, stirring it well in. Mix the whole mixture very thoroughly and put into greased pudding basins, filling them ⅔ full. Cover each pudding with greaseproof paper and a floured cloth and steam for 6 hours.

If you have a slow combustion cooker you can put each pudding into a pan with enough water to come halfway up the side of the pudding, bring the water to the boil and cook on the hot plate for 1½ hours. Then transfer the pan to the simmering oven and leave it overnight.

1820 CHRISTMAS PUDDING

3 lb raisins
3 lb currants
¾ lb orange and lemon peel
¼ lb citron
1½ lb suet
1½ lb flour
¼ lb almonds (grated)
1 teaspoon ginger

1 teaspoon salt
6 eggs
2 nutmegs (powdered)
1 breakfastcup sugar
2 lb breadcrumbs
1 wineglass brandy
1 quart old beer

Mix all dry ingredients together. Add eggs (lightly beaten) and stout or old beer. Brandy last. Preferably, steam for 12 hours.

This recipe, which is the most delicious I have ever tasted, was given to me by the late Mrs May Dixon of Iron Acton, Glos., having been used by her great-grandmother. Mrs Dixon herself died in 1971 at the age of 87.

In 1820 it seems that sultanas were not available, and this was the only alteration I made to the original recipe. Instead of adding 3 lb currants, use half this quantity and introduce 1½ lb sultanas. The quart of 'Old Beer' may be difficult to get in some localities: I found that a glucose stout was a perfectly good substitute. Serve with Brandy Sauce.

Barbara G. Smith

LAST DAYS CHRISTMAS PUDDING

8 oz *sultanas*
8 oz *raisins*
4 oz *currants*
2 oz *chopped peel*
2 oz *grated raw carrot*
4 oz *plain flour*
1 teaspoon *mixed spice*
½ teaspoon *cinnamon*

4 oz *fine brown breadcrumbs*
4 oz *demerara sugar*
4 oz *softened butter*
2 oz *warm golden syrup*
Rind and juice of ½ lemon
2 *eggs*
4 tablespoons *brandy or milk*

Mix and steam for 4 hours; then for 1 hour on the day. This can be made at the last minute, or on the actual day.

CADOGAN PUDDING

This recipe for dark puddings was used throughout the war. Ingredients were varied according to the supply position, and the recipe is still useful. Alternative ingredients are given in order of preference.

½ lb *currants*
½ lb *sultanas*
½ lb *raisins*
4 oz *candied peel or dates or*
1¾ lb *total of available fruit*
½ lb *sugar*
4 oz *golden syrup warmed in*
drop of milk or honey or brown
sugar
½ lb *suet or cooking fat*
½ lb *breadcrumbs*

4 oz *ground almonds or other*
nuts or grated carrot
1 *lemon, rind and juice, or*
1 *orange or 2 teaspoons lemon*
essence
4 *beaten eggs*
1 teaspoon *each salt, nutmeg,*
mixed spice
4 oz *flour*
8 tablespoons *rum, whisky,*
stout or old beer

Clean and prepare dried fruit and chop peel. Grate suet, or if fat is used, rub into flour. Put all ingredients in large bowl. Mix thoroughly with well-beaten eggs and spirit or beer. Let each member of the family stir— this is 'for luck'. Well grease 2 fairly large or 3 smaller pudding basins. Fill with mixture. Steam or boil 8–10 hours, according to size. They should be steamed another 2–3 hours on Christmas Day.

BRANDY BUTTER

3 oz *butter*
3 oz *castor sugar*

3 tablespoons *brandy*

Cream butter, work in sugar and brandy. Pack into pots and store in a cool place, but not the refrigerator.

CHRISTMAS CAKE

8 oz butter
8 oz soft brown sugar
1 tablespoon black treacle
4 large eggs
4 tablespoons sherry, brandy
or cold tea
Grated rind of 1 lemon
$\frac{1}{2}$ teaspoon vanilla essence
4 oz self-raising flour
6 oz plain flour

1 teaspoon mixed spice
$\frac{1}{4}$ teaspoon salt
Pinch of ground cinnamon
Pinch of grated nutmeg
12 oz currants
12 oz sultanas
8 oz stoned raisins
2 oz chopped peel
2 oz halved glacé cherries

Cream butter and sugar until light and fluffy, then beat together treacle, eggs, sherry or tea, lemon rind and vanilla essence, just enough to break up the eggs. Stir a little at a time into the creamed mixture, alternating with the flours sifted with salt and spices. Do not beat the mixture. Add the fruit and mix just enough to distribute evenly; the mixture should be just stiff enough to fall easily off the spoon. Turn into a 10 inch round tin lined with 2 thicknesses of greaseproof paper extending about 1 inch above the tin. Level off the mixture and leave to stand for an hour. Put into the bottom part of the oven set at 300°F (Gas Mark 1) and bake for 4–4½ hours, putting thick brown paper over the top about halfway through cooking if it is browning too quickly. The cake will be done when a depression no longer remains if the surface is pressed gently with a finger. Leave the cake in the tin until it is just warm, then cool on a wire rack. When cold, wrap in paper and store in a tin. The cake is moist, full of fruit and keeps almost indefinitely if not iced.

MRS GLEDHILL'S CHRISTMAS CAKE

This cake can be eaten nearly straight away, if necessary.

1 lb butter
1 lb soft brown sugar
1 lb flour, half self-raising,
half plain

8 or 9 eggs
$\frac{1}{4}$ lb ground almonds
1$\frac{1}{2}$ lb dried fruit

As a rough guide cook for 6 hours at 250°F (Gas Mark $\frac{1}{2}$) but most people know their ovens, some prefer to start a Christmas cake off at a higher temperature then turn the oven down. Mrs Gledhill says the secret of the moisture of this cake is to put a bowl of water in the oven.

RICH CHRISTMAS CAKE

1 lb 2 oz currants
8 oz sultanas
8 oz stoned raisins
6 oz glacé cherries, halved
4 oz peel
Grated rind of ½ lemon
10 oz plain flour
Pinch of salt

½ level teaspoon mixed spice
½ level teaspoon ground
cinnamon
10 oz butter
10 oz soft brown sugar
6 eggs
3 tablespoons brandy

Grease and line a 9 inch cake tin. Chop the peel finely. Mix together currants, sultanas, raisins, peel and cherries. Sift the flour, salt and spices. Add lemon rind. Cream the butter and sugar until light and fluffy. Beat the eggs one at a time into the creamed mixture. Gradually fold in the flour and fruit alternately; towards the end add the brandy. Turn into the prepared tin, spread the mixture evenly, make a slight dip in the centre. Bake in the lower part of the oven at 300°F (Gas Mark 1-2) for 4½ hours approximately; to avoid over-browning of the top, cover with several thicknesses of greaseproof paper after 2½ hours. When cooked, carefully turn out of the tin and leave to cool on a wire rack. Prick the cake with a fine skewer and slowly pour 2–3 tablespoons of brandy over the cake before storing in tin.

LIGHT CHRISTMAS CAKE

6 oz glacé cherries
6 oz currants
6 oz sultanas
4 oz citron peel
4 oz glacé pineapple
8 oz butter
8 oz castor sugar

2 oz ground almonds
4 eggs
8 oz self-raising flour
Grated rind and juice of
1 lemon
3 tablespoons brandy

Grease and line a 9 inch tin with a double thickness of greaseproof paper. Wash glacé cherries to remove syrup. Slice peel thinly. Cut pineapple into small cubes. Cream the butter and sugar until light and fluffy. Stir in the ground almonds. Beat in the eggs one at a time. Add 3 tablespoons of the flour to the glacé cherries, currants, sultanas and peel, toss to coat. Fold these ingredients alternatively with the rest of the flour, grated rind and juice of the lemon into the creamed mixture. Lastly, stir in the brandy. Turn the mixture into the prepared tin. Bake in the centre of the oven or just below at 325°F (Gas Mark 3) for 2½ hours or till risen and just firm to the touch. Turn out and cool on a wire rack.

MATRON'S (ST THOMAS) CHRISTMAS CAKE (1941)

2 lb flour
½ lb sugar
2 lb raisins
A few chopped almonds
1 pint milk
2 teaspoons bicarbonate of soda

1 lb butter or lard
2 lb currants
1 lb peel
1 teaspoon cinnamon
4 eggs

Rub in fat. Mix with other ingredients. Bake 5–6 hours at 275°F (Gas Mark 1).

Lewis' Mother's Cookbook, Mary Horrell, Exeter

CHRISTMAS GINGERBREAD

1 lb plain flour
½ teaspoon salt
1½ teaspoons ground ginger
½ teaspoon bicarbonate of soda
6 oz butter
12 oz black treacle or golden syrup
8 oz soft brown sugar
1 egg
½ pint milk

2 oz citron peel
4 oz crystallised ginger
2 oz sliced almonds
Grated rind of ½ lemon
1 teaspoon coffee essence

Icing:
8 oz icing sugar
2 tablespoons lemon juice

Sift together flour, salt, ginger and bicarbonate of soda. Gently warm butter, treacle and sugar. Beat in egg and warm milk. Pour on to dry ingredients and mix well together. Add the peel and ginger chopped in small pieces, almonds, lemon rind and coffee essence. Mix thoroughly and pour into greased and lined meat tin. Bake at 325°F (Gas Mark 3) for 1½ hours. This cake keeps very well, and it can be iced before using with a mixture of sifted icing sugar and lemon juice.

Mrs Woolner

BILLY-THE-BUTCH'S WAY WITH THE CHRISTMAS TURKEY

To make your Christmas turkey remain in the memory of your guests for years to come, this method of improvement was given by that charming Welsh butcher, Billy-the-Butch of Haverfordwest, some years ago.

When your turkey is nicely cooked and golden brown on top but could do with about 15 minutes more, dish it onto the carving dish and quickly prick the skin all over with a fork. Pour over some green Chartreuse liqueur (or golden if liked) and replace in the oven for 15 minutes. Baste the 'juice' over the bird again just before taking to table, but don't waste any!

JANIE TWENTYMAN'S TIP FOR MINCEPIES-WITH-A-DIFFERENCE

When making your Christmas mincepies, pinch a little of your husband's whisky, enough to dip each top of your mincepies into, before covering up the mincemeat. Sprinkle the tops with a little sugar just before baking and the result is guaranteed to help the Christmas spirit considerably. If you are short of the hard stuff, mix it with a little milk—it is better than nothing, but not as good as 100% spirit.

JACK PAYNE'S WAY WITH FRESH SALMON

For a wedding or similar event. Some years ago, before he started catering for the passing motorist, Jack Payne took a course in cookery at his local Technical College at Bath. Here he learnt how to cook a large joint of beef to perfection, among many other things, and how to cook salmon fresh from the river without its being as dry as old cardboard—such as he had tasted in many a country inn. To this day he still cooks his salmon in this way to serve cold in the buffet section of The Red Lion at Beckington. Many of his regular customers are farmers, as this is bang in the middle of as rural an area as you will find, even in Somerset.

Have ready a fish 'kettle' or large saucepan with cold water, some clean rag, salt and oil. After cleaning your fish, or part of a fish, rub celery salt all over it. Then take your rags—pieces big enough to wrap the fish in, and soak them in oil, cooking oil or salad oil. Stuff one of the rags into the belly of the fish and wrap the other all round the outside of the fish and then place it in the cold water. See that the water entirely covers it. Add cooking salt and bayleaves to the water—12 for a whole fish. Now bring the fish gently to the boil and *no matter how large the piece is* cook it exactly for 10 minutes then take it off the heat. Leave the fish *untouched* in the water until the whole thing is nearly cold. Then it is ready. This method is suitable for using if catering for a wedding party or similar, as it may be done in advance if you have a suitably cold place to keep it in.

GRANNY HONEY'S TRERICE TREACLE TART

Granny Honey was driven out of County Cork as a young girl, with all the rest of her Protestant family, just before the turn of this century. Subsequently she became a lady's maid, but being fortunate in her employing 'family' she was taken into the schoolroom, along with the daughter-of-the-house and educated by the governess. She also learnt a great deal of first-class cooking at the hands of a German cook, who was a real battle-axe but knew her job. She was a wonderful mother-in-law and an exemplary housewife.

For 20 people

Have ready and 'rested' 3 lb pastry (see Mrs Hibberd's Easy Method). Line as many tins as you require having the pastry not too thick nor yet too thin, say $\frac{1}{8}$ inch thick. In a basin mix 8 oz breadcrumbs, juice of 1 lemon and a little desiccated coconut. Stir into this as much syrup as you will need for the total number of tarts, but do not worry if it is not enough at first sight. Share the mixture evenly between the lined but uncooked tins of pastry and tilt the tins to make the mixture spread around the whole surface. Have ready more syrup and fill up any deficiences as may be required. Make patterns with thin strips of pastry arranged on top of the tarts and bake in a fairly hot oven for 10 minutes and at a lower temperature until golden and set.

17 Herbs

Excellent herbs had our father of old,
Excellent herbs to ease their pain,
Alexanders and Marigold,
Eyebright, Orris and Elecampane.

Rudyard Kipling

What long hours
They gloat upon their steepling hollyhocks,
Bee's balsams, feathery southernwood, and stocks,
Fiery dragon's-mouths, great mallow leaves
For salves, and lemon-plants in bushy sheaves.

Edmund Blunden

GROWING HERBS

If we can't manage an elaborate Elizabethan herb garden, most of us can find a tiny patch of soil.

If it is possible to find a piece near the kitchen with small beds and plenty of paths, so much the better. Each herb needs to be near a path for easy cultivation and harvesting.

If you cannot use an isolated patch, try using herbs in flower borders. Angelica, tansy, lavender, sage, rosemary, hyssop and thyme are all decorative and useful.

Neat rows of herbs can be interspersed with vegetables and flowers for cutting to make a French-style housewife's garden, which is much more fun to work in and look at than serried ranks of Brussels sprouts.

A selection of herbs can be grown in windowboxes, tubs, the spokes of a cartwheel or in the pots on the windowsill. The plants do not need green fingers. They like clean, light, well-drained soil in sunny positions.

DRIED HERBS

The best time to gather herbs for drying is when the plant is just about to flower; the day should be dry and the sun should not have reached its zenith. Small leaved herbs, such as thyme and winter savory, can be loosely tied in small bundles in muslin, and hung near the kitchen fire to dry. Large leaved herbs, such as mint and sage, can be stripped from the stalks, any unsuitable leaves can be discarded and after dipping the leaves in boiling water for a minute, they can be dried in a slow oven for about an hour. Alternatively, after gathering, the herbs are washed and put on a wire rack to dry slowly in a warm room or the hot cupboard.

Parsley needs special treatment. It should be dipped in boiling water and immediately put in a hot oven, 400°F (Gas Mark 6), for *one minute* exactly. It is then finished off in a warm place. This method keeps both flavour and colour. The leaves of all herbs, when absolutely dry, are crushed and may be sieved. The finished product should be stored in airtight tins or dark glass jars with well-fitting screw top lids. Light spoils the flavour and colour of any dried herb.

National Federation of Women's Institutes

FREEZING HERBS

Mint, parsley and chives can be frozen, although their flavour will not be strong. They tend to wilt on thawing, so sprigs for garnishing should not be frozen. They should be chopped finely and packed into ice-cube trays, then frozen solid. Each cube can be wrapped in foil, and a number put into polythene bags for storage.

HERB VINEGARS AND JELLIES

Flavoured vinegars can be made which are delicious for mayonnaise and salad dressings but are expensive to buy. A half pint of herbs should be placed in a pint of wine vinegar for 4 days to infuse. Tarragon and fennel make good vinegars.

Most of us make mint jelly, but the same recipe can be used to produce jelly with thyme, sage, parsley and bay leaves. These are delicious with pork, ham and poultry.

HOW TO USE HERBS

Soups and Stews

Parsley, bay leaves, basil, carraway, celery seed, rosemary, lovage, chervil, thyme.

Sauces

Spearmint, parsley, mint, applemint, sage, lovage, fennel, chervil, dill.

Fish

Fennel, parsley, rosemary, marjoram, dill, thyme, basil.

Meat

Tuck sprigs of rosemary under skin of roast lamb and baste well—forget the mint! Knotted marjoram and winter or summer savory makes stews and ragouts succulent.

Stuffing

Thyme, rosemary, sage, alecost, lavender, lemon balm, savory.

Cakes

Carraway, tansy, aniseed, rose geranium (use a leaf in bottom of cake tin. Delicious with apple).

HERBS, SCENTED LEAVES AND FLOWERS AS FLAVOURINGS

Basil: Tomatoes, turtle soup.
Bay Leaf: Beef stews, spaghetti sauces, fish, milk puddings, custards.
Chives: Cream cheese, salads, stews.
Dill: Boiled beef, mutton, cucumber, old and new potatoes, salmon.
Elderflowers (muscat flavour): Gooseberries, custards.
Fennel: Mackerel, salmon.
Garlic: Salads, mutton stew, spinach, savoy cabbage.
Horseradish: Cream, apple sauce, beetroot sauce.
Lemon verbena: Apples.
Marjoram: Potato soup, pease pudding, lamb, pea soup, turnips, marrows, cod, hake, haddock.
Mint: Tomatoes, fresh fruit salad, lamb, peas, new potatoes, lemonade.
Parsley (more flavour in roots and stems than leaves): Sauces, soups, salads.
Rose Geranium: Apples, sponge cakes.
Rosemary: Mushrooms, spaghetti sauces, beef stews, chicken, duckling.

Sage: Duck, goose, pork, beef.
Tansy: Salads, veal.
Thyme: Chicken, turkey, lamb, spaghetti sauces.

HERB BUTTER

Put 1 teaspoon parsley, $\frac{1}{2}$ teaspoon each of mint and chives, $\frac{3}{4}$ teaspoon tarragon, $\frac{1}{4}$ teaspoon marjoram, in as much lemon juice as the herbs will absorb. Allow 4 oz butter to soften in room temperature and cream it. Blend herbs with salted, creamed butter and set aside at room temperature for 1–2 hours so that the herbs can permeate the butter. Store in tightly covered jars in refrigerator. May be kept there until needed.

Use generously on bridge rolls, toast or sandwiches. Garnish hot steak, chops, escalopes, fish etc., with small rounds of really cold herb butter. Shape some herb butter into a roll, diameter approximately $1\frac{1}{2}$ inches, pack into foil, twist both ends, place in refrigerator. Slices of this can be cut when needed.

HERB CHEESE

$\frac{1}{2}$ lb cheddar cheese (shredded) *summer savory*
1 dessertspoon each parsley, *2 tablespoons whipped cream*
chives, thyme, sage and *4 tablespoons sherry*

Blend well cheese, herbs, cream and sherry. Allow to permeate. Can be used immediately or refrigerated for several days.

CHEESE OF THE SEVEN HERBS

This is an old Cumberland recipe and the name dates back at least 200 years. To 4 oz grated cheese, allow 2 tablespoons thick cream, 3 tablespoons sherry and 2 level tablespoons of the following herbs in mixture: finely chopped parsley, sage, thyme, tarragon, chives, chervil and winter savoury, also seasoning to taste. Put all the ingredients into a double saucepan and stir over very gentle heat till the mixture is creamy and pale green in colour. Whilst still warm, fill up small pots with the cheese and use when cold.

HERBY EGGS SERVED IN THE SHELL

Egg *Ginger*
Herbs *Sugar*
Butter *Seasoning*
Saffron

275

Herbs used: Sage, mint, marjoram and other herbs as liked and chopped finely.

Take as many eggs as you wish to cook. Take off the end of egg shell and pour out the egg. Set aside the shells. Take the chopped herbs, fry them in butter, add the beaten eggs slightly seasoned with salt, and cook until set. Break up with fork or chop up on a board adding a little ground ginger and sugar. A pinch of saffron can be used to give a bright colour and failing this use a very little turmeric powder. Fill the shells with this stuffing and put them into the oven to heat through.

A nice way of serving is to cut thick slices of bread, cut out a circle from the centre and butter all over. The eggs can be put in these 'holes'. Place on a baking tin and warm in the oven while the pieces of bread crisp.

HERB LOAF

This is delicious for a winter party. Use second-day tin or sandwich loaf. Cut off crust; cut loaf in thick slices without quite severing at bottom. Spread each side with herb filling. Press loaf back into shape, wrap in foil, tie and bake in moderate oven, 375°F (Gas Mark 5), until slightly crisp on outside—about ½ hour.

Filling

Chop finely such savoury herbs as parsley, chives, rosemary, thyme, mint, fennel, chervil, angelica. Mix well with butter. Fresh herbs are ideal for this loaf, but dried kinds may be used with discretion.

HERB SEASONING

To 2 parts of dried and pounded orange peel add 1 part each of dried thyme, marjoram and hyssop. This can be kept in a well-closed glass jar for months and gives the most wonderful flavour to stuffings and force-meat; it will even cheer up the dullest rissoles.

CONCENTRATED MINT SAUCE

Pick enough mint leaves to fill a breakfast cup when well pressed down, and put ½ pint of vinegar and 3 oz of sugar into a saucepan. Simmer for 2 or 3 minutes after the sugar is dissolved. Put the mint leaves into a colander, pour boiling water over them, and then dry them in a clean cloth; sprinkle them with 1 oz of sugar and chop up finely. Pack into small jars, adding enough vinegar to cover the leaves by ½ inch, and tie them down. When using, dilute with a little more vinegar.

FRAGRANCE FOR LINEN

Fill small muslin bags with equal quantities of rosemary, thyme and bay leaves, rubbed small. Or try 2 parts each of powdered mint and rosemary to one part of thyme, tansy and powdered cloves.

SCENTED PILLOWS

Sleep sweetly on scented silk or satin pillows stuffed with pot pourri mixture. Try well-dried rose petals mixed with a teaspoon each of powdered dried mint and powdered cloves. Or try equal quantities of lavender, lemon verbena and rose scented geranium leaves, with a teaspoon each of powdered orris root and cinnamon.

LAVENDER STICKS

Lavender sticks were used to mark the dozens and half-dozens in our grandmother's trousseau chest, and they keep their fragrance for years. For each stick, take a small bunch of lavender and a length of narrow baby ribbon. Pick the lavender blooms on a fine day, and use them while the stems are still supple. Take an odd number of stems (13 gives a satisfactory 'stick') and tie them firmly together with one end of the ribbon immediately below the flower heads. Turn the bunch upside down and carefully bend the stalks out and down the heads from the point where the ribbon is tied so that the heads appear to be in a cage of stems. Space the stalks evenly, and then starting at the top where the stalks bend, weave the long end of the ribbon over and under the stalks so that the flower heads become completely enclosed in a kind of basketwork of ribbon and stalk. Make the weaving rather tight at the bottom and top of the heads and rather slacker in the centre to give a 'bottle appearance'. When the heads are completely covered, wind the ribbon firmly round the stalks for 1 to 2 inches, then tie in a bow. Leave about 3 inches of stalk below this bow, and trim neatly to an even length with sharp scissors.

POT POURRI

Pot pourri is a mixture of dried flowers, leaves and spices. The secret of success lies in the choice of scents, in correct drying methods, and in the use of the right container. Pot pourri can be used in small quantities to fill muslin bags or cushions, but it is more commonly kept in a jar. The jar needs a well-fitting lid and a stand, and special jars were once made for this purpose. Try a ginger jar, with a wooden lid and stand. The pot pourri should be kept in the shut jar all day, and in the evening should then be turned till pleasantly warm, moved to its stand and left to cool, when the scent will fill the room. When cool, the lid should be replaced till further use.

Roses are the traditional ingredients of pot pourri, but other flowers can be used to give colour and variety to the mixture. The flowers should be gathered freshly after the dew had dried, and the flowers should not be quite full out, as their scent is strongest then. The flowers must be dried, the scents fixed, and the blossoms blended with appropriate leaves, herbs and spices.

A box of fine sand is needed for drying the flowers. The petals should be placed on a layer of sand, then sprinkled with more sand, and so on in layers till the box is full, care being taken not to put too many petals into one box as they may mildew. The sand boxes should be kept in a warm dry place away from sunlight and draughts, and after a few days they will be crisp and retain their shape and colour. Different types of flowers and scented leaves should be kept in separate boxes. When they are ready for use, the sand can be sifted away. Flowers gathered at various times can be kept dried till the time comes to blend them.

If an extra fragrant mixture is required, the petals can be sealed, after drying, into jars with 2 tablespoons of kitchen salt. They should be left to stand for 3 weeks before mixing together. As a final fixative, powdered orris root is used. When the flowers, spices and fixatives have been mixed they should be sealed into jars or packets as required. The following are delightful mixtures:

Mixture 1

In a bowl, put alternate layers of rose petals, bay leaves and the powdered rind of two oranges, sprinkling each layer with a mixture of equal parts powdered cloves, allspice, cinnamon and mace. Finish with a layer of rose petals and a scattering of lavender flowers.

Mixture 2

Use alternate layers of lavender, lemon balm, thyme and mint, sprinkling each layer with a mixture of cloves and cinnamon. Leave for a few days before stirring and mixing together.

Mixture 3

Mix a quart of rose petals with a cup of marjoram, lemon, thyme, rosemary and lavender. Sprinkle with the powdered rind of an orange and a lemon, 6 broken bay leaves, 1 tablespoon cloves and 1 teaspoon allspice.

POT POURIE–GRANDMOTHER'S RECIPE

24 sweet smelling rose petals, 6 stems thyme, as many as possible of the following herbs: some rosemary, lavender, myrtle, balm, bay leaves,

mint, peel of lemon. Dry slowly in sun, rub to powder, put in wide necked attractive container. Add 2 oz each powdered cloves, musk, orris root, cinnamon. Stir well as pot pourie improves with an occasional stir.

Mrs M. E. Sanders, Lostwithiel, Cornwall

HERB OR CAPPALICK TOBACCO

2 oz of Coltsfoot
2 oz of Wood Bottoney
2 oz of Eye Bright
1 oz of Agrimoney

½ oz of Rosemary Flowers
½ oz of Lavender Flowers
2 oz of Lavender Cotton

Dry them in the Sun and rub them fine and mix them with 1 lb of the best Tobacco

Joseph Webb's book, 1823

18 Health and Beauty

Good Huswives provide, ere an' sickness do come,
of sundry good things, in her house to have some:
Good aqua composita, and vinegar tart,
rose-water, and treacle, to comfort the heart.
Cold herbs in her garden, for agues that burn,
that over strong heat, to good temper may turn,
White endive and succory, with spinage enough,
all such, will good pot herbs, should follow the plough.
Get waters of fumitory, liver to cool,
And others the like, or else go like a fool.

Thomas Tusser

CHILBLAIN MIXTURE

Mix 1 tablespoon of honey with equal quantity of glycerine, the white of an egg and enough flour to make a paste—a teaspoon of rosewater may be added. Wash the affected parts with warm water, dry and spread on paste. Cover with piece of linen or cotton material.

FOR CHAPPED HANDS

Every time after washing drop on them a little honey, and rub them together till the stickiness is entirely removed. The same may be applied to sore lips.

Grandma's Book, Mrs Margetts, Leics.

ESSENCE OF SOAP FOR SHAVING OR WASHING HANDS

Take 1½ lbs of fine white soap in thin slices, and add thereto 2 oz of salt of tartar; mix them well together, and put this mixture into 1 quart of spirits of wine, in a bottle which will hold double the quantity of the ingredients; tie a bladder over the mouth of the bottle, and prick a pin through the bladder; set it to digest in a gentle heat, and shake the contents from time to time taking care to take out the pin at such times to allow passage for the air from within; when soap is dissolved, filter the liquor through paper, to free it from impurities; then scent it with a little hergamot or essence of lemon. It will have the appearance of fine oil, and a small quantity will lather with water like soap, and is much superior in use for washing or shaving.

Grandma's Book, Mrs Margetts, Leics.

TO INCREASE THE GROWTH OF HAIR

Hartshorn beat small, and mixed with oil, being rubbed upon the head of persons who have lost their hair, will cause it to grow again as at first.

Grandma's Book, Mrs Margetts, Leics.

NEURITIS

Old remedy, recommended. 1 oz celery seed from chemist, 1 pint of water, boil to ½ pint. Strain, take 2 teaspoons twice daily, in a little water—for a fortnight.

I. Northey, Allet

CORNISH REMEDIES

Rope-yard worn around the legs and wrists for rheumatism and cramp. Hot roast onion in the ear for relief of earache.

New red flannel worn around throat to relieve sore and aching throat.

To cure corns apply fresh yeast on a cloth every morning.

Nettle rash is soothed by rubbing in parsley.

Mrs M. E. Sanders, Lostwithiel

HONEY FOR HANDS

Rub some honey on the sore parts and then cover with cotton gloves. For washing up, and for other wet jobs put rubber gloves over the cotton ones. Honey will soon heal the cracks and will soothe the soreness. Honey is also a marvellous face pack.

Another good thing for the hands is olive oil with just a sprinkle of sugar. If you use it regularly the sugar cleans the hands—and the olive oil makes them soft.

Mrs G. L. Morris, Ludlow

FOR CHAPPED AND ROUGH HANDS

Mix ¼ lb softened lard with 2 egg yolks and a tablespoon runny honey, a tablespoon ground almonds and a tablespoon rose water. Add a few drops of almond essence and work into a stiff paste. Keep in a pot by the wash-basin. This paste is very healing and softening.

AT NIGHT

Olive oil and sugar to clean very sore, stained, ingrained hands. Cover with old tights or bags of rag.

TO REMOVE WARTS I

Rub the warts with the inside of broad-bean pods, after the beans have been taken out.

TO REMOVE WARTS II

Use juice of houseleeks to cure warts and corns. Apply the leaves to the excrescence.

SKIN TONIC

2 oz witch hazel
1 oz elder or orange flower water

1 oz rose water
Few drops tincture of benzoin

Apply with cotton wool every morning before make up.

Mrs Cox, Herts

SKIN BEAUTIFYING MASK

2½ tablespoons pure lemon juice   *1 teaspoon ground camphor*
                                           Few drops glycerine

Mix well. Cleanse skin and apply to face and neck. Leave on for an hour, then wash off with warm water and a good soap. (Use upward movements when washing *and* drying face.) Use once a week—twice, if skin is in poor condition.

Mrs Cox, Herts

MOISTURISING LOTION

Elderflower water is a moisturiser, skin tonic and softener. Put 3 tablespoons dried or fresh elderflowers into ½ pint boiling water. Simmer a few minutes. Cool and strain. Keeps for a week.

FOR A SPOTTY SKIN

Marigold flower water has healing and tonic properties. Make as for elderflower water.

ROSEMARY TEA

Specially stimulating and good for digestion, rosemary tea makes a delicious change. Use a teaspoon of dried rosemary to 1 cupful of boiling water. Just stir and infuse in the usual way. This can also be used as an astringent for the skin, leaving it feeling clean and refreshed, tingling with new life.

LOSING YOUR LASHES?

For falling eyelashes blend together 3 teaspoons of castor oil and 1 teaspoon of rum. Coat the eyelashes with this using a soft, bristle brush and taking care the mixture does not get in the eyes. Repeat every night for as long as possible.

FOR TIRED EYES

Use cotton-wool pads wrung out in strong camomile tea or ordinary tea, or cold milk. Place over closed eyes for 10 minutes.

FOR WRINKLED SKIN AROUND THE EYES

Finely grated raw potato packed between layers of gauze.

AMBRIDGE SOAP

My mother always made her own soap; not only was it cheaper than the recipes suggested, but it also found an excellent use for all the waste dripping and fat removed from the top of boiled meat.

The recipe was:

1 lb caustic soda
6 lb fat, clarified and free
from salt

Mix the soda in 3 pints of rain water and allow to get cool but not cold. Care should be taken not to get the soda on the hands as it boils when placed in water. Dissolve the fat and when lukewarm pour it into the soda water which should be the same temperature, stirring all the time with a wooden spoon until the mixture is of the consistency of honey. Pour into a box or tin lined with wet cloth as this prevents the soap sticking and makes it easier to lift out. Leave until next day, then cut in pieces and store.

Ammonia may be added if rain water is not obtainable, as this will soften the water and whiten clothes in washing.

Colouring and perfume can be added if desired to make a change from the hard, white soap which this recipe provides.

Godfrey Baseley, Ambridge

MISS ALICE ADDINELL'S HOUSEHOLD SOAP

3½ lb any fat   *2 oz borax*
9 pints water   *¾ lb caustic soda*
½ lb resin (powdered)

Boil together for 45 minutes and pour into moulds.
Lewis' Mother's Cookbook, Mary Horrell, Exeter

FOR NAUSEA

Mint tea made with fresh leaves is useful in allaying nausea. Put the leaves in boiling water, in a covered vessel. Let it stand near the fire for an hour.
Mrs Garden, 1847

RASPBERRY VINEGAR

A teaspoon of the above, in a tumbler of cold water, is a cooling beverage in case of thirst, cold or fever. To every pint of best vinegar put 3 pints of raspberries. Let them lie together for 2 or 3 days then mash them up and put them in a jelly bag to strain, but without using any pressure. To every pint when strained put a lb of powdered loaf sugar, boil it 20 minutes and skim it. Bottle it when cold.

Lewis' Mother's Cookbook, Mary Horrell, Exeter

EGG SHAMPOO

Whisk 4–6 yolks (according to thickness and length of hair). Use like an ordinary shampoo and rinse thoroughly. Use tepid water. Eau de Cologne in the rinsing water removes egg smell.

HAIR TONIC

A handful of stinging nettles or rosemary, or sage, boiled in a cup of cider vinegar and one of water. Cool, strain and bottle. Use daily on scalp with a piece of cotton wool.

TO EASE STIFFNESS

3 grapefruit	*2 oz Epsom salts*
2 oranges	*2 oz cream of tartar*
3 lemons	

Squeeze the juice from all the fruits and set aside. Put all the skins, pith and seeds through the mincer, and pour 2 pints of boiling water over it. Add the fruit juice and let it stand overnight. Squeeze through a fine sieve or cloth to extract as much juice as possible. Pour 1 pint boiling water over the Epsom salts and cream of tartar and stir thoroughly. The cream of tartar will not dissolve. Pour this into the juices, keeping it well stirred all the time. Bottle the mixture, stirring well all the time, and store in a cool place. Shake the bottle well before pouring out a dose, and take one wineglass before breakfast each day. Keep this up for a period of 27 weeks, by which time the system will have thrown off all stiffness of the joints. This recipe was given to an old lady in Sussex to give relief from arthritis and rheumatism; she thought it had originated in Canada.

A RECIPE FOR PRESERVING FRIENDS

Select those with round hearts. Don't bruise with unfeeling words. Add a heartful of the milk of human kindness and plenty of tact. Warm with sympathy. Don't overheat or it may ferment mischief. Knead with oil of unselfishness but beware of jars. Keep in a warm corner of the heart. Years will improve the flavour of this preserve.

Mrs Bracewell

MR KINGMAN'S SURE CURE FOR AGUE

2 ounces of Red Bark   *1 ounce of Salt of Wormwood*
1 ounce of Virgin Snakeroot

Put in treacle and take a large tablespoon when the Chills are coming on—and if it does not abate, take again in 4 hours.

Joseph Webb's Book, 1823

ESTHER'S BEEF TEA

1 lb meat cut into dice, all fat taken off. $\frac{1}{2}$ pint of water in a covered jar. Let it simmer—no salt. It ought to look greasy. Leave it 12 hours. Give teaspoon at a time if very ill. Put more water if for common tea.

Mrs Garden, 1847

TO EASE THE BROW

Pour $\frac{1}{2}$ pint of boiling vinegar onto 1 bundle of chopped watercress. Leave for 10 minutes, strain through muslin and keep, bottled, in a cool place until needed. Sponge the watercress vinegar gently over the forehead and temples.

WATERCRESS TEA

Chop $\frac{1}{2}$ bundle of well-washed watercress, put in a jug and pour over $\frac{1}{2}$ pint of boiling water, leave to infuse for 4 to 5 minutes, strain and serve. This can be drunk sweetened, neat, or with a slice of lemon in it.

COUGH MIXTURE

2 new-laid eggs   *1 oz salad oil*
3-4 lemons   *1 pint rum*
$\frac{1}{4}$ lb brown sugar candy

Put eggs into a small basin and squeeze lemons on them. Let them remain about 3 days, turning each day until the shells are dissolved. Beat well together, add the candy, and when dissolved strain through a fine muslin. Add rum and oil, put into a dry bottle and keep well corked. Shake well before taking. Dose: $\frac{1}{2}$ a wineglass night and morning.

ROYAL POSSET FOR A COLD

1 tablespoon groats   *½ pint sherry*
3 tablespoons cold water

Put the wine into a very clean saucepan, when hot pour in the groats mixed to a paste with the cold water. Stir and boil gently 6 minutes. flavour with a few cloves and sweeten with honey. Drink quite hot just before going to bed.

Mrs Page, 1899

ELDERBERRY CORDIAL

A grand stand-by against winter colds. Pick the fruit on a dry day. Stew fruit and stalks in water just to over them. Then strain through muslin, squeezing the bag to get all the juice. To each pint of juice add 1 lb sugar and 10 cloves. Boil for 10 minutes. When cold, pour into bottles and cork.

A MODERN MEAD

1 dessertspoon honey in tumbler boiling water. Stir well, sip very hot. The speedy effect on a tired heart is amazing. The ancient Britons drank mead—fermented honey and water. Recipe is for mead's unfermented counterpart. It helps sleep.

ELIZABETHAN or ELDERBERRY ROB

5 lb of ripe elderberries, simmered with 1 lb of sugar until it is the consistency of honey. Strain and bottle. 1 or 2 tablespoons to be taken at bedtime in very hot water. It is a mild aperient, will stop a cold, and bring on a sweat. It relieves all chest troubles. A tablespoon of whisky may be added if liked. A very old recipe, well tried.

VEGETABLES FOR BEAUTY

Every woman who owns a vegetable garden has a number of beauty secrets ready to hand. The most effective remedies for curing a bad complexion and for improving one's appearance can be obtained from vegetables.

Vegetables freshly cut are twice as valuable as vegetables which have been packed and stored before reaching your table.

The girl who wants a white skin should eat freely of carrots and parsnips. They have a whitening effect on the skin. Spinach and onions purify the blood. An old saying runs 'An onion a day keeps the doctor away'. Lettuce and watercress supply iron to the blood and give colour to the cheeks.

If you lose your beauty sleep—the stalk of the lettuce also has the added virtue of warding off insomnia. If you cannot sleep, you soon grow old and haggard looking. Eat a lettuce and a little thin brown bread and butter before retiring for the night and you will not lose your beauty sleep.

Eat the garnish—when a dish comes to table garnished with parsley, eat the parsley—don't regard it as an ornament. Parsley aids digestion, and you have never yet met a girl with a good, clear skin who suffers from indigestion. Also, if you have been eating onions, parsley will take any taint away from your breath.

Is your skin muddy?—tomatoes cleanse the liver, so the girl with the muddy complexion should count them her best friend. Eat them fresh with a little salt and pepper, but avoid vinegar as much as you can. Too much acid is bad for the complexion. The juice of the tomato is also valuable in removing stains on the hands caused by housework. The girl with a sun-scorched face or a florid complexion can obtain a wonderfully healing and bleaching skin food from cucumbers.

A cucumber wash—take 2 cucumbers, and cut them into small chunks without peeling them. Put into an earthenware basin, and pound to a pulp with a potato masher or other implement. Strain the pulp through a piece of coarse muslin, squeezing out as much juice as you can. Then into a clean enamelled saucepan put both juice and pulp, and simmer (do not boil) for 10 minutes. Strain again, and, when the liquid is cold, add one tablespoon of eau de Cologne to every pint of strained liquid. Pour this into a bottle, and sponge your face with the liquid 2 or 3 times a day.

Some hints from 1916

19 Around the House

Take weapon away of what force is a man?
Take huswife from husband and what is he then?
As lovers desireth together to dwell
So husbandry loveth good huswifery well.
Though husbandry seemeth to bring in the gains
Yet huswifery labours seeme equall in pains
Some respit to husbands the wether may send
But huswives affairs have never an end.

Thomas Tusser

Beechwood fires burn bright and clear,
Hornbeam blazes, too.
Keep the logs above a year,
And they'll be seasoned through.
Pine is good, and so is yew
For warmth through wintery days.
The poplar and the willow, too,
Take long to make a blaze.
Oaken logs will warm you well,
If they're bright and dry,
Larch will of the pinewood smell,
And the sparks will fly.

Birchen logs will burn so fast,
Alder not at all.
Chestnut logs full long will last,
If cut and let to fall.
Logs of pear and apple logs,
Bring scent into the room.
Cherry logs laid on the dogs,
Smell like flowers in bloom.
But ashen logs, so smooth and grey,
You burn them green or old,
Cut them, all you can each day,
They're worth their weight in gold.

Traditional Rhyme

CHEESE TIP

It is always difficult knowing which is the best place for keeping the cheese fresh. The refrigerator makes it too dry and cold and the larder isn't cool enough, so why not try the Flower Pot Way? All you need is a decent-sized clay flower pot which you then soak in cold water before popping the cheese, suitably wrapped, under the pot. In very hot weather, keep a moist cloth over the pot.

BAKING TINS

If possible wash all baking tins and patty tins while the oven is still warm —they can be dried most satisfactorily in the oven before all the heat goes.

FISHY SMELL

The smell and the taste of fish often remain on cooking utensils and cutlery. To cure this simply wash them in water to which a little vinegar has been added and the smell will disappear.

TONIC FOR INDOOR PLANTS

Don't throw away the tea with the tea-leaves; keep it. When it is cool, it makes a good fertiliser for indoor plants, but don't overdo it. Most plants prefer to be kept not too wet.

UNZIPPING THE UNZIPPABLE ZIP

It is so easy to get stuck in an outfit with an out-of-reach zip. To avoid being caught in this predicament, rub the troublesome zip with an ordinary wax candle or a 'soft' pencil—it is the graphite in the pencil which works the magic.

FIRST AID

Epsom Salts are an excellent thing to keep in the First Aid kit; many a farmer has taken the swelling out of a cow's injured foot by bathing it in a good strong mixture. Also this liquid is good for any swelling due to infection. But it is of the greatest help in helping to extract a splinter from a finger—simply soak the finger in a strong, warm solution of Epsom Salts for as long as possible and as often as need be; before long the splinter will easily be removed as the Salts 'lifts' it.

WAX STAINS

Remove as much of the dried wax as possible using a round-bladed knife. Place clean sheets of blotting paper on both sides of the blob of wax. Press with as hot an iron as the cloth, carpet or whatever will stand. The heat melts the wax which is then absorbed into the blotting paper. Any remaining stains may be treated with methylated spirits. If possible follow by washing, or, in the case of a carpet, shampooing.

INSTANT COFFEE STAINS ON CARPETS

The main object is to treat as soon as possible after the spilling. If a soda syphon is handy attack the coffee stain with this at once. Mop up lightly. Spray again and mop again. If this fails to work the coffee right out, of if the stain is of longer standing, use a mixture of alum and water to sponge the spot and dry out as well as possible. Often the vacuum cleaner will pick up the remaining moisture but newspaper placed over and under the spot, if this is possible, will absorb the rest.

MESSY MILKPANS

To make easier the task of cleaning an aluminium milk pan, transfer the milk, as soon as it reaches the required temperature, to another container. Wipe out the hot pan immediately with a soft dish cloth, then fill it with cold water—it will be no trouble to clean.

SAGGING CANE

To brace the sagging cane chair simply scrub it on the seat and under the seat, then dry, if possible, in the sun. It will now have a new lease of life.

SAGGING DRIVER ON LONG JOURNEY

Better by far than smoking (which tends in the end to make one sleepier because of the smoky atmosphere) is to have a supply of 2 kinds of boiled sweets made with glucose—bitter lemons and humbugs make a good contrast. The sugar quickly enters the bloodstream and gives one the necessary stimulus to carry on. However, the wise thing is still to pull into a lay by and have a short nap.

SCORCHING

A badly scorched garment or cloth can never be cured, but for milder damage try using a warm solution of borax and water—½ oz borax to ½ pint water.

FURNITURE POLISH

Equal parts pure turpentine, vinegar and linseed oil.

Mrs F. Miller, Dorset

'Feed' oak on linseed oil and polish with plenty of grandma's recipe of grated beeswax and turpentine melted carefully over low flame.

Mrs N. E. Pow, Somerset

FLIES HATE BLUE

Are you troubled by swarms of flies? Then did you know that flies hate blue? Change your colour scheme to blue and you won't be bothered again. One farmer's wife tried this out and remarked that, though they had flies in every room in the house, she had no flies in the blue room. She told this to a friend of hers who said that this is fairly well recognised and in Holland many stables are painted blue inside to keep those pestering flies away from the horses. But no one has yet explained why blue is so effective.

CLEANING PEWTER (1900)

A thin paste of olive oil and powdered whitening rubbed on and left to dry, then polished.

FURNITURE POLISH FROM BEESWAX

3 oz beeswax
1 oz whitewax (½ a candle)
1 pint of white spirit
(turpentine substitute)

1 pint of hot water
1 tablespoon of washing-up liquid (more in hard water areas)

Using old saucepan or large tin stood in saucepan of boiling water, melt waxes. Remove from heat and gradually stir in the white spirit. Add washing-up liquid to hot water and then add to the waxes, stirring well. Stir occasionally until cold. Pour into suitable screw-top jars and label clearly.

TO PREVENT STEAMY WINDOWS IN KITCHEN

Soak a clean duster in a strong solution of detergent, allow to dry without rinsing. Use to clean windows; the film of detergent deposited will break down steam and leave windows clean for hours.

Mrs M. E. Sanders, Lostwithiel

IN THE GARDEN

St George's Day (23 April) is best day for picking *dandelions*—if the sun is shining.
Potatoes are traditionally planted on Good Friday—because the working man had this one day off as a holiday.
Runner beans should be planted on 1 May—May Day.
Apples should be picked by Marlborough Little Mop Fair Day (the Saturday before 11 October) and never later than Big Mop Fair Day (the following Saturday).
Blackberries must *never* be picked after 30 September, otherwise the Devil will have spat on them. (Irish and Cornish belief.)

TO TINT LACE

A few drops of coffee added to the rinsing water will give that creamy tint which is often spoken of as 'old'.

TO STIFFEN LACE

Never use starch for fine laces. A little borax dissolved in the rinsing water will give the desired stiffness. Or rice water is equally good for this purpose.

TO IRON LACE

Lay the lace on your blanket with the wrong side uppermost. Then with a cloth or a flannel placed directly over the lace it should be ironed. In thick lace, any raised flowers should be pulled into position with the tips of your fingers, taking great care not to tear the lace.

Miss L. A. Wheway, Hinckley, Leics.

TO WASH COLOURED EMBROIDERIES

Coloured embroideries, such as silk crewel work, should never be washed with soap, or the colour will come out. Have 2 basins of bran water. This is made by tying a lb of bran in a bag and putting in a saucepan of water. The bran may be used several times. Put the embroidered article in 1 of the basins and press it until the water is dirty. Then repeat the process in the other bowl of water. If the embroidery is very dirty, more than 2 bowls of water will be needed. Finally rinse the article in cold water, squeeze out as much water as possible, and hang it up. When it is nearly dry, iron it quickly on the wrong side with a hot iron.

Miss Mabel Nield

A GOOD WAY TO DRESS RICE

Soak the rice in cold water and salt for an hour; have ready a saucepan with boiling water, throw in the rice and let it boil briskly for 10 minutes, then drain it in a colander. Put it in the oven for a few minutes and then serve. The grains should be double the usual size and quite distinct from each other.

SCOURING POWDER

Shake up 1 lb whitening, 1 lb pumice powder and 1 lb soap powder. Store in clean, dry jars.

Mrs R. Evans, Merioneth

FOR PLANTS

Infusion of elder leaves poured over plants preserves them from caterpillars.

Mrs Garden, 1847

FOR CLEANING

For ormolu dip a soft brush in water, rub a little soap on it and brush the article for a minute or 2. Then work clean and rub dry near the fire. Finish with burnt bread nicely powdered. Mother of pearl should be washed in whiting and water—soap destroys its brilliancy. A solution of alum will clean ivory and bone.

Mrs Garden, 1847

HOMEMADE TRANSFER INK

3 teaspoons castor sugar
1 teaspoon hot water

1½ teaspoons powdered
laundry blue

Mix in a cup and stand it in hot water to dissolve the sugar. For a dark material, use the same method, but substitute 3½ teaspoons powdered whitening for the blue.

Mrs Corrie, Burnside of Auchegool, Kirkcudbrightshire

MRS BOMPAS' WAY TO BOIL COCOA

A tea-cup full of nibs and a quart of water. Simmer them gently for 4 hours then pour off the liquid. Add to the same nibs a pint of water and simmer for 4 hours more. Put the 2 liquors together and warm it when required.

Mrs Garden, 1863

CAKE AND PASTRY MIX

3 lb self-raising flour
1½ lb sugar
1 lb butter
½ lb lard

Mix and store in plastic bag in refrigerator. I find the dewbin ideal.

For Pastry:
3 lb self-raising flour
1 lb lard
½ lb butter
Mix dry and store as for cake mix. Saves a lot of time.

Mrs Haynes, Isle of Man

REMEDY A FRUIT CAKE WITH A SUNK MIDDLE

by leaving it upside down on a wire tray in a warm room overnight.

Mrs Butcher, Cambs.

ALMONDS ON CAKES

Before putting the blanched almonds on the top of a Dundee cake, I dip them in milk. This keeps them tender and crisp and prevents them burning while the cake is baking.

Miss Christian Milne, Fraserburgh

BROWNING FOR SOUPS AND GRAVY

Take $\frac{1}{2}$ lb of coarse brown sugar, a tablespoon of salt, and nearly $\frac{1}{2}$ a pint of boiling water. Place the sugar and salt in a frying-pan with a very small lump of dripping, and stir well over a clear fire, till of a *dark brown*, then add the water; boil well, and when cold bottle for use.

Lewis' Mother's Cookbook, Mary Horrell, Exeter

GRASS AND MOSS STAINS

During the summer grass and moss stains are common, and as these are unsightly, especially on white garments, steps should be taken to remove them as soon as possible.

If the stains are on white material, damp the affected parts with cold water, then sprinkle with a mixture of equal parts of salt and tartaric acid. Allow the mixture to remain on the material until it is quite dry, then brush off lightly with a pad of soft cloth, or with a soft brush. Should any traces of the stains remain, repeat the process.

For coloured materials, rub the affected parts lightly with pure glycerine. Allow this to remain on the material for an hour or so, then wash the article or garment in the usual way. If the stains are old, it may be necessary to repeat the process 2 or 3 times.

ONION REMEDIES

The usefulness of the onion as a cooking agent is known to most house-keepers, but that it can be used for general household purposes is not so well known.

Rust stains on steel knives can be removed with the juice of a raw onion. Rub a slice over the affected parts, then polish in the usual way.

Try the juice of an onion for removing burnt foodstuff that clings to the sides of an aluminium saucepan. Rub well into the metal, then fill the pan with water and boil briskly for $\frac{1}{2}$ an hour. This will loosen the burnt food, leaving the inside of the pan quite clean.

Onion juice can be used for polishing tinware. Allow it to dry on the metal, then polish in the usual way.

Linen that has become slightly scorched through faulty pressing should be rubbed with slices of raw onion. Rub the juice well into the fabric, leave for a few minutes, then wash in a warm soapy lather and rinse in tepid water.

Index

298

300

A Selection of Historical Fiction from Sphere

THE BLACK PLANTAGENET	Pamela Bennetts	30p
BORGIA PRINCE	Pamela Bennetts	35p
THE BORGIA BULL	Pamela Bennetts	35p
THE GAME OF KINGS	Dorothy Dunnett	40p
QUEENS' PLAY	Dorothy Dunnett	40p
THE DISORDERLY KNIGHTS	Dorothy Dunnett	60p

The Six Wives Series

ANNE BOLEYN	Margaret Heys	30p
KATHERINE OF ARAGON	Julia Hamilton	30p
ANNE OF CLEVES	Julia Hamilton	30p
JANE SEYMOUR	Frances Clark	30p
KATHERINE HOWARD	Jessica Smith	30p
KATHERINE PARR	Jean Evans	30p

The Golden Sovereigns Series

AN UNKNOWN WELSHMAN	Jean Stubbs	40p
THE SPANISH TUDOR	Freda M. Long	35p
VICTORIA	Evelyn Anthony	40p
SON OF YORK	Julia Hamilton	35p

Sphere Books Beginners Guides Series

STAMP COLLECTING	Kenneth Anthony	40p
PAINTING IN OILS	Barbara Dorff	40p
WATER COLOUR PAINTING	Barbara Dorff	40p
TROPICAL FISH AND FISH TANKS	Reginald Dutta	40p
COARSE FISHING	Arthur Hardy	40p
ROSE GROWING	Cyril Harris	40p
RIDING	Veronica Heath	35p
COIN COLLECTING	Howard Linecar	30p
BRIDGE	Norman Squire	40p
BUDGERIGARS	Philip Marsden	40p
BETTER WINEMAKING AND BREWING	B. C. A. Turner	35p

All these titles are illustrated

A Selection of Cookery Books from Sphere

POOR COOK	Campbell & Conran	60p
GREAT DISHES OF THE WORLD (Illus)	Robert Carrier	95p
THE ROBERT CARRIER COOKBOOK (Illus)	Robert Carrier	£1.30
THE FOUR SEASONS COOKBOOK	Margaret Costa	75p
THE GRAHAM KERR COOKBOOK (Illus)	The Galloping Gourmet	95p
JAMS, MARMALADES AND SWEET PRESERVES	Mary Norwak	40p
FRENCH FAMILY COOKING	Eileen Reece	50p
FARMHOUSE COOKING I (Illus)	Norwak & Honey	£1.00
FARMHOUSE COOKING II (Illus)	Norwak & Honey	£1.00
DEEP FREEZING MENUS AND RECIPES	Mary Norwak	30p
CALENDAR OF HOME FREEZING	Mary Norwak	60p
DEEP FREEZING	Mary Norwak	40p
A-Z OF HOME FREEZING	Mary Norwak	40p
MIXER AND BLENDER BOOK	Mary Norwak	35p

The 'Cordon Bleu' Series
The following titles fully illustrated in full colour at 90p each

MEAT COOKERY	SUMMER COOKERY
MEMORABLE MEALS	SUMMER DESSERTS
PARTY COOKING	CASSEROLES
SALADS	POULTRY AND GAME

All Sphere Books are available at your bookshop or
newsagent, or can be ordered from the following address:

Sphere Books, Cash Sales Department,
P.O. Box 11, Falmouth, Cornwall.

Please send cheque or postal order (no currency), and allow
7p per copy to cover the cost of postage and packing
in U.K. or overseas.